Simon & Schuster

New York   London   Toronto   Sydney   Tokyo   Singapore

WILD THING

the BACKstage, on the RoAd,
in the stuDio, ofF the chaRts

meMoirs of iAn cOpelanD

WARNING:

parts of this book contain gratuitous sex and violence

SIMON & SCHUSTER
Rockefeller Center
1230 Avenue of the Americas
New York, NY 10020

SIMON & SCHUSTER and colophon are registered trademarks
of Simon & Schuster Inc.

Designed by Elina D. Nudelman
Photo design by Irving Perkins Associates

Manufactured in the United States of America

10   9   8   7   6   5   4   3   2   1

Library of Congress Cataloging-in-Publication Data
Copeland, Ian, date
    Wild thing: the backstage, on the road, in the studio, off the
charts: memoirs of Ian Copeland.
    p.   cm.
    Includes index.
    1. Copeland, Ian, date.   2. Concert agents—Biography.
3. Rock music—History and criticism.   I. Title.
ML429.C642A3   1995
338.7′6178′092—dc20
    [B]   95–31760
                                                  CIP
                                                  MN

ISBN 0-684-81508-7

To my lovely daughters,
Chandra and Barbara

Do as I say, not as I do.

CODT

ENTS

CHAPTER 1

Ten Copeland's Tales

As we walk in fields of gold . . .

—Sting

January 17, 1994—Hollywood, California:

I WOKE UP this morning at 4:15 with a feeling that something was wrong. I'd set my mental alarm clock—which rarely fails me—for 5:30 A.M., giving me plenty of time to pack my bags and catch the 8:30 A.M. flight to Tokyo, where I'd be joining Sting for the start of his world tour 1994. I needed to pack since I planned to be out on tour for nearly three months. Five-thirty, therefore, was perfect. So what in the hell was I doing wide awake at 4:15?

I went to the bathroom and came back to bed. I lay there with the lights on, knowing that if I fell back to sleep there was a good chance I'd miss my flight, yet I was exhausted from being up late finalizing the details of the tour. I couldn't resist the allure of my soft pillows. Just as I was dozing off, the earthquake hit. It threw me out of bed and onto the floor.

I crawled to my bedroom door frame and stood there while the house shook with incredible force. My bedside lamps crashed to the floor and all the lights went off at the same time. In the darkness, I could hear glass breaking and things falling all over the house. It sounded like a freight train was running through the downstairs. Five or ten seconds into it, a second earthquake hit with a bone-shuddering jolt that threw me up in the air and nearly knocked me to the floor a second time. The quivering intensified and grew in ferocity, and I knew the house was coming down. I grabbed a pillow from the bed and bolted for the front door, running barefoot through the broken glass and out to the street. Some of my neighbors were already gathered there. I joined in the conversation that was taking place on a million sidewalks all over the city: "Are you okay?" "Where were you when it hit?" "In bed." Someone laughed and said, "Ian . . . ?" I looked down. I was stark naked.

In thirty seconds the earthquake was over. Aftershocks kept coming, some of them quite severe, but my house, which had once belonged to Rita Hayworth, and later to Ben Vereen, did not come down—much to my amazement. Between the tremors I was able to get back in the house, get some clothes and a flashlight, and go check on the neighbors, including one with whom I had just been battling in court over his complaints about my wild parties. Relieved that no one was hurt or in danger, I went back to my house to inspect the damage. What I found was a mess. Medicine cabinets and kitchen shelves had emptied their contents. Antiques and artifacts I'd collected from around the world had fallen from their places on bookshelves and mantelpieces and smashed on the floor. My framed gold and platinum albums, which only weeks before I had mounted on the wall after months in storage, were strewn around the living room. It looked as if someone had walked through my house with a mighty grudge and a baseball bat, breaking everything in sight. I would later find that virtually every wall was cracked, my chimney was on the verge of collapse, and my swimming pool had been lifted out of the ground. The whole city of Los Angeles was without power, and because of the aftershocks and the danger of leaking gas lines, I knew it was unwise to light candles. This put me in a peculiar predicament. Despite the darkness and confusion, I still had to pack my suitcase. As it turned out, I packed all the wrong clothes and forgot several essential items, like my razor.

The drive to the airport was like a scene from a big-budget disaster movie, complete with fires from broken gas lines, floods from busted water pipes, and streets strewn with bricks and debris from collapsed buildings, fallen walls, and toppled chimneys. All of the traffic lights were out so I took the precaution of stopping at every intersection, but there were no other cars on the road. In some areas the sidewalks were filled with crowds of frightened people, many wrapped only in blankets or sheets. As the car radio began to report some of the damage caused by the earthquake, which measured 6.8 on the Richter scale, I could see for myself that the disaster was real; this was no Hollywood movie. The broadcast warned that the freeways were destroyed and the L.A. Airport was closed. I soldiered on regardless. Come hell or high water, I couldn't miss the first show of Sting's world tour.

January 18, 1994—Tokyo, Japan:

After some delay, the L.A. Airport was opened for outgoing flights, and mine was the first to leave. The local promoter met me with a limo at Narita Airport and for the two-hour ride into Tokyo he brought me up to date. Sting had gotten sick on the last tour of Japan and most of the dates had been canceled, so fans were skeptical this time; the three shows at the Budokan in Tokyo had sold out almost immediately, but some of the other cities had been slow. Now that Sting was in the country doing press and television promotion, however, ticket sales had started to pick up and it looked to be a sold-out tour. Since Sting was getting a percentage of profits, this was particularly good news to me.

Japan had always been a "flat deal" in the past, and bands never received a percentage over and above their guaranteed fee. Years ago it was the same in the States, but promoting shows had become more of a science since then, and it was common for a band to get both a guarantee and a percentage of profits. When I had suggested we do the same in Japan, the promoters were reluctant to set the precedent. That's putting it mildly. They flipped out and flat refused.

But I insisted, demanded, and threatened to cancel the tour unless I got it. Since the promoters with whom I was working had already announced that they had procured the Sting tour, they didn't have much of a choice. If I wasn't bluffing and canceled the tour they would lose face. To the Japanese businessman, there's nothing worse than losing face.

While checking in at the lobby of the hotel I bumped into Dominic Miller, David Sancious, and Vinnie Colaiuta, Sting's guitar player, keyboard player, and drummer. After exchanging greetings I inquired as to Sting's health. The week before they had played a series of shows at London's Albert Hall, and I heard reports that his voice had been giving him trouble, and that some of those shows had come close to being canceled. The worried look on their faces told me that we weren't out of the woods yet despite the fact that all the shows did play. Considering the canceled dates on the last tour of Japan, it would be catastrophic if Sting lost his voice this time. On the previous tour the promoter had failed to take out insurance, so he lost a fortune and virtually went out of business. As a result of those cancellations it was now cost-prohibitive for the promoters of this tour to take out insurance. If we canceled this tour we would have to return our deposits (100 percent of the guarantee up front), but the promoters would still have to eat the cost of hotels, building rents, ticket printing, advertising, truck rental, salaries, equipment hire, and a multitude of other expenses adding up to millions of dollars, or should I say millions of yen. Aside from the loss of income, we had a lot to lose too. Band and crew salaries, shipping costs and international flights, and so on. An incredible dollar amount hinged on the state of Sting's vocal chords.

I dropped my bags in my hotel room and called Billy Francis, the tour manager. There was no answer in his room, and there was no answer in Kim Turner's room either (Kim co-manages Sting with my brother Miles). Since Sting would be registered under a false name I couldn't call, I went to check the gym, the most likely place to find Sting when not in his room. Sure enough, he was there in the steam room.

"Leroy!" he said, calling me by my nickname, "It's good to see you. How the hell are you?"

"A bit jet-lagged, I suppose, but more to the point, how the hell are you?"

"Never felt better in my life," he said, but his voice was husky and a bit hoarse. True enough, I'd never seen Sting in better physical shape, the result of his relatively new fascination with and devotion to yoga. Sensing my concern, he added "I've been doing interviews all day, and I've got a bit of a cold, but nothing to worry about."

"Well, why don't you skip soundcheck and rest your voice?"

"No. I'll be fine. We need to do a soundcheck 'cause we've got a new sound system." That was final, I knew. You can suggest things to Sting, but in the end he'll do what he wants to do.

At soundcheck he sounded good, much to my relief. To save him from going out again into the freezing cold, Billy Francis decided to keep him at the venue until the show, and arranged for him to do his two hours of yoga in the dressing room, followed by a massage. Kim Turner and I spent the time counting the seats in the hall and checking the turnstiles to make sure the promoter's ticket counts were accurate. Everything was fine . . . until just before Sting went on stage. The Japanese interpreter, a particular woman we had insisted the promoter employ, gave Sting a couple of cold pills to dry up his sinuses. Bad move. They also dried up his throat.

After a few songs it was obvious Sting was in trouble. His voice was cracking, and on the high notes it was giving out altogether. For a while he covered up by letting the audience sing the familiar choruses, and in between each line of his songs he would gulp down some lemon tea with honey. It helped some, but halfway through the set he surprised us all by walking up to the mike and announcing a short intermission. He came off the stage and went to his dressing room where he gargled copious amounts of an herbal concoction that had been given him for just such an emergency. Ten minutes later he was still in pain, but he went back on stage and continued where he'd left off. The crowd loved it, and when he managed to sing a near perfect "Roxanne" I knew we were home free. At least for the night.

The Japanese promoters were shitting themselves. We had been arguing with them about the many press interviews and after-show meet-and-greets they'd scheduled relentlessly each day. We now had no problem convincing them to cancel all but the most important of them. Sting spent the whole next day in bed and that night he was fine. On the third night he was in top form, and for the rest of the tour there were no more problems. At the end of the seven-date tour we made a considerable amount on the percentage deal, which to me was a major victory. I had broken new ground and contributed to the modernization of the Japanese music business. In any case, the Japanese promoters were so relieved at the tour's completion that they were more than happy to pay it.

With everything going smoothly, I decided to let the band go on to the two shows in China without me, and I flew home to L.A. to deal with the damage to my home, and to take care of some major clusterfucks that had cropped up with the dates in South America that I was booking in March.

January 22, 1994—Hollywood, California:

L.A. was still recovering from the earthquake, and it took me an unusually long time to get home from the airport. All the major freeways were damaged and cars were being rerouted onto streets that couldn't handle the extra flow. The traffic was murder.

So was the week ahead. The tail end of the tour which was to be in South America was falling apart. In Peru the Shining Path guerrillas announced a campaign of violence during elections, and everyone agreed that a large concert might be too tempting a target. We had the same problem in Guatemala. In Caracas, Venezuela, we lost our venue at the university because a local homeowners group had managed to have concerts banned in the stadium we had been planning to use. So we were forced to find an alternative site, a place that required extensive preparations to make a show possible.

The promoter in Brazil, after losing his ass on a series of INXS shows, decided that the economic climate wouldn't support the large shows we were planning to do in Rio de Janeiro and São Paulo. We solved that problem by coming up with a double bill with James Taylor, still a big attraction there owing to a hit he had with a song about Rio. But in order for that to make sense for James Taylor, we had to add him to our shows in Argentina and Chile. That created another problem: the larger venues there were available only on dates that were back-to-back, and that meant a logistical nightmare for the road crews. The same promoter would be doing both cities, however, so I made him guarantee at his own risk that the shipping of equipment could and would be done even if it meant hiring his own airplane to do it.

The rest of it was relatively simple. In Puerto Rico the only problem was choosing between two promoters. The one I preferred happened to be offering almost twice as much as the other one, so I didn't have to think about that too much. Mexico City was offering a king's ransom because the last time Sting played there he sold out four shows in a twenty-thousand-seater, and on this tour we had time for only two. We had never done Costa Rica, so I put that in even though the money wasn't quite what we were offered elsewhere. I routed it between Mexico City and Caracas so that it made good sense anyway. And just to be safe, I had all the promoters send their money up front.

January 31, 1994 — Manila, Philippines:

Getting out of L.A. again was a joy. The continuous aftershocks (there were hundreds of them in the weeks following the big one) were seriously messing with my nerves. It didn't help, however, to discover in the travel guide I read on the airplane that the Philippines were the earthquake capital of the world. Sting had insisted on playing cities on this tour that were slightly off the beaten path, places he'd never been, or even better, places where no band had been before. Manila had hosted quite a few shows before so it wasn't exactly virgin territory, but it was still a new city for Sting and for me, so I didn't know quite what to expect.

What I found was worse than I could have imagined. The road crew had flown in the night before, and when I spoke with Tam Fairgrieve, the production manager, he had nothing good to say about the venue or the promoter. The stage was still under construction, the equipment was substandard, the sound system inadequate, and worst of all, there was no electricity at the venue. I called the promoter and he promised that everything would be taken care of, but I'd heard that one before and it did nothing to calm my fears. I had a hard time dealing with him right from the start.

In most places I could choose between several promoters and take the best bid for my act. In Manila there were only two, and one had such a notoriously bad reputation I couldn't even consider him. The one I was dealing with, therefore, had a virtual monopoly. And he knew it. When I asked him to provide me with a detailed list of his expenses he told me to mind my own business. As he put it, "I don't want anyone to know what I'm paying people, and besides, how can I document all the bribes I have to pay to the government and everyone else in order to make the show happen?" When I tried to get him to agree to the percentage deal on top of our guarantee he just laughed in my face. In the end he agreed to pay us a bonus if the show did well, but he would decide that after the show was over and all was said and done. "Trust me," he said. Oh my God! But Sting wanted to play Manila.

When I walked into the venue my heart sank. I had been told the capacity was twenty thousand. What I found was a baseball stadium that could easily hold at least twice that, and I was told by everyone from the taxi driver to the bellhop at the hotel that it was sold out and impossible to get tickets. Since I had based our guarantee on the number of tickets for sale, obviously we were being ripped off. When I stormed into the promoter's office and demanded an explanation he assured me that the show was not sold out, and that he had been forced to give away thousands of tickets to government officials and sponsors and advertisers. "You don't understand how it works here in my country," he kept saying. "This is the Third World, my friend, and we have our way of doing things. You have to accept it." I was enraged, but I had the distinct feeling he didn't give a shit.

At that stage there was nothing we could do. If we threatened not to play we faced the certainty that our equipment would never get out of the country, and neither would we. I'd be bluffing anyway, since Sting would never opt to disappoint his fans. The only thing to do was grin and bear it, and promise to make sure everyone I knew in the business was made aware of the situation so at least they could avoid the same mistake.

When Sting went on stage there was still a huge flow of people coming in the front gate to the stadium, and Kim Turner called me up there to see what was going on. I'd never seen anything like it. There were so many people trying to get through the one entrance that the police and security people were having to beat them back with batons, even though it seemed all of them had tickets. Kim and I estimated that fifteen thousand people or more were still outside trying to get in. When they heard Sting's music begin they surged forward en masse and it looked extremely dangerous. It was certain that people were going to be crushed and trampled. Just then Billy Francis joined us at the gate and saw what was going on. Billy was a veteran of the road, having tour-managed just about everyone from Rod Stewart to David Cassidy, and he was not one to stand around and watch when something was going wrong.

"Kim," he said, "unless we do something soon we're going to have blood on our hands."

"What can we do?" asked Kim. "It's definitely out of control. Can we stop the show?"

"We can try," said Billy. I don't know how he did it. We were a long way from the stage, and it wasn't easy getting through the crowd, but somehow he managed to get to Sting and make him aware of the situation. Sting then went back to the mike and explained the problem to the audience, and announced that he was going to take a break and come back on when it was safe to do so. If he hadn't, a few thousand people would be still coming in by the end of his set, and then there'd be riots for sure. The crowd, once they were all in, went nuts when Sting returned to the stage, and he gave one of the best performances I'd ever seen him do.

The next morning as Sting and I had breakfast I explained the situation with the promoter. I told Sting how I'd been screwed by him, but I pointed out that we had few other choices, that it was a Monday night and the routing was perfect between the last show and the

17　　　　　　　　　　　　　　WILD THING

next, and that, in fact, our guarantee was more than anyone had ever been paid in the history of shows in Manila.

"Coolbreeze," he said, "it was a great crowd, and I enjoyed it immensely. As for the promoter, I guess we'll know better next time." Then he winked at Billy Francis, and said to me, "But as for you . . . you're fired."

FEBRUARY 2, 1994—KUALA LUMPUR, MALAYSIA:

Coming from the pollution, poverty, and filth of the Philippines, Kuala Lumpur was a Garden of Eden. A pleasant surprise indeed. Chosen as a place to play almost solely because few major acts had ever played there, I had expected it to be primitive. Instead it was well organized and the promoter was professional, at least to the degree that there were no major malfunctions. The venue was an indoor stadium with a capacity of eighty-five hundred, and the crowd was the most responsive of all so far. They sang along with every song, and the roar of applause was deafening. The band played great. It was an extra-special show. When I went back to their dressing room I found a room full of long faces and all of them moaning about what a lousy performance they'd delivered. Hence, a word of advice to any budding agents: never walk into a band's dressing room and exclaim "Great show, guys!" Quite often the band won't think so, and they'll think you're full of shit. I made that mistake once early in my career and for almost two days I was frozen out by the band for my poorly timed praise.

While I'm on the subject of things you shouldn't do, if you're ever out with a celebrity make sure you don't wear anything or do anything that will draw attention to who they are. If you're wearing a T-shirt or jacket with their name sprawled across it, they won't appreciate it. It's hard enough for them to lead any semblance of a normal life, and it's easier if they can remain anonymous. As a result, the days of the outrageous rock star are a thing of the past. Without thinking, during the earthquake I packed only one warm jacket for my trip, and it had STING in bold letters on the back. Until I got rid of it I was shunned from all social occasions.

The very last thing you want to do is fall asleep on the airplane when anyone else is still awake. If you miss your meal you needn't worry because it will most likely turn up in the pockets of whatever you're wearing. And if you take your shoes off before napping they'll either go missing completely or be filled with toothpaste or shaving cream. One time, our accountant (not Theirry Pouchain but his boss, Mike "The Goon" McGinley) fell asleep on a flight, and Billy Francis took a thick black Magic Marker and carefully wrote GOON in big letters across his bald head. It wasn't until he got to his hotel room and looked in the mirror that he noticed, but meanwhile he had to wonder why everyone was laughing at him at the airport and why the clerk at the front desk was cracking up when he checked the band into the hotel. "Hi! I'm The Goon," he had said, as he always did. "Yes," replied the clerk, "I can see that."

FEBRUARY 3, 1994—SiΠGAPORE, SiΠGAPORE:

Singapore is perhaps one of the most beautiful cities in the world, and certainly one of the cleanest. You're not allowed to spit or even chew gum on the sidewalks, and there's a distinct lack of graffiti. The punishment for those crimes can be a caning administered by a martial arts expert. And if you're caught with drugs, it's a death sentence. On the flight into Singapore, Billy Francis, displaying his perverse sense of humor, warned everyone in the band and crew that anyone caught with drugs would be fired.

Like all of the top touring bands, Sting travels with a small army of professionals who take care of everything and make the show run smoothly, many of whom have worked with him for a long time, some from as far back as the days of The Police. The chain of command goes something like this: my brother Miles is the manager, in charge of all aspects of Sting's music career. He rarely goes on the whole tour, but often shows up for the important concerts or when he has business to discuss with Sting. Kim Turner was the tour manager for The Police from the very beginning, and is now partners with Miles, representing management on the road, responsible for

WILD ThiΠG

everything to do with the tour overall. Billy Francis, the tour manager, had also been a tour manager for The Police, and he is responsible for taking care of everything involving Sting and the band before and after the show, including getting them from country to country, arranging their travel and hotel accommodations, getting their visas and work permits, and generally looking after all their needs while on tour.

For this tour, the production manager, another Police veteran, Tam Fairgrieve, did the same thing for the crew and the equipment, and working under him were Jimmy Bolton, the stage manager; Nick Sholem, the set and lighting director; Mike Keating, the sound engineer (mixing the sound that comes out of the PA to the audience); Tom Herrmann, the monitor mixer (mixing the sound that the musicians hear on stage); Bill Spoon, rigging engineer and Kabuki backdrop expert; Andy Perrin, carpenter and set builder, Matt Dean, who worked for the PA company; and Rich Locklin, who worked for the lighting company. Additionally, each musician had his own technician to take care of him on stage: Danny Quatrochi (a Police vet) for Sting, Donnie FitzSimmonds for Vinnie Colaiuta on drums, Phil Docherty for Dominic Miller on guitar, and Peter Lorimer for David Sancious on keyboards. Then there's the accountant, Theirry Pouchain, who took care of payroll, paid the hotel bills, and settled up with the promoters after each concert. Including Sting, the band, and myself, there was a total of twenty-one people on the road.

My work as agent in setting up the tour is done months in advance, so as long as everything goes according to plan, it's not an absolute necessity for me to travel on the tour other than to show support. To keep from feeling like the proverbial "spare dick at a sailor's wedding" I become a sort of self-appointed morale booster and social director for Sting and the band, and generally help out wherever I might be needed. I booked us into the Singapore Indoor Stadium, a modern state-of-the-art venue holding just over seven thousand people, and it had sold out well in advance. We were using the same promoter that did the show in Kuala Lumpur, and I was confident that there would be no unexpected problems. So in Singapore I didn't even go to soundcheck with the band. Instead, I did the tourist thing, and took off to the country to play a round of golf. It did me a world of good.

February 5, 1994 — Jakarta, Indonesia:

Flying into Jakarta gave me flashbacks of a flight twenty-five years before, a flight I'll never forget. From the window of the airplane I could see water buffaloes and rice paddies and people in the fields in black pajamas and sampan hats. But there was a world of difference between now and then. Now we'd be met at the airport by a mob of screaming Sting fans, and we were flying into an idyllic situation; then it was Vietnam in '68, and I was flying into war.

I took advantage of a day off to go shopping and discovered a gigantic department store with floor after floor of local handicrafts and art. I was followed around the store by a constantly growing crowd of giggling girls who were convinced that I was Sting despite the fact that I denied it. It was especially ridiculous because Sting wore his hair in a crew cut and my hair was past my shoulders. I don't look anything like him, but then I suppose we round-eyes all look alike to them. Eventually I signed an autograph for one of them and that started an avalanche of requests for more. They were so thrilled that I felt obliged to sign them all, and frankly I really enjoyed it. My little moment of stardom. I signed them "Leroy Coolbreeze" and in smaller letters "Sting's agent." The next day I showed Sting some of the things I'd bought, and told him where I'd done my shopping. His son's birthday was coming up so he had me take him there to look for presents. I was concerned that there might be mob scenes when he was spotted, but my fears were unfounded. Instead it turned out to be a rare treat for Sting because for some reason we were mostly ignored. I suppose the mob had been fed—they thought they already had his autograph so they left him alone.

February 7, 1994 — Sydney, Australia:

A day from hell. Make that two. I flew with the band back to Singapore to catch our connecting flight on to Brisbane, Australia, but that flight was canceled. Instead of staying there overnight with the band I decided to fly directly to Sydney to meet with Michael

WILD THING

Gudinsky, our Australian promoter, with an ulterior motive of seeing an old friend from my childhood days in Beirut, Lebanon, who had since immigrated to Australia and opened a club called The Cauldron, one of the most happening nightclubs in Sydney, and a small hotel called L'otel. It was a red-eye flight, a long one, and together with the flight from Jakarta and the layover in Singapore the total trip took nearly twenty-four hours. Just to add insult to injury, I was singled out and strip-searched at the airport upon arrival in Sydney. I found L'otel easily enough, but when I inquired about my friend, the owner, I was told he was out of town until the end of the week. The young lady at reception promised to get a message to him, so I went up to my room to try to get some sleep. As soon as my head hit the pillow, the phone rang and it was my office in L.A. with a host of new problems that needed to be sorted out, mostly to do with some of the other bands on my roster.

I stayed on the phone until lunchtime when I met with Gudinsky. We discussed the tour and resolved all remaining issues, so at least that was worthwhile. But when I returned to the hotel for another attempt at getting some much needed shut-eye, no such luck. They were remodeling the next room and the hammering made sleep impossible. I called downstairs to complain and was less than courteous to the poor girl in reception. I felt bad about it afterward so to make amends I called her back and invited her to dinner. To my surprise she accepted. But it was not to be. She later called with apologies and blew me off. So there I was, sleepless in Sydney with nothing to do. I took a cab out to the famous Bondi Beach, and wouldn't you know, it started to rain. I went back to the hotel, only to find a pile of faxes from the office with more problems to deal with. In my frustration I decided to book a flight for the next morning back to L.A. I spent the rest of the evening by myself getting drunk in the bar downstairs.

Just so you know, my life is not always so miserable. The next day started out in a much better light. The receptionist called and invited me to join her for breakfast. After that, she came up to my room to help me pack my suitcase. I'd already packed.

I gained a day by crossing the International Dateline, so I arrived in L.A. before I left Australia. By now the earthquake and aftershocks were old news, and this time I was glad to be home. At the office, my desk was overflowing with correspondence and so many demo tapes of bands looking for representation that there was no way I could listen to them all. Instead, I concentrated on current clients and their problems.

The Squeeze tour, for instance, had to be almost completely re-booked. They had asked us to book a tour that began in May, then, when it was nearly planned, they had us move it to June, and then finally to July. What began as a six-week tour was later whittled down to three weeks, then to two, and eventually a total of only ten days. It also started out with a Squeeze lineup that included most of the original members, and that's how we presented it to promoters. Then the bass player and drummer dropped out, and it became a "Squeeze Unplugged" tour, which meant our going back to the promoters and making them change their advertising. No sooner had we done that than Aimee Mann was added as a member of the band, and also as a special guest to the show, so we had to go back to the promoters yet again and add her to the bill. We also had to put on an opening act, which required us to look for a solo artist due to the lack of remaining room on the stage.

I don't mean to imply that Squeeze is disorganized; that's just the way it often is with most tours and most bands. This is what the agent has to live with. So many factors can cause a tour to change, such as a change in recording schedules, unforeseen television opportunities, developments in other markets, decision changes at the record company, health considerations, and so on. Even during the tour it can continue to evolve in response to chart positions and radio airplay. The agent has to monitor that and be able to make changes in the tour if necessary.

Another thing I had to deal with had to do with an artiste I signed before she had a record deal or even a manager, a somewhat unusual practice for an agent. I first saw her on a television show called

The Real World on MTV, in the original version filmed in New York. It involved a diverse group of artistically inclined young adults, all in their late teens or early twenties, thrown together in a house and filmed as they interacted with each other and pursued their various ambitions. Becky represented the young budding musician, and she attracted my attention even though she performed a song that was still in the making, and therefore not particularly exceptional. There was simply something about her. By a curious twist of kismet, the following Saturday I attended a party held by InterTalent in a large bowling alley, and in the crowd I spotted a person, a young lady, that gave off an aura I was irresistibly drawn to. A friend introduced us, and I talked with her for quite a while before it twigged that she was the same girl I'd seen on MTV. She told me her name was Rebecca Blasband. She gave me a tape of her song, now a finished version. I played it in my car on the ride home. I thought it was brilliant, and decided to take her on.

At that stage she had no band and no plans to tour, so my first job was to help her get a manager, a lawyer, and a record deal, in whatever order I could. I sent the tape to various people in the business, including my brother Miles, who not only runs a management company but also a record company called IRS. Miles said he was interested and liked the tape, but he wanted a band that could tour before he could get involved. Numerous other managers took notice, and Becky met with several, eventually settling on Art Collins, the manager of Iggy Pop and Marianne Faithfull. This lasted for only a short time, when it became obvious that Art was too busy with his other clients to be of much use to a new artist looking for a record deal. A few of the people I contacted from record company Artist & Repertoire departments responded with interest, but none with actual offers; it was always "We want to hear more material," or "When can we see her live performance?" To the former, I sent out a new tape with three new songs, and for the latter I set up a gig at CBGB's in New York so we could showcase her in front of an audience.

Meanwhile, I also heard from Paul Schindler, an attorney in New York who represents a host of major music business clients including Madonna, Bruce Springsteen, Michael Bolton, and Sting. Schindler expressed a great deal of interest so I set up a meeting on my upcoming trip to New York.

March 1, 1994—New York, New York:

It was no coincidence that Sting's concert at the Meadowlands Arena in New Jersey and his four shows at the Paramount in Manhattan were scheduled to coincide with the Grammy Awards ceremony in New York. Sting instructed me to arrange it that way when I first started booking the tour. An agent's worst nightmare. It meant coming all the way from Australia to Florida, where we had some makeup dates to do, then straight to New York. He had been asked to perform at the Grammy ceremony as a previous recipient of a Grammy Award, ten of them in fact. Sting received a short-list ballot for 1994's competition, and from it he felt confident that his current record stood a good chance of at least getting a nomination. I think even he was surprised, however, when he was nominated for a total of six awards: "Album of the Year" and "Producer of the Year" for *Ten Summoner's Tales;* "Single of the Year/Performance," "Song of the Year/Writer," and "Best Long-Form Video" for "If I Ever Lose My Faith"; and "Best Rock Performance/Male" for "Demolition Man."

R.E.M., a group I discovered and signed more than twelve years before, were also in New York for the Grammys, and were up for some of the same awards as Sting. The night before the ceremonies we all got together and took over the bar at their hotel, keeping it open long after normal closing time. It's a surprise to me, knowing how I felt the next day, that any of them were able to perform.

The ceremony itself was a major bore, if only because I'd been to several previously over the years, and the process during rehearsals and filming is long and drawn out and not very interesting to anyone not actually involved. Sting shared a dressing room with some of the other guests on the show, including Billy Joel and Garth Brooks, and the crowded backstage area was a complete Who's Who in both the music and acting worlds. As soon as I could, I left to watch the event on television in the company of some childhood friends from Beirut.

While in New York, I met with Paul Schindler regarding Rebecca Blasband. I filled him in on the interest that Becky and I had been

WILD THING

generating at various record companies, which he agreed to follow up on, and I asked him to help convince Miles to manage her. It had been proven to me a long time ago, with R.E.M. in fact (more about this later), that I could not take my relationship with Miles—or anyone else for that matter—for granted, and that I couldn't expect him to sign anyone merely on my say-so. As is usually the case with anyone, it would be necessary to get as many people talking about Becky as possible. Paul, fortunately, was eager to help. Things don't always happen in this way—in fact they rarely do—but this time around it worked. Paul did convince Miles to sign Becky for management, and between the three of us I knew we could get her a good record deal.

Now the ball was really rolling. I realized I could solve two problems at once. I was able to fill the opening slot on the upcoming Squeeze tour with Becky, and at their prestigious show in New York I could showcase her again to the growing list of interested A&R people.

After a busy week in New York, I accompanied Sting and his band to Puerto Rico, and on through Central and South America, ending the tour in Chile at the end of March. I next visited New York for a Save the Rain Forest charity show at Carnegie Hall organized by Sting and his wife, Trudie Styler, at which Sting performed with an eclectic collection of artists including James Taylor, Whitney Houston, Pavarotti, and Elton John. One of the highlights of the evening for me, however, was sharing a table at a dinner reception after the show with none other than the infamous and hilarious talk-show host Howard Stern, together with his effervescent sidekick, Robin Quivers. Being made fun of on their radio show the next morning was an added bonus.

A few weeks later I was invited to attend the International Film Festival in Cannes. I went at the expense of Lumiere Pictures, ostensibly to help them promote their upcoming film *Fresh* that starred one of my young actors, Sean Nelson. In reality I was there to protect my client from the other agents likely to be buzzing around like flies on shit. The film, which coincidentally was sound-tracked by my brother Stewart, was already winning all the advance film-critic awards, and Sean, a handsome and talented thirteen-year-old, was receiving rave reviews across the board. As a result, the vultures were sure to be out in force.

After a wild and crazy week in Cannes, I was beat. Every day was filled with a multitude of press conferences, "get acquainted lunches," and endless "photo opportunities." Each evening we attended one star-studded film premiere after the next, and every night we spent in the opulent harbor, yacht-hopping from party to party. By the end of the festival I was absolutely exhausted. When it was over I returned to Hollywood, only too glad to be back to the quiet and peaceful business of music.

On the morning of June 22, 1994, I woke up early as usual and made my calls to Europe. With eight hours' time difference to England, and even more for calls to the Continent, I was catching people just before they ended their day, or not at all. For some reason I encountered nothing but headaches, cancellations, and disappointing offers in calls to Europe and then the U.S. It was a day I should have stayed in bed. To compound my problem, I had been working overtime to finish this manuscript. I had only to finish this chapter, but I'd developed a serious case of writer's block. I had spent much of the previous week staring at the screen of my computer with nothing coming out. This day was the same. On a wild hair, I decided to take off and do something I hadn't had time to do in the three years that I'd lived in L.A. I decided to go to the beach and just lie on the sand in the sun.

At about five o'clock I left to go home, but as I passed Gladstone's 4 Fish my stomach began to growl, so I pulled in for a quick bite to eat. I took a booth on the outside deck overlooking the ocean and ordered a meal. And who should sit down in the next booth? Bruce Springsteen. The Boss!

Coincidentally, it was the second time I'd seen him in less than a week, having been introduced to him only a few days before by Trudie Styler, Sting's wife, at the showing of a documentary film she'd produced about the ill treatment and human rights violations of dissidents in China, *Moving the Mountain*, written and directed by Michael Apted. It was a star-studded charity affair attended by the likes of Dustin Hoffman, Branford Marsalis, Julian Sands, my brother Stewart, and of course, Bruce. I was honored to meet him, if only briefly, and what made it all the more poignant was the fact that I had been listening to the CD of his latest single almost nonstop for the few weeks prior to this. I have an annoying habit of playing my current favorite song over and over again until it drives people crazy. It so happened that Bruce's "Philadelphia" was the current top of my hit parade.

So when he sat down and took off his dark glasses, our eyes met, and there was a glimmer of recognition. I didn't think he'd remember, so I reintroduced myself.

"Yeah, hey, good to see ya again," he said. "Why dont'cha c'mon over and join me?"

"You sure you want company?" I asked. I hadn't meant to intrude on his space.

"I've been locked in the studio so long I was goin' nuts," he said. "So I jumped on my motorcycle just to get away, and I just ended up here at the beach. Been by myself all day. Yeah, I could use someone to talk to."

"No shit?" I said. "Same with me. Don't mind if I do."

I sat down at his table and we shot the shit for over an hour. It was small talk mostly, but it was casual, like we'd known each other for a long time. We talked about O.J. Simpson's murder charge, and the crazy car chase down the freeway watched by people all over the world on TV. We talked about the earthquake, and laughed about how we still suffered from aftershock paranoia, how every time we felt a heavy truck go by outside or a pet jump on the bed in the middle of the night it made us jittery. We talked about the riots and hysteria that followed the Rodney King trial, and I told him how I had been roped in by my nervous neighbors to set up armed roadblocks at the bottom of our hill. We talked about what we liked about living in L.A., and what we didn't. I thought it bizarre that here I was, the boy from Beirut with The Boss from New Jersey, sharing experiences that made us bona fide citizens of Los Angeles.

Just then, one of three ladies in the next booth asked Bruce if he'd mind having his picture taken, explaining, as if it might make a difference, that they were from "back east," and that they were big fans. Bruce graciously accommodated them, and invited them into his booth for the snapshot. They didn't expect it, and from their squealing it was obvious they considered themselves the luckiest people on earth. They were so excited and thankful, and kept saying "Oh my God! Nobody back home's gonna believe this!"

After our meal, I remembered I was due at a screening and it was time to go, so I paid the bill and said good-bye to Bruce.

"Nice talkin' with you, Ian," he said. "See you around."

As I rode back to Hollywood the three ladies kept coming back to mind. I realized that their chance meeting with Bruce was a special moment in their lives, a story they'd tell for years to come. "Nobody's gonna believe this," they had said, and I suddenly felt the same way. Not just about meeting Bruce, but about all the other chance occurrences that have happened in my life. My life has been like that. A peculiar series of events that seem like they could only happen to someone else, but, in fact, happened to me. My life has been unusual. This is my story.

Born in the CIA

Wild thing . . . you make my heart sing.
—The Troggs

BEFORE I WAS born, my father planned to blow up the American Embassy, but I screwed that up. Right from the start I was trouble for my parents. I nearly killed my poor mother. While pregnant with me she contracted toxemia, a rare ailment which just happened to be particularly uncommon in the Middle East and a complete mystery to the Arab doctors in Damascus, Syria. My unborn body robbed her of the oxygen from her blood, which eventually caused her to faint and go into a deep coma. She was rushed to the hospital on April 25, 1949, and I was born prematurely, saving her life.

With a police escort and sirens blaring she was taken to the hospital in a limo belonging to the head of Syrian Security, a ruthless individual known as Colonel Adib Shishakly. It so happened that my father had been plotting with him at our house when I was persuaded to make my untimely arrival.

Dad's plan called for a few relatively harmless sticks of dynamite to be placed on the roof of the American Embassy. As the local CIA representative, a gambler in the game of nations, he simply needed to create an incident which could be blamed on the Communists, and thereby show that the current Syrian government was too weak to protect its foreign diplomats. His ultimate goal was to give friendly Colonel Adib Shishakly an excuse to stage a coup d'état and install a government that would cooperate with Uncle Sam by making peace with Israel.

My early arrival caused the whole plan to be moved up by two weeks, since both my father and Adib had conspired with the doctors to concoct their alibis, and instead of blowing a few tiles off the roof of the embassy, Dad chose to stage a raid on our now-vacant house on the embassy compound. The hastily revised plan called for a few thugs, employed by my dad, to pump a few pistol shots through the window, while Pop was safe in a center room, conveniently on the phone to Washington. But something, apparently, went drastically wrong.

Instead the assailants showed up heavily armed with submachine guns, and they didn't quit after a few shots. It soon became obvious that they were hell-bent on actually assassinating my old man. Dad had been double-crossed. Faded newspaper clippings in the family scrapbook describe how Dad held off the attackers armed with only a pistol, and one of Dad's lines from the event is still told on the Washington cocktail circuit. If I remember it rightly, he was on the phone to Kermit Roosevelt (a grandson of President Theodore Roosevelt) at CIA Headquarters in Langley, Virginia, when he realized his plan had backfired: "Sorry," he said. "I'll have to hang up now. They're shooting at me personally."

In any event, the raid lit the fuse that started the revolution that put Adib's man in as prime minister of Syria (Husni El Za'im, for anyone interested in Syrian politics). And so I was born to the sounds of rolling tanks and pounding artillery.

Before my first birthday, Colonel Adib Shishakly decided to seize the reins of power for himself. On the morning of August 14, 1949, a group of Syrian army colonels, fronted by one Sami Hennawi but actually led by Shishakly, surrounded Za'im's house and killed him. Exactly four months later, Shishakly jailed Hennawi and ran the country himself, eventually electing himself president of Syria. As if to show his great appreciation of my father's covert talents, he promptly threw the whole Copeland family out of the country.

This was not the last time we were forced to flee a country due to my father's clandestine activities. From Syria we returned to the United States to reside in Alexandria, Virginia, close to CIA head-quarters in Langley. When my youngest brother Stewart was born a year or so later, we were relocated to Cairo, Egypt, our home for the next four years.

Growing up in the Middle East made its mark on me. From what I'm told, my babyhood was one long horror story. The start was modest enough, although somewhat symbolic: I peed all over my father the first time he tried to change my diapers. When I was a little older I fell out of a window from the second floor of our house and landed unhurt only inches away from a jagged tree stump. Then I fell into a snake-infested lily pond in our backyard in Cairo, and was rescued by the family dog, whose barking alerted my older brother, Miles. According to family lore, Miles pulled me out seconds before a poisonous snake (an asp perhaps?) was able to sink its teeth into me. One day, while playing cowboys and Indians in the shadows of the Sphinx, I crawled under some barbed wire near the pyramids, and fell—or almost fell—into one of the air shafts leading down to the as yet undiscovered tomb of some nameless pharaoh. All this doesn't add up to *Romancing the Stone,* but as infant adventure it was exciting enough.

My dad, meanwhile, was having adventures of his own, but at the adult level. A Good Old Boy at large in the political fun house of the Cold War Middle East, Dad was purposefully vague about his vocation, making oblique references to us kids about oil company "interests." What he was really interested in was that particularly nasty brand of hardball The Company excelled in during the glory days of the mid 1950s. And what he couldn't tell us then came out years later in his three books—*The Game of Nations, The Real Spy World,* and *The Game Player*—cowboy operatives orchestrating assassinations, coups, palace revolts. The plum of his portfolio was the overthrow of the Iranian prime minister Mohammed Mossadegh, setting the stage for the Shah's return to his "rightful" perch on the Peacock Throne and two decades of oil-fueled Westernization culminating in the revolt of the Mullahs.

In the fall of 1947, while serving as CIA station chief in Damascus, my father became the first Westerner to get his hands on the Dead Sea Scrolls, the oldest biblical manuscripts in existence.* One day an Arab Bedouin showed up at the American Embassy with a burlap sack full of moldy old parchments he wanted to sell. As was often the case, my father suspected them of being clever fakes made to peddle to tourists. But they seemed authentic, so he took a team of cameramen up to the roof of the embassy and had them photographed. Unfortunately, it was a windy day, and several pieces of the precious parchment blew away, but the rest of it was documented for the first time in history.

For obvious reasons, throughout our childhood we never knew what Dad did for a living, and we were not encouraged to ask. Years later when I was old enough to read and understand old newspaper clippings about him that he'd saved I realized he'd been quite a character.

He was born in Birmingham, Alabama, where his father was a doctor and his mother was a schoolteacher. Due to a long childhood bout with tuberculosis, he spent a good deal of time at home as a kid. While confined to bed he learned to play trumpet, and later spent most of his youth traveling around the South playing in various jazz bands. He played with the Glenn Miller Band, though I should mention that it riled him when we'd brag to friends about it; he'd say he'd played with lots better, some bands I've never heard of. My father was a real muso.

During World War II, as a member of the Office of Strategic Services, he'd played the role of a German spy just to find out what a real German spy might accomplish in spite of the American Army's security controls. He did this first in Washington, then in London, and when General Eisenhower's forces invaded Europe, he went along as part of a team seeking out German intelligence officers who could help us do some spying in the next war. Already, with World

---

* *The Dead Sea Scrolls Deception* by Michael Baigert and Richard Leigh: Touchstone Books, published by Simon & Schuster, 1991. Page 10.

War II not yet won, the U.S. was preparing for the Cold War with the Russians.

Somewhere along the line, he met the daughter of a prominent doctor from Edinburgh. A pretty Scottish lass, Elizabeth Lorraine Adie was working for British Intelligence in the planning of sabotage missions behind enemy lines. As an agent for SOE (Special Operations Executive) she specialized in blowing up bridges and derailing German troop trains. After a few months of wartime courtship, the two were married in a fashionable church in the West End of London, and one year later my older brother, Miles, was born in a war-damaged hospital in Hampstead.

With London as the pivot point, the family traveled extensively for the next few years, back and forth to Washington, where my sister, Lorraine (Lennie) Leonora, was born, and where my father helped the postwar government to organize the best elements of all the various secret services, and form the Central Intelligence Agency. From there he was sent to fight the Cold War in the Middle East, and from 1947 to 1957 he planned, directed, or otherwise participated in fourteen "political action operations" in Africa and Asia. "Political action," an essential part of the CIA's mission, included the following:

- Rigging elections—or, in some cases, preventing the rigging of elections;

- Organizing coups d'état, or assisting governments in power in preventing being overthrown by coups d'état;

- Boosting carefully chosen political groups or individual politicians, either by secret financial assistance or by covert propaganda to help them or to damage their enemies;

- Other types of covert activity designed to bring about, in any country or geographical region, political circumstances favoring "peace and security in the area"—i.e., immunity to Soviet or pro-Soviet influence, or protection of American interests in general.

In Egypt his mission for the CIA was to find and establish a "suitable" leader to replace the highly unpopular King Farouk. In other words, someone sympathetic to Uncle Sam. They thought they had found such a candidate in Gamal Abdel Nasser, a bright young colo-nel in the Egyptian army, and through him organized a coup d'état that overthrew the monarchy in July of 1952.

As is typical of the kind of thing my father would do, he made Nasser my godfather, and maintained a friendship with him that lasted until Nasser became president, at which time Dad became one of his "advisors." At the same time, he was running around the globe on various other missions for the CIA, organizing coups d'état and playing with politics. In 1953 he helped to organize the over-throw of Mossadegh in Iran.

But I wouldn't know it if I hadn't researched it. At the time I was concerned with kindergarten, and making friends, and normal things that kids do. My older sister and I spoke Arabic before we spoke English, partly as a result of being brought up by Palestinian nannies. Instead of candy we ate dates, and we ate our cereal with goat's milk, and instead of playing Monopoly, our favorite game was a board game named "al hayah w'al sulum," which could be trans-lated into either "snakes and ladders," or the game of life.

Our spell in Egypt came to an abrupt end when, feeling betrayed by the Americans after Israel, France, and Great Britain invaded the Sinai, President Nasser closed down the U.S. Embassy and expelled the entire staff. A friend on Nasser's staff warned Dad of a plot to assassinate him, so we were evacuated from Cairo with less than a day's notice. From there we relocated to another Middle Eastern capital, the bustling city of Beirut, Lebanon.

Beirut was a center of intrigue and espionage, and at the same time an intellectual center (four universities), banking center, and fun city for rich folks of all nationalities who came there to enjoy the beach clubs, discos, nightclubs, boutiques, gourmet restaurants, lux-ury cinemas, Levantine architecture, and all the fleshpots they'd find in the South of France, only lusher and more colorful. Lebanon in those days was not the place one thinks of today. To the contrary, it was heaven on earth, and Beirut, right there on the still unpol-luted eastern end of the Mediterranean, was a wonderful place in which to grow up. The environment was somehow suitable for the nurturing of the "problem child" I was set to be.

As it was, the sultans and sheiks of neighboring Arab countries, eager to enjoy their wealth, found this seaside paradise particularly attractive. Strict Moslem laws threw a serious damper on the social scene in most other places, so oil money flowed like water in Beirut, the capital of the only Christian Arab country. On the surface it looked as richly Western as, say, San Francisco. But a visitor didn't have to peek very far beneath the surface to find "the mysterious East," complete with bazaars, ancient mosques, coffee houses, and mezze places with belly dancers. I guess everyone needs a place to have their childhood, and I couldn't have picked a better one from the pages of *Arabian Nights*.

Behind Beirut stood majestic Mount Lebanon, one of a rocky range of mountains stretching from the northern end of the country all the way down to Israel. In the spring you could be sunning on one of the sandy white beaches along the Mediterranean, and only a few hours later be skiing on the slopes, slaloming through those Cedars of Lebanon mentioned in the Bible. When we weren't in school, our parents took us on picnics all up and down the Lebanese coast and across to Syria and Jordan. We'd play hide-and-seek in the ruins of old civilizations while the old folks admired the scenery, and while kids back in the States were playing cowboys and Indians, we were playing Crusader and Saracens, in real Crusader castles.

Along the coastline to the south there were ruins at Tyre and Sidon, once thriving Phoenician seaports, and to the north the remains of an ancient civilization at Byblos, which gave the Bible its name. My favorite was Baalbek, in the Bekaa Valley, a whole city of remarkably preserved Roman temples. I kissed my first girl there in the Temple of Jupiter, a cute little English girl named Anne Philby. Her parents, Eleanor and Kim Philby, were my folk's best friends, or so I thought, and were frequent companions for picnics. While the parents were wandering around taking photos, Anne and I would sneak off together in the ruins, to do a little exploring of our own.

Neither Anne Philby nor I knew it, of course, but *both* our fathers were spies. Kim Philby was once a high-ranking official in MI6 (Britain's equivalent to the CIA). American Intelligence, however, suspected Philby of being the traitor within British Intelligence passing secrets to the Communists, infamously known as "The Third Man." British Intelligence refused to believe it, but they were pressured to put him to pasture. He then became the Beirut correspondent for two British newspapers, *The Observer* and *The Economist*, while main-

Wild Thing

taining his connections with MI6. From 1956 until early in 1963, the CIA was paying my dad to watch him.

Early on the evening of January 23, 1963, my mom and dad went to collect the Philbys on their way to a cocktail party, only to find that Kim wasn't coming. He said he was tired, and that they and his wife, Eleanor, should go on without him. He said perhaps he'd meet them there later. But he never did show up at the party, and he wasn't home when they returned to drop off Eleanor. Nor was he ever seen again this side of the Iron Curtain.

My mother, through all of this, became a highly respected Holy Land archaeologist and pre-historian. In fact, she looks on anything this side of 30,000 B.C. as contemporary. She's written several books on her subject, but they're written for other archaeologists and are full of highly technical data. You wouldn't want to read them unless you were extremely interested in what man was doing back before the Ice Age. Which isn't much. Mom's bag is flints and what Stone Age man did with them, but she also has a professional understanding of the ancient civilizations, rulers, and invaders that left their ruins, monuments, Crusader castles, Moslem forts, Phoenician seaports, Greek temples, and Roman baths all over the Middle East.

With Mom's interest in archaeology, and Dad's working for the CIA, the Copeland family lived and socialized on the intersection between university people and Beirut's "real world" of high-powered businessmen, fast-talking promoters, intelligence operatives, white slavers, and shady characters of a dozen varieties. When Anthony Quayle, the British writer and Shakespearean actor, visited Beirut to get material for a novel he was writing, he asked Dad's help in getting to meet some of the leading figures in Beirut's underworld, and Dad said, sure, we'd have them all to dinner. Mr. Quayle noted Mom's hesitation, and he said, "Oh, I wouldn't ask you to have such people in your home," and Mom replied that having them in our home was not the problem. The dilemma was one of protocol, a delicate matter of seating arrangements at the dinner table. The owner of the biggest brothels in the Beirut area was an archimandrite of the Greek Orthodox Church, the leading trafficker in drugs was a member of the House of Parliament, the head of the Lebanese Mafia was a minister-without-portfolio in the government, and so on. In Beirut, the "best people" ran all the vice and crime.

As foreigners in Lebanon we lived in a glass bowl, enjoying a privileged existence. The Lebanese were a mercantile, friendly people, with a great sense of humor. They had been doing business with foreigners for centuries, and probably sold Chiclets to the Crusaders. Tourism was serious business in Lebanon, and since foreigners brought wealth, they were provided a special status as welcome guests.

I certainly had no complaints. In fact, I grew up thinking we were stinking rich. We certainly lived like we were. Our house, Villa Tarazi, was a virtual palace, and we had a large staff of maids, cooks, chauffeurs, and gardeners to serve us. Dad's monthly income was more than an ordinary Lebanese citizen could earn in a year, so we lived like kings. Or so it was explained to me at the time. I had no idea that one of my father's missions was to pry secrets from foreign dignitaries and such with lots of booze and lavish parties, and that we were most likely operating on some sort of CIA "lush fund." As for myself, I got an allowance that was more than I could possibly spend. Can you imagine such a thing as too much allowance?

I would spend nearly ten years in Beirut, which made me an expert on the myriad array of illicit kicks available. That, and perhaps the fact that I had an excess of mischievous energy, made me popular with my playmates, some of whom were Arabs but most of whom were from the large communities of Americans and Europeans. Most of these were embassy brats who'd stay for only a year or two, then move on as their parents were reassigned elsewhere.

My friends at the American Community School, where I started in third grade, stayed mostly to themselves and behaved as though they were back in Dallas, Texas, or Arlington, Virginia, or any other American town. A large percentage were boarders, the sons and daughters of American oilmen in Arabia and surrounding Arab countries, and rarely mixed with the locals. Since I knew my way around the country and spoke Arabic, I was pretty much the "Big Man on Campus," second to my best friend Tom Najemy, who was an even bigger smart aleck than I was in class, and who'd been in Beirut longer than I had.

In the Moslem section of Beirut where we lived it was different. The kids on my street were of many different nationalities, since ours was one of the favorite areas for foreign embassies. Not all of

WILD THING

the same tongue, we kids had to communicate by way of sign language most of the time, and our games were all a sort of "follow the leader." As we got older this grew into a "Daredevil Club," a group of ten or twelve of us whose leader was the one most willing to dare, like climbing the farthest up the side of a building to the highest floor. I remember I topped everybody off in that game. I scaled up about ten floors. Then I made the mistake of looking down, and in sheer panic, I broke into a strange apartment. The gang all thought that I had been incredibly brave going into the apartment, but I was just too scared to climb back down. After that, though, I was always expected to go one step closer to the edge than anyone else.

It drove my mom crazy. Especially since Stewart, who was almost three years younger than I, insisted on following me around and doing all the things I did. I'd beat him up all the time but he'd still keep following me. (As I look back on it, I think I was careful to hit him in a perfect rhythm, which may account for his ability to keep the beat so perfectly in later years.) But we soon found a use for him. Mom found out we were training him to sneak ice cream from the local grocery store, and she got Dad to get the belt out. He'd give me the old "Believe me, this is going to hurt me more than it's going to hurt you, son." Yeah, right. Like hell it is.

It was a tough neighborhood, by any definition. We were constantly getting into fights with the Arab gangs from the nearby refugee shanty towns, where Palestinians dreamed of vengeance in shacks made of flattened oil drums and cardboard. These were kids whose parents were routed from their homeland by American-made tanks and bombers, and they weren't too fond of us Yankees, or foreigners in general. The fight would almost always start with some kid running up to say "You shut up," which, for some reason it would take an anthropologist to explain, is the first phrase an Arab kid learns as he tries to pick up English. Anyway, it's considered a terrific insult by the Arabs, and its use normally causes an outbreak of the Lebanese national sport—a friendly exchange of flying boulders, any one of which could crush your head, but backed up, all the same, by accurately aimed slingshots. Let me tell you, most Arab kids are pretty good with a slingshot.

But it was all good clean fun most of the time, for a while anyway. Then, when I was almost ten, it began to get nasty. The skirmishes with the refugee kids grew into pitched battles, then all-out war. Whereas we used to take a dirt path lined with cactus through the refugee camp to get to Smith's Grocery Store, where all the American candies were sold, now we had to take the long way around or we were sure to get jumped. Friends of mine were getting beat up all the time. I would have understood it better if I knew what my father knew, because it all had to do with what he was up to.

The grown-ups were getting serious too. It was 1958, and various local events, most of them trivial, combined to set off the first Lebanese civil war, with Moslems shooting Christians, Christians shooting Moslems, Moslems shooting Moslems, and Christians shooting Christians. Nasser attempted to topple the existing government in order to install a puppet regime that would join his plans for a United Arab Republic, which the current government opposed, and the fighting soon spread to the masses. A government of sorts remained in power, and in frantic attempts to "Do something, anything!" just to show it still existed, it imposed curfews, put soldiers at street corners, set up roadblocks and sandbags, and raced fire engines and ambulances up and down the streets, sirens wailing.

To us kids, it was all a pain in the ass, with the occasional gun battle interfering with our games of kick-the-can and hide-and-seek, but when we got used to it, we saw new opportunities for fun and mischief. We walked the walls at night while heavy curfew was on, tossed the odd brickbat at passing police cars, and continued to steal chocolate bars from Smith's Grocery Store and to commit the other kinds of mischief that constitute normal behavior for nine-year-old kids in an anarchic environment like that of Lebanon.

As things grew more dangerous, the U.S. Embassy ordered all American families to evacuate the country immediately, and most of my friends were shipped to Athens or Rome temporarily, though some were sent home to the States and I never saw them again. For some reason, though, our family stayed in Beirut.

Day by day the situation grew worse. When Smith's Grocery Store went up in smoke, having taken a direct hit from a bomb or a mortar, I began to realize how serious things were. There was a real honest-to-God revolution going on! It got worse. One morning we woke up to the sound of gunfire and tanks tearing up the roads. One tank pulled into the driveway that led to the parking lot under our building and began firing away. Fearful that it would attract return fire, my father went downstairs and bribed the tank driver to find another spot.

Then, a bomb went off in the building next to ours and blew out most of the glass from all the buildings on the block, including ours. Our particular building was high on a hill overlooking the city, and we were protected from direct hits by inset balconies, but our main balcony was a ringside seat from which we could see across the fields all the way down to the beach, and the area where most of the action was taking place.

We stayed holed up indoors for several days, with only the occasional trip for provisions, or to walk the dog, who refused to acknowledge there was a war on and wouldn't shit in the apartment to save his life. The phones didn't work much at the best of times, and now they didn't work at all. Our only form of communication with the outside world was through a monstrous ship-to-shore radio, which Dad stayed glued to most of the time.

On the morning of July 4, 1958, we saw what the old man was waiting for. We looked out to the Mediterranean to see it filled with a whole fleet of U.S. Navy ships extending all the way to the horizon, an awesome sight indeed. Battleships, cruisers, destroyers, and a flotilla of transport ships crowded the sea. Coming from them were a hundred or so LST boats carrying U.S. Marines, all screaming when they hit the beach in the way they'd been taught to do in boot camp.

In Lebanon, however, screaming is only a minor art form. The Marines came prepared for battle, and came charging up the beach expecting to meet a hail of bullets. Instead, they were greeted by swarms of merchants, ragged-ass kids selling Chiclets, and others with the Lebanese knack of recognizing commercial opportunities when they saw them. It took less than a day for the whole Beirut beachfront to turn into one big makeshift marketplace, and only a few hours more for the Marines to turn from warlike to peaceful, and then to lustful. To answer their needs, the nightclubs took to staying open twenty-four hours a day, and in no time Beirut returned to business as usual.

As it happened, I too was afforded the opportunity to profit from the situation. Not that I'm too proud of it, actually. I was down at my parents' beach cabin, checking out the action, when a Marine approached me and offered to pay what was to me a huge sum of money just to take a hike for fifteen minutes and let him and his "girlfriend" use the cabin. Pretty soon I was making a fortune renting the place out. As I look back on it I realize, with some shame and a touch of embarrassment, that for my first business enterprise I was basically running a whorehouse.

CHAPTER 3

Boys in Beirut

I was living in a . . . fool's paradise.
—Ricky Nelson

WITH THE PRESENCE of the United States Marines, a certain semblance of order was restored in Beirut, and Dad was allowed to take leave. He took the opportunity to take his family to London, to show us off to our relatives on my mother's side of the family. It was in London that the Copeland family "got its act together," as Dad was to say thirty years later when he sat down to write the family history. We developed into "a true Copeland cast of characters, all individuals but related to one another like parts in a play."

Dad put us in a mansion-sized house in snooty St. John's Wood overlooking Lord's Cricket Ground, and, over our strong objections, enrolled us in the American School of London in Regents Park. Not that there was anything wrong with the school; it was just that we thought we deserved a vacation, and dropping into school at the end of term made it hard to make friends.

As it was, each sibling was now separated from the individual support systems, our own friends and gangs, and we were forced to turn to each other in what was, at least to us kids, a strange land. The other thing about our stay in London was that we got to see a lot more of the old man. In Beirut he was away from home much of the time, traveling all over the Middle East and Africa. Even when he was home he was often too busy partying to pay us much mind. But now that we were in London, he spent all his time with the family and we got to know each other better than had been possible in Beirut, where life had a powerful centrifugal force.

For the first time, Dad talked to us about the world and what was going on in it, painting even the wars and the bloodshed as inescapable facts of life. He tried to give us a perspective on the life ahead of us. There were many things I didn't agree with, but there was one thing I *did* agree with. He said that everyone should have an interest outside himself, an obsession, something he or she can be better at than everyone else, even if it's only stamp collecting or tap dancing. It was around this idea that our family developed, and we spent six months in London cultivating it.

Well, the others did, anyway. As for myself, I spent most of the time in London vegging out in front of the TV set. Television was taken for granted by other kids, even in England where there were only two channels, with boring gardening shows and horse races until late in the afternoon—but there was no TV in Beirut. For the first time, I was actually able to see what life was like in America, and like so many others around the globe whose only view of America was through television, I thought it was all *Leave It to Beaver,* or *Dennis the Menace.*

My sister, Lennie, divided her time between reading good literature and dissecting frogs. She was the scholar in the family, the intellectual, but she also had an adventurous streak, and she always gave as good as she got in any family feuds. She never took any crap from us boys—or any other boys, for that matter. In London, Lennie took on the task of teaching piano to our youngest brother, Stewart, employing what I call the "Hitler Method" of instruction. Stewart absolutely hated it, but Lennie would force him to sit for hours at the keyboard to ensure that he learned the basics. When he refused to practice, Lennie would deprive him of dinner, only to serve it to him for breakfast—cold. As much as he hated it, this was Stewart's first introduction to music, at the age of six, and it served him well in the years ahead. From then on, no teacher was too tough to endure.

Miles had two "obsessions," as Dad called them. One of them was music. He spent much of his time in London hanging around the record store near our house, soaking up as much new music as he possibly could. Records were unavailable back in Beirut, so Miles knew he had to stock up while he had the chance. I've heard people ask: "If you were stuck on a desert island, and had to chose ten records, which would you choose?" It was like that for Miles. He would listen for hours to all the 45s on the hit parade, including the B-sides, just to select the best of the bunch for his precious collection. On one trip to the store, he let me pick out a single, my first record. Much to his dismay, and over all his objections, I chose "Fool's Paradise," a wimpy love song by Ricky Nelson.

His other "obsession" was judo. Every morning, rain or shine (I seem to remember it was mostly rain the whole time we were there), he'd march down to the Budokwai to learn judo throws from a Scotland Yard bobby who had won his black belt in Japan. Before we left London Miles had worked his way up to a brown belt, and when we got back to Beirut it took him less than a year to get his black belt.

In school, Miles was never more than a solid B-average student, but only because he was so distracted by his other interests. Instead of studying, he was busy collecting ancient artifacts, or inventing elaborate board games. To me and my friends back in Beirut, he wasn't a normal teenager at all. While other kids were partying, going to movies, or getting themselves entangled in various mischievous enterprises, Miles would be down at the gym practicing his judo and karate, two sports that were at the time virtually unheard of outside of Japan. He took his judo to the extreme, taking up Shinto philosophy, diet and all. He would eat only yogurt, carrots, and tomatoes, and no "poisons" such as coffee or chocolate. He nearly caused a revolution in the Copeland household when he made all the servants give up smoking. (At age ten, I had been the first person in my class to give up smoking, but when Miles made a big issue of it, I started up again as sort of a one-child protest movement.)

He almost caused another revolution in his gymnasium when he refused to take bribes from the other judokas to let them win their

47   WILD THING

matches every now and then. He was only sixteen when he got a summer job training the Lebanese army in self-defense, taking me along to serve as his dummy, the fall guy. As it turned out, I ended up with an orange belt in judo myself, along with a few black and blues.

At the end of the summer, a local wrestling promoter put on an exhibition match between Miles and a Lebanese opponent named Khalil Abu Khalil, who was the current World Champion of Pungras, a sport popular in Greece and the Middle East that combines boxing, wrestling, and ordinary street-style dirty fighting. A ten-year-old school friend of mine and I were the opening act, going over big because we made a kind of Three Stooges thing out of it, throwing each other around in a way calculated to amuse the audience. Then Miles came into the ring, and the crowd turned deadly serious. His muscle-bound Lebanese opponent, having been the World Champion for years, was their hero, and the script called for Miles to lose to him. But Miles, the incorruptible, would have none of it. Instead, he whipped the guy's ass so badly that by the time he tried to leave the stadium an angry mob had gathered outside, and we had to be whisked away through a back entrance and into an embassy car.

If Miles could whip the World Champion of Pungras, it followed that he could lick anyone else in Lebanon, but this didn't make Miles a bully. To the contrary, his confidence showed so clearly that he didn't feel a need to prove himself.

I looked up to Miles, but I think even then I sensed the difference between us. Miles was wound tight, focused and driven. I was all over the place, like an accident waiting to happen

In the fall of 1962, Miles went off to the States for his freshman year at Birmingham Southern College in Alabama, and I didn't see him again for several years. With him gone, and Dad now always away from home, I suddenly found myself as the male head of the family. Not that this made me any more responsible. In fact, just the opposite. I had nobody to keep me in line.

I never took school very seriously, at least not academically. School was for clowning in class, fighting in the playgrounds, and getting into the kinds of trouble that our inventive minds could concoct. My behavior didn't please the teachers, though, so I was a regular visitor to the office of our infamous principal, Dr. Knox. He was a tyrant of the first order, who was determined to make ACS the highest-rated school in the world just to ensure his getting a better job back in the States. His method of doing so was simply to get rid of anyone with bad grades or a rebellious nature. I was terrified of him at the time.

The American Community School in Lebanon made the same pretense of democratic student government as all schools like it make, and student democracy was *one* feature of the school that I did take seriously. Miles had been president of his class the senior year, and I decided I would try to carry on the family tradition. Miles had made the grade in student politics in spite of his constantly being at odds with Dr. Knox, so I saw no reason why the old tyrant should stand in the way of my ambitions.

But he did. I won our eighth-grade election for class president, but on the grounds that I was both a lousy student and a troublemaker, Dr. Knox arbitrarily disqualified me. He compounded this tyrannical act by replacing me with some nerd who, on his own, couldn't have gotten himself elected as school toilet cleaner. I was outraged. I'd tolerated the old fart's messing with me, but now he was messing with *democracy!*

I wasn't the only one who was outraged. I was at Sheik Salim's coffeehouse with ten or twelve friends, celebrating my supposed victory, when we heard the bad news. We didn't take the tidings at all well, and my classmates and I proceeded in mob formation to the ACS assembly hall where we staged a "peaceful protest." Well, it was supposed to be peaceful, anyway, but it soon got out of hand.

The next thing I knew, I was standing up before Dr. Knox in his office. This time he called in my parents, so I knew my goose was cooked. I didn't find this out until many years later, but what happened was this: Mom went into the principal's office first, while Dad parked the car. When he came in, Dad found Dr. Knox sitting back with his feet propped up on the desk. He was playing with his ruler, making a helicopter by spinning it on his fingertip, while lecturing Mom on what a bad kid she'd raised. Dad told Dr. Knox he'd do well to take his feet off the desk, get off of his fat ass and stand up when a guest entered, and act as though he had some manners with a lady in the room. Knox didn't move fast enough to suit Dad, who took

WILD THING

Mom by the arm and left the office without a further word. I was expelled from school.

Since I was unaware of what had happened in Dr. Knox's office, I believed that this expulsion was all my own doing, and Dad made the most of it. To start with, not only was my allowance docked, and any privileges I had rescinded, but I was forced to spend that whole summer locked in my room reading books. I didn't just have to read them, I had to give in-depth reports on each one. To me at the time, this was the worst punishment possible.

But, as they say, every cloud has a silver lining. Most of my friends thought being thrown out of school was pretty cool. It gave me a certain notoriety, and in the Beirut of 1961, notoriety was better than fame. I was bad, with a double *D*. I suppose that's when I started to gravitate to, as Dad would say, the "wrong crowd."

I next did time at an English school called Manor House, in the hills just outside of Beirut. It was very different from ACS. Suddenly the emphasis shifted from algebra, chemistry, and sports to Latin, Shakespeare, and poetry. We had one class called "general knowledge" which was essentially a course on trivia. All the tests were essay instead of multiple choice. It was a much smaller school, without all the facilities we had at ACS—no gym, no theater, no football field, and no student's lounge to hang out in after school. As a result it was less insular than ACS had been. The students at Manor House mingled with the Lebanese society to a much greater extent than the pampered students at ACS.

The kids of Beirut, Arabs and foreigners alike, were already divided into groups by age, language, and cultural background, each group having its favorite hangouts. But there was a lot of overlapping. On any given day of the week, from dawn to the dead of night, there was a party going on somewhere, if not at the Neptune Bar & Grill, where the cultured heirs of English ambassadors drank themselves into a stupor, then over at the Al Hamra Bowling Alley, notorious hangout for the Aussies, or at Le Carousel, the French pub of choice. The surfing gang hung out at whichever beach had the waves, or wherever there was even the hint of a party. Then there were the motorcycle gangs who congregated at various coffee shops such as Uncle Sam's and Sheik Salim's, where they just sat around shooting the shit and looking for parties to crash. It helped that there was no minimum drinking age in Lebanon.

The mood in Beirut then was peaceful. The natives were quick to cater to the whims of the Westerners, and so they started to form bands to play at parties, discos, and beach clubs. These were mixed-national groups playing copies of Western hits, and even though most of them couldn't understand the lyrics or speak the language, they still managed to reproduce the songs we heard on BBC World Service, broadcasts of the British hit parade. In 1963, The Beatles landed at Beirut Airport as a stop on their world tour, causing such a commotion that Beirut was never the same afterward. There were mob scenes and screaming girls, and it nearly caused a riot. From then on, nearly every kid in town picked up a guitar or grabbed a microphone or a pair of sticks, and bands were being formed all over the place.

The most popular band was called The Nomads, a group of teen-agers whose drummer was Ahmed Mamlouk, a Syrian kid living in exile in Lebanon while his father, a former prime minister of Syria, was in jail in Damascus. The Nomads were unusual in that they had an American in the band, and Pete Wybro, the bass player, was a friend of mine, so I often went along to the gigs to give a hand with the equipment and to help Ahmed set up his drums. Usually I spent my time at the gigs doing nothing more than checking out the girls, but I soon inherited the job of collecting money owed to the group after it had gone on stage. This was my first taste of the music business, and before long I'd mastered every trick a club owner can use to avoid giving a group their full payment.

Ahmed, the drummer, was a very special character. Nicknamed "Blondie" since he'd bleached his hair blond and let it grow long, he was the coolest kid in town—so out-cooling me, in fact, that he swiped my first girlfriend, a pretty Scottish lass named Fiona McRobert. The macho mentality reflected by his long blond hair (on a dark-skinned Arab) somehow fitted the rebellious mood in Lebanon at the time, and Blondie became a cult figure overnight. He and I became best friends, and before long, business partners.

Blondie was one hell of a politician, Middle Eastern style, and he

WILD THING

knew everybody in Beirut who had any connection with the youth scene. It was only natural that at one point the two of us should be approached by the owner of Le Fin du Monde, one of Beirut's largest and most popular stereo clubs (i.e., discos), to help him work out special means for attracting customers. Le Fin du Monde already had flashing lights and effects, a great dance floor, and a brilliant sound system, and it was situated on Al Hamra Street, the Sunset Strip of Beirut. But there was a new disco across the street that had invested in a bigger mirror ball, or something like that, and the owner of Le Fin du Monde was losing out to it—so much so that he was about to go broke, leaving The Nomads without a venue. In coming to Blondie and me, he'd come to the right people.

After a bit of take-it-or-leave-it negotiating, the owner put us in charge of turning the place around for him, and agreed to a deal whereby we'd get a big share of the profits. After having a few friends redecorate the place, we threw an opening rave party that was the talk of the town, helping to get the club reestablished as the "in" place for all the gangs and their girlfriends.

Naturally, The Nomads were the featured group on opening night, but just to make it a very special event we also put on two other local bands, The Black Knights and The Vultures. We promoted it as "Beirut Rocks—Lebanon's First Rock Concert." Between bands, we played records of all the latest music, whatever we could get our hands on from England and the States, with Blondie and I taking turns as DJ. On opening night it was packed, and it stayed that way for months, until we fell out with the owner.

To begin with it was great, and Blondie and I strutted around like we owned the place. Club owners at the age of fifteen! Then one night Blondie and I sat down with the real owner to settle up. We learned Lesson Number One in the business: *never*, never make a deal by which you are paid out of net instead of gross. Week after week we could see the money rolling in, but when it came time to settle up, the club owner gave us a pile of phony bills and a lot of bullshit to explain why we were barely breaking even. There was no net profit, or so he claimed. Out of the goodness of his heart, he gave us each a hundred Lebanese pounds.

Blondie and I decided we'd been had. So the following week we moved to another stereo club, an even glitzier place called The Montezuma, and we took our crowd with us. Within two months, Le Fin du Monde closed down for good.

Meanwhile, the music business was developing a family angle. Blondie got word that his father was dying in prison, so he had to leave abruptly for Damascus. The band, naturally, turned to me to replace him. There was only one problem; I couldn't play drums. "No problem," they said, "anyone can do it."

Well, anyone, perhaps, but me. It took me no time at all to learn that I couldn't hold a beat, and I didn't have the patience to keep practicing. Little brother Stewart, though, was fascinated by the exercise. From his bedroom he could hear me, playing along to a record and trying to figure it out, and it amazed him that I was having so much trouble. He picked up some sticks and began to play along on tin cans and cardboard album covers, and, lo and behold, he could do it with ease.

From then on, while I was flailing away at the drums, he stood lurking over me, like a vulture waiting for the lions to leave so he could get at the meat. But of course this only made me practice longer. When I finally would give up on Blondie's kit, he'd jump on the drums and beat them as though he'd been practicing for months. For the first time in his life, Stewart had found something he could do that his big brother couldn't.

When it came time for rehearsal, I convinced The Nomads to give Stewart a shot, and he easily got the gig. A few weeks later he performed with them at the American Embassy Beach Club, his first-ever live performance. The band went over extremely well, and they were called back for several encores. Immediately after the show Stewart was invited to become a permanent member. Fortunately for Stewart, it was his night for firsts. Later that evening he was hauled off to the beach by a sixteen-year-old groupie, and introduced to one of the perks that goes with being in a band. For the record, Stewart was twelve.

CHAPTER 4

THE KING OF DEATH

The leader of the pack...
—SHANGRI-LAS

In MY TEENAGE years I was afforded a fair amount of freedom, mostly because my father was almost never home. His CIA assignments kept him chasing off to Egypt, Iran, Iraq, or some obscure country in darkest Africa, and this kept him away for several weeks, sometimes months at a time.

More often than not, Mom was left to watch over Lennie, Stewart, and me (Miles being away at college), but she, too, was busy doing her own thing, becoming internationally famous as an archaeologist (at least to other archaeologists). Mom had little time for persons and problems of the here and now. She didn't exactly *ignore* us kids, but so long as she remained unaware of any problems, she left us alone.

I had a way of getting anything I wanted from Mom, since I knew exactly when to ask for it. Timing was everything. If you waited until she was in her "museum" at the back of our house, absorbed in her flints and artifacts, you could ask Mom for just about anything and get it. And that's exactly how I got my first motorcycle at the age of fifteen.

The purchase of my first bike, a shiny new Ducati 275 cc, made me officially a member of the much older motorcycle gang. This was the most elite of all the gangs in Beirut, since we could go where we wanted and do most anything. Our mobility was a passport to mischief.

The leader of the motorcycle gang was a great big guy from Texas, named John Wybro (brother of Pete Wybro, bass player of The Nomads). Aged nineteen, six feet tall, weighing about 220, and strong enough to push a car up a hill, he was leader not because of his physical qualifications but because he was the kind of lunatic that kids in Beirut admired. His motorcycle was only a Honda 300, but it was the fastest on the road at the time, and the way he rode it gave him opportunities to show just how crazy he was.

But if Wybro was "the leader of the pack," there existed in Beirut another character who stood above him in our eyes. If we were able to watch television in Lebanon, we would perhaps have recognized him as the Fonz but instead we knew him as Malakan Moot, which translates from Arabic to "the King of Death." He was an Armenian refugee kid who had a reputation among the older gang members for being even cooler than John Wybro, and as a new recruit I heard wild stories of him that made him into an almost mythical character, none of which I fully believed until the first time I saw him for real. We were loafing with the gang at Le Carousel, a popular sidewalk cafe, when the King of Death came riding down one-way Al Hamra Street—the wrong way. Standing straight up on the seat of his motorcycle with his arms folded across his chest, he was riding a BSA 650—the baddest bike we'd ever seen, and the loudest, as a result of having no mufflers. Without a word, we all jumped on our bikes and went after him.

The King of Death played with us. He'd let us catch up, or nearly, and then he'd zoom off again, leaving us to putter in the dust. The power of his 650 put our smaller bikes to shame, but it was his driving that blew us away. Totally ignoring all one-way street signs, stop signs, traffic lights, pedestrians, oncoming cars, or obstacles of any kind, he seemed oblivious to danger. And when he finally got bored with the game, he led us to El Nahr, ending the chase.

Even we knew better than to follow him into El Nahr, the Armenian refugee camp. When the Armenian Christians were driven out of Turkey and Russia, they were encouraged by the Christian-dominated minority government to settle in Lebanon as a way to increase their numbers, but they were blocked from actually becoming Lebanese citizens, so they set up in Beirut this enclave, a city-within-a-city, surrounded by hostile Lebanese Moslems. Sticking together tightly for protection, the Armenians organized their own police force and supplemented it with a kind of private army with which to fight the outside world when the necessity arose. Inevitably, El Nahr become sort of an Armenian Casbah, a redoubt area for fleeing criminals and social dropouts. It was so infested with professional killers, drug dealers, white slaves, and other forms of social outcasts that even the licensed-to-kill Lebanese security forces, the dreaded Squad Sixteen, dared not go there.

Now that we knew he actually existed, and especially because he had eluded us the King of Death soon became a hero to us all, John Wybro included. We were in absolute awe of him, and our already wildly exaggerated stories of him grew with each telling. In no time at all, he was a demigod. When we finally saw him again, he was flying full throttle down Rue Bliss, by Uncle Sam's, dodging trolley cars and traffic like he was on a slalom course. No sooner had he disappeared down the road when a Squad Sixteen police car came roaring past, sirens wailing. The King of Death was on the run, and we had one more story to add to the legend.

We did finally meet him. Big John Wybro and I were cruising along the corniche on our bikes one day, when the King of Death pulled up next to us. He spoke no English and very little Arabic, and neither of us knew a word of Armenian, so it was hard to communicate with him at first. He didn't say much in any case, but this only added to his mystique. The King had charisma, a kind of uncontested coolness; like the Fonz, but with James Dean's economy with words. He was a mystery to us before, but now that we'd met him, he was even more of one. We found out his real name was Tony, but he got his morbid nickname from surviving motorcycle accidents that others didn't.

Tony had long been running from the Lebanese cops as a result. As an Armenian refugee he couldn't get a driver's license, nor could he register his motorcycles, so he drove them without any plates. That was reason enough for the police outside of El Nahr to give chase every time they spotted him. But nobody could catch the King of Death. His BSA 650 cc Golden Flash couldn't outrun the gendarmes on the highways, but maneuvering through the narrow streets of Beirut he had always managed to evade them. Ironically, what particularly pissed off the police was that Tony had constructed his bike from old police bikes that he'd rescued from the junkyard after the police ditched their BSAs for more powerful—and more cumbersome—Harley-Davidsons.

So we became friends, and together we wasted away the summer of 1965, bumming around and hanging out, sometimes down in El Nahr, just cruising or toying with the bikes. From the six or seven bikes Tony had rescued from the scrap yard, we managed to piece together two more bikes that worked, one of which was even faster than the first. Tony agreed to sell the fast one to me, and I raised the money by selling my Ducati and hitting Mom up for the rest. John Wybro, not wanting to be left out, and now too embarrassed to be seen on a Honda, bought the other one. We didn't find out until nearly a year later, but, to come up with the money, he stole his stepmother's diamonds and pawned them off down in the souk.

Just before school started, in what would've been my senior year, Miles came home to Beirut from college in America. Since Dad was away from home a lot, and since, as he figured it, he'd spent a fortune on Miles's education, Dad came up with the bright idea of making Miles the head of family finances. So, Miles was put in control of the entire household, and from then on it was up to Miles to decide what we could spend, where we could go, and what we could do in the way of amusement. Inevitably, that led to problems for me, and for Lennie and Stewart as well. Whereas it had been easy to get money from Mom, with Miles controlling the purse strings the answer was always "no." In short, Miles became the family shit.

It got worse week by week. When I went to him for my weekly allowance, Miles would whip out my report card from the previous semester and start jumping in my shit. He'd inform me that he did not approve of the company I was keeping, nor did he think I was spending my time wisely, and since my report card was so bad, I was grounded. Then he confiscated my bike keys. Naturally, I was outraged, but there wasn't much I could do about it, since Dad was obviously going to stand behind his decision. Anyway, I thought the restrictions would only be temporary. Furthermore, I figured Miles could kick my ass if he wanted to, so I decided to go with the program for the time being.

But then I got a phone call from a friend at the American Community School, asking me what was wrong with my motorcycle.

"Wrong? With my bike?" I asked. "What, are you nuts? There's nothing wrong with my bike."

"Then how come you're selling it so cheap?" he asked.

"What are you talking about, douche bag? My bike's not for sale, not at any price."

"Then why in hell is it posted for sale on the school bulletin board?"

I went down to ACS to see for myself, and there it was. Miles had put my motorcycle up for sale. I charged home and got into a horrendous shouting match with Miles, but it did no good, and he could not be moved. He said that from then on I could regard the motorbike as past history, and that I was banned forever from seeing my "loser" friends. Worst of all, he threatened to take me down to the barber shop for a haircut he considered normal length, which I knew meant a completely unfashionable all-American crew cut. And, of course, I was sent to my room.

That night I waited until everyone was asleep before creeping out of the house. I left a tearfully maudlin note to my mother saying how much I loved her, apologizing for the unhappiness I must have caused her. Then I crept into the garage, hot-wired my bike, and ran away from home.

I took off to El Nahr, planning to use the King's bike shop to hide out in for a while. It should have been the perfect place for me, or so I thought. But in less than two days the old man found me, to my utter disbelief. I was deep in El Nahr, sitting outside the King's bike shop, enjoying my rebellious freedom, when a scrawny little man rode up on a bicycle and gave me a note from my father.

My confidence was shaken by Dad's finding me, so I followed the instructions in the note and met him at Sheik Salim's. Humbled as I was, I still wanted to negotiate. I figured if he wanted me to come home he'd have to give in to some demands from me. But Dad said, "No deals. You live in my house, you live by my rules."

"And if you want to run away," he continued, "you're going to

WILD THING

have to run a little farther away than El Nahr." If I thought I was going to be able to negotiate any terms for my return home, I was in for a rude surprise. Dad told me for the first time that he was a high muckety-muck in the CIA, with contacts in police, intelligence, and security agencies all over the Middle East. So long as I was in Lebanon or any of the neighboring countries, I couldn't wiggle a finger without his knowing about it. At the same time, however, I could imperil the rest of the family if I was running around like a loose cannon in Beirut, especially down in El Nahr. "So if you *must* run away," he said, "you'd better get entirely off my patch. In Lebanon you're just a kidnapping waiting to happen. I don't want to wake up one morning to find an envelope sent by some terrorist organization containing one of your ears and telling me what I've got to do to get you back."

Fully expecting to call my bluff (he told me years later), he gave me my passport and a handful of Lebanese lira, and suggested that I follow up on my threats to make my way to London. He threw out some more advice, none of which I even heard, and then he left, leaving me dazed and confused.

Wondering what to do next, I returned to El Nahr to confer with John Wybro and the King of Death, only to find that while I was meeting with Dad, John had been fighting with his parents also. No doubt they'd discovered the missing jewels, but John gave us another reason. In any case, he was now a runaway too, so I now had a sort of partner in crime, and though it occurred to me that Dad's suggestion was only a bluff, the thought of going to England was now an option we could seriously consider. John and I started getting excited about the prospect, and Tony too. We were getting carried away, but I'm not sure how serious I was, since in the back of my mind I was actually thinking of a way to go home gracefully.

Sometime soon after that, however, events took a turn for the worse, and fate mapped out our course for us. Tony's motorcycle died on him, for lack of a vital part, so he took to riding on mine. John and I took John's bike to raid my family's beach cabin at the Sands to pilfer some food, and when we got back with the loot, we found Tony cowering in a darkened shop, shaking from head to toe. His hands were bandaged, and his torn pants were drenched in blood. We could tell just by looking that the King had been in another accident.

According to Tony, while he was cruising down the corniche, minding his own business, a policeman stepped out in front of him, in an attempt to flag him down. He did the best he could, but was unable to avoid the cop. He said that my bike was a mess, and though he wasn't absolutely sure, he said he thought he might have killed the policeman.

In Lebanon you can kill just about anyone without getting into *too* much trouble, but killing a cop will put a price on your head. John and I decided we'd better take a ride into town to see just what had happened.

We found the scene of the crime easily enough. There were spots of blood all over the street, and still the remnants of a crowd. We found a little old man at a *shawirma* stand who claimed to have seen the accident, but no one who could verify Tony's hunch that the cop had not survived. We then set out to find the bike, and eventually located it inside a police station parking lot where they'd dragged it after the accident. It was not a pretty sight. Everything we saw in our cursory examination spelled disaster.

It was clear that the King had to leave the country immediately, and our toying with the idea of going to London became a reality. The question was, since we now had only one motorcycle, who would go with him, John or myself, and who would stay behind? I was eager to be the one to go, but John was absolutely adamant, *insisting* that he be the one to go. He claimed to have a reason that he couldn't talk about, and he accused me of "getting us into this mess in the first place." I still haven't figured that one out, but in the end, as I always did, I gave in to John.

It was also clear, upon inspection, that the one motorcycle we did have—John's—wasn't going to make it very far. We'd have to retrieve my bike for some essential parts. So without any more conversation, John and I headed for the police compound, intending to rescue my bike. I had serious reservations. It seemed that we were slowly but surely being sucked into situations more and more on the wrong side of the law. I couldn't see how we were going to get my motorcycle past the guards without knocking them out. Surely, even a nut like John Wybro wouldn't expect us to go that far.

But when we got back to the lot, there wasn't a guard. We went right in and, in the middle of the night, stole my bike back from the cops. Considering what an unwieldy mess it was—front forks twisted, the front wheel crushed, and the handlebars bent in two directions—it was incredibly lucky that we were not caught.

We got it back to the King's bike shop and worked on it all night. By morning we had put the two BSA's together beautifully: basically, my engine on John's frame. And, after doctoring the paperwork to make the identification numbers match, Tony and John said good-bye and took off for Europe.

Now there was only one more tiny, insignificant matter to attend to, which was what to do with my life.

CHAPTER 5

Runaway Child

I'm free . . . to do what I want.
—The Rolling Stones

I HAD RUN away from home to protect my freedom, but without my buddies and without my bike, being free was not much fun. My once-perfect world was now a mess. As I saw it, I had but two choices. I could either follow John and the King to London, hitch-hiking through Europe by myself, or I could return home with my tail between my legs, submitting to conditions laid down by my older brother.

The first choice was a dream, really, a plan that had more substance when the three of us had been together. I would have followed my buddies anywhere. Now that the others were gone, however, reality began to creep in on me. As for going home, I had already lost my bike, so now it was more or less down to getting my hair cut. It shouldn't have been such a big deal. But in those days my long hair meant so much to me; it defined my individuality. I felt that if I gave in I was giving up my identity. By today's standards, it wasn't even all that long.

I had another close friend in Beirut whom I could ask for advice, a resourceful English kid named Paul Mulligan who was sixteen or seventeen, a year or two older than me. Paul was the local playboy whom I often turned to with my girlfriend problems (until I noticed he was stealing them from me), and who later became my sort-of guru. Badly needing someone, anyone, to talk to, I caught a tram across town to Sheik Salim's, where I knew I'd find Paul holding court.

Paul's solution to my problem was simple. His older brother was a pilot for Middle East Airlines, and Paul claimed it would be easy for him to sneak me aboard a flight to London. But Paul had a history of seemingly simple solutions to complex problems that often fell apart in their execution, and I was more than a bit skeptical. In my particular predicament, however, I was ready to try anything.

And so the very next day I went along with Paul and his brother to Beirut Airport. Even as I was being ushered through customs and onto a plane bound for London, and even as I watched Lebanon disappear from view below, I couldn't really believe it was happening. I had never thought the plan through to the end, and I felt like I was being guided not by my own will but rather by a chain of events, forces outside of my control.

Once at Heathrow, I had no idea what to do next. My only assets were my money for taxi fare into London, and a letter from my old girlfriend, Fiona McRobert, who had moved to England with her family several months earlier. I gave the address on the envelope to the cabbie, and he took me all the way out to Ilford, Essex, on the opposite side of London. Like cabbies the world over, he knew a sucker when he saw one, so by the time I arrived at Fiona's house the meter registered almost all of the money I had. That is when it first occurred to me that my move lacked proper preparation and planning, a thought that became even clearer when I landed on the McRoberts' doorstep, thinking that my arrival would constitute a pleasant surprise.

It was a surprise all right. I was a hit for about a day. I naively expected from the McRoberts the same kind of hospitality they'd always shown me when I visited their spacious home in Beirut. I'd practically *lived* there, and I assumed that it would be much the same in London. But in London, the whole family, including a pair of crabby grandparents, was crowded into a tiny house with only three bedrooms and one toilet. The McRoberts' accommodations were uncomfortable before I got there, but the addition of myself made life in their house next to intolerable.

Apart from the grandparents, however, the McRoberts were great. Immediately, Fiona set about finding me a place where I could stay permanently, and she soon found a friend whose folks were looking for a lodger. She introduced me to Eddie Coltham, whose family lived in a two-story brick house on Ilford High Road. It was attached to a whole row of working-class cottages just like it, all with their neat little walled-in gardens in the back. Well, I was about to find out just how pampered life had been for us in Beirut.

The Colthams offered me a bed-sit, which meant I had one room to myself and had to share the kitchen and bathroom. The room was small, but it was clean, and under the circumstances, I was lucky to get it. I almost froze my balls off, though, since the paraffin stove gave off more foul odors than heat, and it warmed only a small area. There was also a problem with the electricity. To keep it going I had to feed shillings into a meter in the corner, and when the shillings ran out, the lights went out. Being broke, I had to learn how to live in the dark, and go to bed early. But the Colthams let me watch television and use the family room whenever I wanted, so I lived like an adopted member of the family. Eddie, coincidentally a biker like me, was one of the funniest guys I'd ever met and we soon became good friends.

Next I had to find a job. With no experience of any kind, with no credentials, no references, and no work permit, this was nearly impossible. I beat the streets, following up ad after ad in the newspapers, but nobody would hire me. Finally, when the traveling circus came to town, Eddie offered to take me down to the Barking Fair and get me a job. "Eddie," I said, "I didn't run away from home to join a fucking circus!"

But a job was a job, and the one Eddie landed for me wasn't bad. I operated "The He-man Hammer," one of those contraptions where you hit a wooden block with a huge hammer and a metal pellet shoots up a "Power Meter" shaft to ring the bell at the top. I'd yell at the crowd, "Are you a man or a mouse? If you can't do it, your girlfriend can!" I got in lots of experience goading customers into paying for things out of which I could make money. Most customers, or punters as they were called in the trade, would take the hammer and bust their guts pounding the block, only to watch it go no more than three-quarters up the shaft, showing they were less than 100 percent he-men. Of course, there was a trick to it. No matter how strong you were, if you hit the shaft from an angle, most of your effort was absorbed by the block. But if you hit it straight down, all the power went into sending the pellet flying, and it was easy to ring the bell. You could ring the bell just by gently dropping the hammer, as long as you dropped it flat.

With a little practice, I learned to do it with just one hand. I'd flip the hammer, catch the handle, whirl it around once or twice, then bring it down and ring the bell every time. Since I was quite skinny, it would piss the he-men off when they couldn't do it like I could. I used to keep some fairly big lugs going at it for hours.

After only two weeks, however, I was sorry to learn that the circus was to close down for the winter. When I went to get paid, the boss, a gypsy, told me, "Look 'ere, mate. I want to be the first one out of 'ere. If you could see your way to come early in the mo'nin', and if you 'elp me load up my gaff, I'll not only pay you wot I owes you, but I'll give you an extra week's wages on top of that! 'Ow's that then?"

When I got there in the morning the gypsy was long gone. When he said he'd be the first one out he wasn't kidding. All the other rides were still breaking down and loading up, but there was just an empty space where the hammer-and-bell contraption once stood. Another valuable lesson in business: get your money up front.

Now I was desperate. Eddie's folks felt sorry for me, but they needed the rent, and I needed to eat. So back I went, all over town, looking for work. But there wasn't any to be had. I finally found a job working on a building site, where there was a job opening for a hod carrier. There was always an opening for hod carriers; it was the worst job on any site. I had to "carry the 'od" full of bricks on my shoulder, and climb the ladders up to the top of the building. Up and down, all day— like an ant. They paid you by the brick, so you were always trying to carry an extra load. The hod was heavy, but the cold was the killer. The rungs on the ladder wore holes in my hands, and the cold made them numb—increasing the chances of my falling from a great height.

Every day after work we'd climb onto Eddie's motorcycle and ride out to the Ace Cafe, where the bikers hung out, and I first learned about "mods" and "rockers." You had to be one or the other. If you were a mod, you dressed up in a parka like a pansy and you rode a motor scooter all decked out in chrome and mirrors, probably with learner's plates. You listened to The Who and The Hollies behind little white pills. If you were a rocker, you wore leather and you rode a motorcycle, you greased your hair back, and you listened to Elvis Presley and The Animals over a pint of beer or a lager. The rockers were mostly manual laborers, mechanics, and factory workers, while the mods were office workers, clerks, and shop assistants. And, for reasons I never understood, mods and rockers were supposed to beat each other up whenever they came upon one another in uneven numbers. Eddie and all of his "mates" were rockers. So therefore so was I.

In time I'd saved enough to make a down payment on a rickety old Royal Enfield 750 cc that took up more of my time in fixing it than actually riding on it. On weekends, Eddie and I would ride out to one of the other cafes in the area, going up the dual carriageway at a hundred miles an hour (called "doing the ton"). We spent our days just sitting around drinking beer or coffee and admiring each other's bikes.

I can't even remember how it all came together, but there came the big day, an event that was to the mods-rockers war what the Battle of Waterloo was to Napoleon or the Tet Offensive was to Vietnam. On the bank holiday of May 28, 1966, all the bikers from Ilford, and from the surrounding towns of Romford, Dagenham, Barking, and Seven Kings, converged on the parking lot of the Ace Cafe. From there we headed down to Brighton, a seaside resort on the south coast of England, about fifty miles out of London, where we'd been hearing rumors of hostility between the mods and rockers. On the way down, we ran into other groups of rockers roaring their motorcycles through quiet English towns, and before we knew it we had what amounted to a real Spanish Armada, ready to invade Brighton in force.

No sooner did we hit the edge of town when we began to see mods everywhere. They had gathered forces just as we had, and were set for a showdown. The kickoff was at a little sidewalk cafe just off Connaught street, where some of the rockers we'd rode into town with saw a lot of mod motor scooters parked in front and began kicking them over. One of the rockers set fire to one of the scooters, and it went up in flames. Mods came from every direction, and all the rockers in the neighborhood—including my group—poured into the fray, and there was a free-for-all as good as any Hollywood movie bar brawl. The fight soon spilled out onto the street, and eventually spread through the whole town.

I was getting my ass kicked by a bunch of mods when I was saved by the arrival of policemen. In fact, a horde of policemen began to arrive, some on motorcycle and some in squad cars. As soon as they waded into the fight, swinging their clubs, the mods and the rockers joined forces and turned on the policemen with blind, senseless fury so taking them by surprise that they had to fall back, dragging their wounded along with them. Meanwhile, the riot was spreading all along the corniche and into the side streets, and there was a wave of looting and destruction that was later estimated to have cost several million pounds.

The Brighton riot continued for the whole weekend, and died out as we all went back to work and returned to the real world. But not before it had become a big deal all over Britain. There were hundreds of arrests. A flood of news reporters took trains from London as soon as word of the riot reached there, and so did more mods and rockers. The riot was News of the World. But this was in the middle of the mad sixties, when youth was in rebellion everywhere. The Watts riots had taken place in Los Angeles less than a year earlier, destroying twenty blocks of the main commercial center for the area, and the upshot was a condemnation of police brutality, not of the rioters. On a somewhat smaller scale, the upshot of the Brighton riot was similar. It is perhaps ironic that Sting's first movie role would be that of a mod leader called Ace in the Brighton riots.

The rest of the summer passed peacefully enough, then an early winter came and construction work in Ilford slowed to a minimum. Most of the workers were laid off, even the hod carriers. In any case, the last to be hired was the first to be fired, so I was out of a job. For a while, I couldn't find work anywhere, but I finally got a job with a prefab construction factory by agreeing to work for half the normal salary. I had to scrape and oil the molds, then fill them with concrete and stack them in the yard to dry. When the concrete hardened, the molds were broken open, scraped, oiled, and filled again. It was boring, monotonous, and backbreaking work, and at the end of the day I was cauliflower.

Every day it was the same thing, in the ceaseless rain and the frightful cold. The epitome of drudgery. But, can you believe it, I loved it! There was always something to laugh about, both at work and on weekends, and life was simple and, for that very reason, pleasant. But I couldn't see going on like that. Eddie and his mates, whom I rarely had the energy to see anymore, had quit their jobs and gone on the dole (social security), making just as much from it as they would have made from jobs. They seemed content with their lot, but I wasn't content with mine. I felt that life must have more in store for me. On top of everything else, I was terribly homesick.

But I still wasn't ready to give up; I had something to prove, although I didn't know quite what it was. I was truly a "rebel without a cause." I didn't realize that I was trying to impress my father, or maybe prove that I was Miles's equal. Whatever it was, I knew what I was doing wasn't getting me anywhere. One day, I saw a newspaper advertisement about a computer programming course that guaranteed a job at the end. I flipped. I remembered Dad saying that computers were the wave of the future, and that advertisement, I thought, showed me a way out of the rut I knew I was in. I thought to myself, here's how I'm going to impress the old bastard.

The course was in London, so when I'd saved up enough money, I packed my things, quit my job, and said good-bye to Fiona and my biker friends in Ilford, who all thought I was nuts. I contacted an old friend from Beirut, a French kid named John Joujoura, but for no apparent reason called "Gorgeous" by his friends, who had served as my only contact with the old gang from back home. I knew him as a truly amazing character, although trapped in a nerd's body that made him look like a nuclear scientist. He was studying at Royal Holloway College, and was as homesick for Beirut as I was. His pad was also a bed-sit, but it was enormous compared with my old one in Ilford. Gorgeous told me I could stay with him as long as I liked, or at least until I found my own place.

As fate would have it, I was there about three days when John Wybro showed up out of the blue. Like me, John had maintained

WILD THING

contact with the old gang through Gorgeous, but it had been a long time since he'd been in touch, and he had one hell of a story to tell. He'd come all the way through Europe from Beirut, dropping the King off in Norway where he'd gotten a job racing motorcycles. They'd been forced to abandon my bike in Yugoslavia, having blown a tire which they couldn't get fixed, Yugoslavia being a Communist country where it's next to impossible to get *anything* fixed. He and the King had finished the trip by train.

It was good to see my old partner-in-crime, and we had a great time bringing each other up to date on our respective fortunes. As is often the case with people like John and myself, one plus one can add up to more than two, and we hadn't gone far in our exchange of stories before we were "thinking big," as Miles and Dad would say. We decided to take London by storm. To start with, we'd move Gorgeous out of his bed-sit in Muswell Hill, and the three of us would find a decent pad in trendy Kensington, or a "flat" in Earls Court, where several other ex-Beirutis now resided.

John had no money, of course, but that was no problem. He swore his folks were sending some from home once they knew where to send it. I was glad to hear him say that, although I didn't believe him 100 percent, because I needed all my own money for the computer course. But John was confident it was coming, and I wasn't very bright at this stage of my life, so we all went off to the pub to celebrate our reunion and ended up spending nearly half of my money showing John the nightlife in London. After many a drink, we came back and crashed out on Gorgeous's floor.

Early in the morning, the landlord let himself into the flat, found John and me sprawled out in a mess of empty beer cans, soiled clothes, etc., and instantly changed all our plans by kicking the two of us out on our asses— literally.

Wybro and I were suddenly homeless. I was the only one who had any money, and very little at that. I could already see my computer course going down the drain, but John assured me that his money was due any day. I hadn't yet wised up to the old "the check's in the mail" dodge, so I foolishly spent whatever I had left on food and necessities for the both of us. We spent the days bumming around and riding the underground trains to keep warm. When these closed at night we slept on park benches at night, or in train stations when it snowed, and every now and then managed to sweet-talk some dodgy old boilers into letting us crash with them.

My money eventually ran out completely, and it became obvious that John's folks had no intention of sending him any. By now we were starving. We kept ourselves going by waiting for the milkman to pass, then we'd pinch a bottle of milk from somebody's doorstep. That was our breakfast and lunch. For dinner, we scrounged whatever we could from Gorgeous or the girls.

But John Wybro, being big and rough, eventually fell back on his biggest asset: brute strength. One day, with me tagging along, he went over to Gorgeous's college to bully the poor guy into giving us some money for lunch. Gorgeous said he didn't have any money, so John lost his temper. "Come on, you frog bastard," he said, "you're holding out on us." He had Gorgeous quaking in his shoes, but Gorgeous kept insisting that he didn't even have enough money to buy lunch for himself. "On my mother's grave, I promise, I haven't got a penny to my name," he said.

That convinced us, and we left him to return to his classes. It was snowing heavily that day, so we went to hang out in the college gym, which was at least warmer than the subway stations and park benches. We weren't bothering anyone. But some college kids came in to play basketball and decided bums like us had no business being there, so they kicked us out. John put up a fight but, realizing that he couldn't take on a whole basketball team, he eventually let me talk him into backing down, and we left. But on the way out we stopped off in their locker room and liberated their wallets.

Now filthy rich, we went straight to the college cafeteria for a feast I'll never forget. We piled our trays high with more food than either of us could possibly eat. It so happened that, while we were stuffing ourselves, Gorgeous came into the cafeteria. He didn't see us until he'd filled his tray and came looking for a table. When he saw us sitting there his eyes nearly popped out of his head, and then when he saw the mountains of food on our trays, he nearly dropped his load. He was furious.

"You bastards!" he shouted. "How'd you pay for all that food?"

"We might ask you the same question," John threw back at him. "I thought you said you were skint!"

Gorgeous accused us of finding the place in his flat where he had hid his money, and thought that we'd stolen it from him. At that suggestion, it was John's turn to blow up. "Aha!" he said. "You *have* been holding out on us." But it was difficult for him to sustain his anger when it had dawned on us that now we had money available to all three of us.

The money we had was nowhere near enough to solve our problems, so John, in his wisdom, decided we might as well spend it and have a good time. So that night we all went out on the town again, starting in Soho and ending up in the back-alley dives. At one place, we had no sooner entered when one of the nicest-looking girls in the room asked me to dance. I couldn't believe my luck. It was a slow dance, and she was unnaturally friendly. We were holding each other tight, when I noticed my friends motioning to me, and pointing at my dance partner behind her back. I assumed they were egging me on, and that they were jealous, so I held her tighter. About then I became conscious of an unusual bulge in her groin area, and as I looked around the room I suddenly realized that most of the girls there weren't girls at all.

This finding bent John Wybro all out of shape, and he began behaving the way he always behaved when he'd had too much to drink, starting with a few loud comments about faggots in general. Then someone in the club spat in his face. John started swinging, and suddenly it seemed as though everyone in the place was jumping on us. Even the bouncers came down on us, and we had to fight our way out of there.

When we made it out of the club and onto the street, John took off his leather jacket and we saw that his shirt was soaked in blood. John had two knife wounds in his back, but, bull that he was, he didn't even know he'd been knifed. We took him to the Goodge Street Hospital for examination and bandaging, and waited for ages until the doctor on emergency shift could see him.

But John is one of those people who simply don't know when to cut their losses and give up. It was six in the morning when we left the hospital. John was determined to go back to the club.

"You're nuts!" I said.

"They've got my wallet, with all our money."

"John, you win some, you lose some," I said, trying to cool him out. "Easy come, easy go. C'mon, John, it's not like it was really our money to begin with." I tried to convince John that there was no chance of ever seeing it again. But he wouldn't be budged, so off we went to Soho to look for the place we'd been mugged. Since all such places look pretty much alike, and none of the streets look the same in the daylight, we had a hell of a time finding it. But we finally did. It was all closed up, as were all the other places in the alley, all being nocturnal establishments deserted from dawn until eight in the evening when they all come back to life.

John refused to get the picture; all he thought of was getting back his wallet. He banged a while on the door, but, naturally, no one answered. Again, I tried to talk sense to him, arguing that it was the club bouncers who were beating us up, and that John hadn't *lost* his wallet, they'd *taken* it and there was no way they'd think of giving it back. Besides, if there were any bouncers hanging out in the place during the day they'd soon tire of John's banging and come out to beat us up again.

John remained unmoved. "I'm not going to let them knife me in the back and steal my wallet without doing something about it," he said. "No fucking way! I'll *make* those bastards answer the fucking door." He then proceeded to find a trash can full of garbage and paper, drag it back to the club, and with his trusty Zippo, he started a fire in the club doorway. Then we ran like a bat out of hell.

The entire episode served to convince both John and me that our partnership in London was leading nowhere, and that one or both of us needed to do something about it. John decided it was time for us to go home to Beirut. Since this would involve a three-thousand-mile journey through nine different countries in the dead of winter, I said "John, we've got no money and no transportation. Just how in hell do you propose to get there?"

"We'll hitchhike," he said.

WILD THING

CHAPTER 6

THE GREAT ESCAPE

I'm on the road again.
—CANNED HEAT

It NOW SEEMS apparent that my father tricked me from the start. He had predicted the war in the Middle East between the Arabs and Israelis, and plotted to move the family's center of gravity from Beirut to London long before I had actually done so. Back when he called my bluff in Beirut, Dad knew that at worst I'd get to London before them.

About the time I had hit rock bottom in London, I received word from home that Dad, Mom, and Stewart had moved into an apartment in Regent's Park that they used as a base while seeking a residence in St. John's Wood appropriate to the family's sudden (and as usual, temporary) upgraded financial status, the result of one of Dad's many short-lived successes in private business. Miles, I learned, stayed behind in Lebanon to finish his M.A. thesis at the American University of Beirut, while Lennie went to America to attend the prestigious Vassar College.

As soon as I was able to get their phone number, I called my mom. She said Dad was out of town so I went right over to put feelers out about coming home. But Mom set me up. Before I got there, Dad arrived "unexpectedly." Though clearly glad to see me, his attitude was strictly "I told you so." I did my best to convince him that things were going great for me, but after a lifetime in his chosen profession, he recognized bullshit when he saw it. He stood it as long as he could, but blew up when I told him I would "consider" going back to school, but only under the right circumstances. "Right circumstances?" he said. "Look here, you little twerp. You're coming home, and that's that! There will be no deals. This experiment is over."

There followed one of those confrontations that have become traditional in the Copeland family.

"Experiment?!" I cried. "After all I've been through? Now you call it an experiment!" Perhaps realizing I'd been duped into coming to London as part of the old man's plan, I rebelled against the concept, considering it a great insult to my manhood.

"We tried it your way," he said, "and you blew it. Now we're going to do things my way. We are going to put that wayward ass of yours in a good military academy," Dad said decidedly.

"No way," I protested. "I'm going back to Beirut."

"The hell you are. It's not safe in Lebanon."

"Well, Miles is there."

"Miles is a responsible adult. You are the family fuckup."

"So who's fault is that?" I whined. "You've never given me any responsibilities. Always Miles and Lennie, but never me. All I get from you is punishment, and those bloody book reports!"

The argument, if that's what it was, went on like that for over an hour until Dad, with the air of one pronouncing the final word, said, "Look, you are not going back to Beirut to those bums and losers you call friends, and that's final."

"How are you going to stop me?"

That shut him up. Strangely enough, it cooled him down. He thought for a minute before he spoke. In a calm voice, as if speaking to a hysterical child, he said he honestly thought I was off my head, and that something in it had snapped. "Tell you what I'll do," he said. "I've said I wasn't going to make a deal with you, but now I can think of one that'll settle this whole thing. We'll have an impartial judge, someone I know who's an expert on family fuckups, and he'll look you over. If he says you've got enough gumption and enough sense of responsibility to be trusted back in Beirut, you can go with my blessing. But if he says you're a nut, a case of arrested development or whatever, you'll stay right here in London and go to school. Okay?"

This being the first "deal" Dad had ever been willing to make with me, I couldn't refuse it. And what I knew, but he didn't, was that if I was going to go with John Wybro back to Beirut I needed his signature on an application for a new passport, as mine was about to expire. One way or another, I needed his blessing. "Okay," I said, just to get him off my back, "when do I see this quack?"

Without a second's delay, Dad went to the telephone and called an old friend of his in M16, the British intelligence service, and told him he had an "emergency" on his hands in the form of a rebellious son who was "about to do something drastic" unless he could be talked out of it by a competent psychiatrist. He gave his friend the impression that I was poised on the edge of a roof on a ten-story building and about to jump. All the same, it never occurred to me that the "psychiatrist," or whatever he was, would show up before the next morning, by which time I was planning to be long gone.

But, no, in just over an hour the doorbell rang and we let in a distinguished-looking gentleman in evening dress, who explained that he'd been called away from a dinner party in Mayfair but was all the same ready to be of any help he could. To my father, he put on a look of concern to show that he appreciated the seriousness of the situation, then he turned to me with a patronizing smile to say, "Ah, yes, young man. What seems to be the trouble?"

If Dad's experience had taught him to recognize bullshit when he saw it, mine had taught me to recognize assholes when I saw them, and this "psychiatrist" was a prime example. But I knew he was smart enough to understand that it was Dad, not me, who would be paying his bill, so I had no intention of respecting his opinion. We went into the next room, and he began to ask me questions, apologizing for their personal nature but explaining that doctors have to ask personal questions to get to the bottom of their patients' problems.

"When was the last time you wet your bed?" he asked.

"When did you stop beating your wife?" I said.

Maybe it wasn't *exactly* like that, but it was that sort of thing.

Anyway, it went on like that for half an hour, getting nowhere, until the psychiatrist wound things up by saying, "Now, I'd like to play a few games. Do you like games?"

The game he had in mind was something I later learned was the famous Rorshach test, in which the examiner holds up a series of cards with ink blots on them and asks the person being examined what each suggests.

The first ink blot was just a round blob. "That's the sun setting over the Mediterranean as you can see it from a beach in Beirut," I said.

The next one was long and thin. "That's a shish kebab," I said.

The next one was a camel. The one after that a mosque, and the next one was a Lebanese notable with a fez on his head buggering his man servant.

On that note, the psychiatrist gave up and began to lecture me with a lot of high falutin' psychiatrist's terminology, dwelling on the notion that I was suffering from a multitude of "traumas." He never came right out and said I was crazy, but he did say that I needed "prolonged psychiatric consultation," and that was what he was going to recommend to my father.

After a few words with my parents, he left. Mom fixed some hot chocolate and the three of us sat down for a few minutes of normal family conversation about how things were going for the family in general. As our last words for the evening, we agreed to save for the next morning a discussion of what, if anything, we'd learned from the psychiatrist.

I couldn't sleep that night for thinking. I badly wanted to come home, but I couldn't get over my father's cutting words. Had this all been only an experiment, merely a test? If so, then I had failed, it was true. And that was something I didn't want to suffer with for the rest of the foreseeable future. My dad would never let me live it down. I began to feel that I had no choice but to follow through with my bluff, and I genuinely believed that I would meet with a greater chance of success if only I could just get back to Beirut. Beirut was, after all, my turf, my hometown. So that night, when everyone in the apartment was asleep, I put on my clothes as quietly as I could, and crept out of the house.

Stewart woke up as I was sneaking out and tried to stop me. He was extremely upset. I tried to explain to him why I was leaving yet again, but I really didn't know myself. For the first time in my life I realized how much we take our brothers for granted, and how we don't realize how much we need each other. Stewart insisted on giving me his favorite scarf, and the only money he had. Exactly one pound, British sterling.

Once out on the street, I found a telephone box from which I called the girls in the Muswell Hill apartment to tell them to wait up for me so I could get into the flat, but the one who answered told me that John had packed his stuff, borrowed some money from Gorgeous, left a note for me, and taken off for Beirut. He'd been gone only about half an hour, and he was on his way to Dover to catch the ferry for Europe.

I couldn't believe what I was hearing. John had taken off without me. He was like that. He'd get a wild hair about something, and off he'd go. Nobody I knew was crazy enough to try and stop him. But now what was *I* supposed to do?! I couldn't return home. I didn't even have a key, and I couldn't face the thought of waking up the old man to let me in. It was as simple as that. One way or another, I was out for the night. I remembered that the train to Dover left from Victoria Station, so I decided to head down there on the slim chance I might find John. As late at night as it was, there wasn't much chance of that, but at least I knew Victoria would be a warm place to spend the night.

When I got there I found that I'd just missed the last train to Dover, and the next one didn't leave until morning. Thinking that John had caught the train, I began to consider either going back to Beirut on my own—because once John got to Dover he could chose from several different destinations on the European continent and I would never be able to find him—or going back to my parents.

Victoria is an enormous train station, one that John and I had passed the days away in while bumming around London. I knew of a warm place where we used to crash, and headed over there to wait for morning. And there was Big John, slouched in the subway where it was warmer than in the waiting rooms. I woke him up and told him my story.

He was as glad to see me as I was to see him, but a few minutes of consultation revealed that we didn't have enough between us to pay

WILD THING

for a trip across the Channel to Europe. In fact, we had just enough for two of the cheapest ferry tickets from Dover to Ostend, Belgium, but not enough for the train fare to get to Dover.

"And you know what?" said John. "Your ol' man is going to be lookin' fer you, and it wouldn't surprise me if they're waiting for us at the border."

"Well, then we better get a move on, and hope to get out before he knows I'm gone." So, in a cold drenching rain, we had to hitchhike our way out of the city and down to the coast. It took all night and most of the next day to get there, and we caught the last ferry with only seconds to spare. With our last few shillings we bought one thin British Rail cheese sandwich and shared it between us.

We arrived in Ostend at ten o'clock that night, to find it snowing so hard that any more hitchhiking was out of the question. We asked directions from a guy in the Ostend terminal who looked like he knew what was what, and he told us our situation was hopeless. There was no hope of getting any kind of a free ride anywhere or anyway; in Belgium hitchhikers were considered dangerous vagrants.

But having no better ideas, we stood out on the highway in the driving snow, trying to hitch a ride with one of the cars coming off the ferry. They all passed us without even slowing down. We watched as the last one went by, and then all activity on the highway ceased completely. The next-to-the-last train left the station, and as it went off down the tracks, it seemed to me like a giant zipper had closed us up in the darkness. With only one train left, there was no choice. We had to jump on it.

Once aboard it, we discovered that it was bound for Aachen, over the border into Germany. This seemed a bit of good luck, but the luck didn't last long, and we were by then too tired to think straight. To avoid having to pay the fare, we had locked ourselves in the toilet, forgetting that this was a dodge that had been used by vagrant travelers since trains were first invented. When the ticket collector came knocking on the door and went on, we might have made it if we'd moved on right away to another car, but some of the passengers finked on us and pointed to the knapsacks we'd left on the shelf in the cabin. When we finally decided to let ourselves out of the toilet, the railroad police were waiting for us. They'd already confiscated our bags, and next they took our passports away from us, and when we got to Brussels, they threw us in a Belgian jail.

I'd never experienced anything so demoralizing as the sound of that cell door clanging shut. The time went so slowly that minutes seemed like hours and hours like days. Friday night became Saturday, then Sunday. An orderly brought food to our eight-by-ten cell, which we shared with two other bums that spoke only Flemish. The cell was covered in graffiti in several languages. There was only one lightbulb hanging from the ceiling, and it was kept on twenty-four hours a day. We had blankets and coverless pillows that I wouldn't let a dog sleep on. The bed was a concrete slab that came out from the wall with no legs, and the toilet was a hole in the floor in the corner of the cell. Toilet paper? You must be kidding.

On Monday afternoon we were taken handcuffed from our cell and transported to the American Embassy, where we were bailed out by a kindly old lady, a vice consul or something. I gave her my whole sob story, how I ran away from home and all, only when I told her I was trying to get home to Beirut I left out that my parents weren't there anymore. She renewed my passport for me, then told us we were required by the Belgian authorities to leave the country by midnight. She then took us by car to the Brussels city limits and dropped us off, wishing us luck.

We barely made it to the German border post at Aachen by midnight, and then it took us all the next day and most of the night to get to Bad Godesberg, Germany, where John said he had a friend. Our new plan was to get some work, and earn enough money for a train ticket for both of us; at least as far as Istanbul, where we would take a service-taxi on to Beirut.

John's German friend turned out to be less than pleased to see us. The minute he grasped our situation he began to throw cold water on us. He told us there wasn't any way he could get us any work, and that he had enough troubles of his own without adding ours to his. John was really pissed off, but I saw the guy's point. If we couldn't get work in England, the chances of our getting work in a country where we couldn't speak the language were less than zero.

Discouraged though we were, we next took off toward Simmern, a small village in the Bavarian mountains, to look up another friend from Beirut, Mike Van Bose, whom we knew to be a nice guy with

WILD THING

a reputation for being generous to a fault. Just as we'd expected, he was overjoyed to see us and he took us into his house without a single question about our troubles. He led us into the dining room where he gave us a good meal over which we laughed for hours over old times. And he gave us some good news. He said that his girl-friend's father ran a ski lodge, and that he'd heard from the father that the lodge was looking for workers in the wine cellar. Just our sort of thing.

We got the job, and for a while it was fine—the job, the pay, the pleasant little village and living at Mike's place, where we stayed until our vibes told us we were about to wear out our welcome. Then, with the lodge owner's permission, we moved into the wine cellar to sleep on straw on the floor. It was otherwise okay, but nights were unbelievably cold in that mountain village and we had to drink the wine to stay warm. One night, John Wybro got plas-tered and began chasing me around the wine cellar, threatening to hit me over the head with a wine bottle. When he couldn't catch me, he hit Mike Van Bose over the head instead, and knocked him out cold.

This was the end of *that* particular episode. By this time, Mike was regretting the day he had met us. One day he came and told us we'd have to leave. But by that time we hadn't saved up enough money to get very far, so John called his parents and asked them to send us some money. I listened in on the phone call this time, and heard for myself that it was arranged for us to pick it up at one of the banks in Frankfurt.

So, more hitchhiking. We made it to Frankfurt only to find the banks closed for the weekend, so we had to sleep rough until the following Monday. The warmest place we found was in the under-ground walkway outside the train station, but the police came along every couple of hours to clear us out, along with the other bums. On Monday, we went to the bank, and the money hadn't arrived. Then Tuesday, and still no money. The money didn't arrive for a whole week, during which time we walked around in the snow to keep our circulation going so we wouldn't freeze to death. Finally, the money came on Friday.

The arrival of the money had a strange effect on John. He went all sentimental, to the point of actually weeping. On the way to the train station we stopped in a store to get out of the rain and catch a bit of warmth, and John began looking at all the Christmas goods. Then he started pricing them. I was stunned by the prices, and since John's folks had sent him barely enough money to get us back to Beirut there was no question of our buying gifts. But John had made up his mind that he wouldn't appear back in Beirut without Christmas presents for his parents, so we had one hell of an argument trying to convince John that his mere arrival back home as the prodigal son would be the best present he could give them—and that if he bought the presents we'd never make it by Christmas anyway. I was wasting my breath. By then, John had worked himself up into such an emotional state that he bought not one, but *two* presents—at least partly, I thought, just to piss me off.

"Way to go, Wybro," I said. "*Now* how are we going to make it back to Beirut?"

"Fuck you!" he replied. So now we didn't have enough money to get to Istanbul by train, and it looked like we were going to have to thumb it again. But I came up with a bright idea.

"Where did you say you left my motorcycle?" I asked.

"In Yugoslavia," he said.

"No shit, Sherlock. More specifically."

"In Ljubljana, at the train station."

"I mean, was it in a parking lot, or garage, or what?"

"No, we left it right on the street in front of the station."

"Might it still be there?"

John said he hadn't the faintest idea, but he pointed out that Yugoslavia was behind the Iron Curtain, and that if he hadn't been able to get a tire to replace the one he'd blown, then it was unlikely that anyone could. Besides, we figured, a BSA 650 would look pretty conspicuous in a country with nothing but bicycles, so if anyone had walked off with it he'd instantly be spotted as a thief. The tire was all that the motorcycle lacked, although it may have deteriorated somewhat from having sat there for several months. So there's where my idea came in. It was a long shot, but I thought we could buy a tire right there in Frankfurt, and take it with us to Ljubljana. From there, we would simply pick up the bike and ride back to Beirut in style.

And so, off we went. We still had to hitchhike to Munich to catch the train to Vienna, Austria, and from there on to the border with

Yugoslavia. Once we got there, the Communist border guards, with their machine guns and grim faces, couldn't quite figure out what two American kids were doing on their way to Ljubljana, Yugoslavia, and we had a hard time explaining it to them. Not knowing what else to do with us, and not wishing to hold up the train any longer, they eventually let us through, and the train took us up the steep slopes of the Alps and over to Ljubljana, where we arrived just before nightfall. We went straight out to where the bike had been left several months before. It wasn't there.

I spent that night feeling more down than at any time on the whole journey, including the time in jail. We slept, or tried to sleep, huddled together with a bunch of snoring Slavic peasants around a broken wood stove in the waiting room of the train station. I was too cold to sleep, fearful that I might wake to find some part of my body had frozen and fallen off. At around five in the morning I got up and went outside to take a piss, rounded the corner, and there was my bike leaning up against a wall. To my astonishment and joy, after a few kicks it started up. I ran to get John, and, after changing the tire, we took off for Beirut.

Neither of us had the right clothes for a motorcycle trip through the Alps in wintertime. We made it on one meal a day, consisting, more often than not, of a watery bowl of soup and some kind of heavy black bread that the locals ate.

The roads were icy and the wind was freezing. Twice the bike slipped on the ice and threw us off. We were forced to stop and switch drivers every half hour or so to keep whoever was driving from suffering frostbite. As we descended the mountains, alongside the Danube River to Belgrade, and on to Nis, the roads got better but the weather got worse. By the time we reached the border with Bulgaria it was a full-scale blizzard, and it became so cold that we just couldn't go on. We took refuge in the border post for two days. On the third day some friendly Bulgarian truckers came through who let us put our bike in the back of their truck and ride with them all the way to their work camp, a Communist commune in Sofia, Bulgaria, where they lived. They were thrilled to make contact with Americans, and they couldn't do enough for us. They advanced us food coupons, on the understanding that we'd have to work for them. There were blue coupons for food, green ones for clothing, yellow ones for household items, and so on, something like that. They provided John and me with one bunk between us, so we had to take turns sleeping and working.

After we'd worked for a few weeks on the commune, mostly shoveling coal, the weather finally took a turn for the better. So we ate as much as we could hold, then traded the rest of our food coupons for gas for the motorcycle, said good-bye to our Communist friends, and took off for Turkey. When we finally made it to the Turkish border, the Turkish officials gave us an incredible hassle, claiming we lacked the proper paperwork for the motorcycle. What we lacked was the proper bribe.

So we were forced to abandon my motorcycle, and we went back to holding out our thumbs. On the outskirts of Istanbul we were picked up by some Lebanese businessmen, who happily agreed, for the little bit of money we had left, to take us all the way to Beirut, and off we went again.

Crossing the tundra in Turkey was, for anyone thinking of going there, an absolute living hell. Since most of Turkey is a high altitude plateau, in the summer it's a scorching desert, in the winter it's colder than the North Pole. This meant that the windows were closed and the heater was on full blast for the whole trip, and John and I smelled so bad that the Arabs were ready to ditch us before we even got to the Lebanese border. It wasn't until we entered Syria that the climate began to change for the better, and it improved more and more the closer we came to Lebanon. But at the Syrian border, before we could enter Lebanon, we ran into another slight problem. My passport showed that I was born in Damascus, Syria, and the chief official accused me of dodging the draft. With Syria preparing for war with Israel, a lot of Syrians were crossing into neutral Lebanon, and the official seemed to think I might be one of them.

It was clearly time for another bribe, and I asked John to offer them the Christmas presents he bought in Germany. To my dismay, John refused. "John," I said, "what could possibly be more important than keeping me out of the Syrian army?"

"You still don't get it," he said. "Do you remember when you asked me how I was going to buy my bike from the King of Death? Well, I got the money by stealing my mother's diamonds."

He went on to explain that he'd gone into his stepmother's jewel

85   WILD THING

box, dug out the most expensive-looking items in it, and sold them to a fence in the Basta. His stepmother knew very well that John was the thief, and that was why they hadn't sent money to England. But by now they'd forgiven him, and just wanted him to return home. "So, you see," he said, " I just can't go back home without some token of gratitude."

"John," I said, "I'm beginning to see you as a jinx." Then I waited until John wasn't looking, took his gifts, and gave them to the Syrian official. If there was one thing I was more afraid of than John Wybro, it was the goddamn Israeli army.

CHAPTER 7

İ Fought the Law

Cruisin' along in my automobile . . .
—CHUCK BERRY

JOHN WAS FURIOUS with me for a spell, but it did the trick, and we arrived back in Beirut on Christmas day. Despite the fact that he came without gifts, John was welcomed home with open arms by his loving parents, so I was forgiven.

When we landed back in Beirut, I expected my problems to disappear miraculously, and to some extent, they did. I moved in with Blondie, my old friend from The Nomads. He had returned from Damascus in my absence and, as the result of getting a "real" job, got himself a one-room apartment on fashionable Al Hamra Street, which he was more than happy to share with me on the condition I found somewhere else on the nights he got lucky. Unfortunately for me, Blondie was lucky a lot, so I often spent nights on the beach. But that didn't matter to me. Hey, the Kid was back in town.

After the Christmas holidays, however, most of my friends went back to school, and I was left to hang around with others like myself who had nowhere to go and nothing to do, bumming around as a way of life. I didn't even try to get a job, and I was always broke. But it somehow didn't matter. You could sit for hours over one cup of coffee at most of the hangouts, and my friends seemed happy to pay my way to movies, discos, and whatever. Beirut was that kind of town.

My friends in school, amazingly enough, envied me and my idle buddies. But I knew better. Bumming was boring. One day a bunch of us were sitting around at Uncle Sam's, looking for something to do, when a misfit named Mustafa Bamyeh suggested that we go skiing. Mustafa was a rich kid from Jordan that nobody liked, an insufferable nerd who was less popular in our crowd than a pork sausage at a Jewish wedding, but who desperately wanted to be one of the gang. We barely tolerated him, but when he offered to borrow his sister's car and take us all skiing we sat up and took notice. Lebanon had some of the best skiing in the world, but getting to the slopes posed a problem. So, taking Mustafa at his word, John Wybro and I, and an Armenian kid called Berge Bedrossian, and some of the other bums of Beirut all rented skis, and made ourselves ready to go.

What we didn't know was that Mustafa was a liar. We walked up and down the block where Mustafa said the car would be, and there was no sign of it. Mustafa put on this big act, like he couldn't understand what could have happened to it, as if there had been some mistake. We were just about to thump Mustafa then dump him, when he suddenly spotted his sister's car. Dipping into his pocket, he brought out a huge collection of keys and began mumbling about how his sister must have given him the wrong set. When none of those keys worked, he broke the vent window on the driver's side, reached in, and opened the door.

I looked at John Wybro, he looked at me, and we both remembered what a fruitcake we'd known Mustafa to be. No way could that be his sister's car. It wasn't even the right color; we'd been looking for a green Fiat, this one was brown. When Mustafa started trying all his keys on the ignition for the second time, John and I took a walk down the road.

"John, do you get the feeling," I asked, "that this is not his sister's car?"

"You think this dude even has a sister?"

"Well, what are we going to do? He's stealing that car!"

"Yeah, he's crazy," John said. "If he's going to jail, at least he should do it for stealing something decent, like this car here." He was eyeing a Facel Vega sports car parked just up the street from the heap Mustafa was working on. I'd never seen anything like it—a rare beauty of a car, up-market Italian and looking brand-new. John tried the door and found it unlocked. He opened it up and climbed in on the passenger's side.

Before I knew it, I was in the driver's seat, pulling out the wires under the dashboard. I'd figured out how to do it once when I lost the keys to the family Opel; you simply cross the ignition wires, push the car off, and slam it into second gear. It was all too easy. We drove around to the others, and watched Berge's eyes bulge out of his head when he saw us sitting in the fancy sports car. "Got room for one more!" we said. Berge piled in the jump seat, and we took off down the road, leaving Mustafa still fumbling with the Fiat. Feeling guilty, we came back for him a few minutes later, and so, with four of us crammed in a two-seat sports car, off we went to the Lebanese resort of Faraya for a great weekend, racing all the way up the mountain.

When the weekend ended, our euphoria turned to paranoia. As we came back down the mountain, the thought grew on us that by now the owner of the car would have reported its loss to the police, and that the police might be on the lookout for it. So, John got a bright idea.

"Let's drop this car off before we get to the city," he said.

"So how do we get home?"

"We'll just get another one." And so we did.

After that, "joy riding," as we called it, became our favorite pastime. Almost every night we went out looking for cars to "borrow." Naturally, we nicked only the best; why bother with Volkswagens when the streets were crowded with luxury cars? We were soon in a contest to see who could come up with the coolest wheels; Wybro'd grab a Rolls, light-fingered Berge would come back with a Maserati, I'd top them with a Ferrari.

It was a dangerous sport, especially in a part of the world that had a long tradition of summarily chopping off the hands of thieves. The prevailing political situation didn't help much either. Our joy rides ran the constant danger of running smack into a military roadblock, where edgy guards with itchy fingers would check identification papers and search suspicious cars for weapons. One time I was out for a ride in a stolen Cadillac with Berge Bedrossian when we ran right into a roadblock.

There was no way we could stop, and the soldiers were sure to ask to see papers for the car. It was obviously stolen: no key in the ignition, and wires hanging out all over the place. So, without thinking, I stuck my head out the window, and yelling "Americani! Americani!," I stepped on the gas and drove straight through the barricade and between a row of sand-filled barrels. The soldiers were stunned. But as we took off down the road, I could see in the rearview mirror that they had begun to chase after us on foot, shouting profanities in Arabic, and waving their guns. "You see, Berge," I said, as we rounded the bend in the road, leaving the soldiers far behind, "all you gotta do is bluff your ass off."

"You crazy motherfucker, you almost got it *shot* off!" he said.

But the danger of what we were doing never occurred to me at the time. That's not what bothered me, or even the fact that we were breaking the law. As a foreigner I felt (foolishly) that I was immune to serious punishment, and I also felt we were just having harmless fun, robbing from the rich, sort of like modern-day Robin Hoods. But then something happened that changed my whole way of thinking.

We were cruising around in a stolen Buick Skylark, when Wybro pulled into a gas station. It looked shut down, but there was a light on in the office and a man asleep inside. Some hungry-looking dogs were roaming around guarding the place, and although they made a hell of a racket at our arrival, the man inside the office continued to sleep through the ruckus. Wybro began to honk the horn, and eventually the man woke and came outside. He scattered the dogs with a few swift kicks and came over to the Buick on the driver's side.

"Fill 'er up, would you," said Wybro, "and check the oil while you're at it."

The attendant put the nozzle in the tank and began to pump gas. Then he eagerly put in a quart of oil and washed the windshield. While the car was still filling up, he came for the money. He wanted ten pounds, Lebanese.

"Oh, dear!" said Wybro. "I'm afraid I only have a hundred pound bill, and I'm sure you don't want to give me all that change. You wouldn't have change for your other customers. I tell you what," said Wybro, "you go into your little shop there, bring me a carton of Marlboros—no, make that four cartons, and a couple of bottles of whiskey. Then there'll be less change to give me." The man went running off to get the goods thinking this was his lucky night.

Well, it *wasn't*. When he returned, Wybro had him put the stuff on the back seat, and when he went to shut off the pump and re-move the nozzle, Wybro rammed the car into gear and stomped on the gas pedal. With a squeal of tires and the smell of burning rubber, he pulled out of the station and took off down the road, with the gas hose, yanked out of the Buick, spewing gasoline all over the place. And the little old man just stood there, watching us disappear down the road with his goods. We laughed uproariously at the whole thing as we drove away, but I couldn't help remembering the look on the poor old man's face. It was beginning to dawn on me how seriously wrong this was. This wasn't robbing from the rich, this was robbing from the poor, and it sure as hell wasn't harmless.

A few nights later we went for a joy ride, and another thing hap-pened to sober me up, and make me realize the error of my ways. This time, when we were done cruising and went to ditch the car we'd stolen, one of the guys, a Lebanese called Freddie Nassar, started stripping the car, removing the radio and anything else he could sell for a profit. That was it for me. Joy riding in some rich Arab's car was one thing, but making money out of it was beyond my moral limitations. That's when I decided that my career in crime had come to an end.

Miles, meanwhile, had moved into an apartment on Rue Bliss, across from Sheik Salim's Coffee Shop, and was taking courses at the Amer-ican University leading to completion of his M.A. thesis. The word around town was that he had become quite a swinger, although he was spending most evenings in the Beirut office of Merrill Lynch,

WILD THING

the New York stockbrokers, increasing the family fortune. I hadn't been to see him since I arrived back in town, though, and I didn't think he even knew I was there, since I went to great lengths to avoid him. He was doing well while I wasn't, and I didn't want to hear him rubbing it in, or lecturing to me about my "slimy" friends.

I surprised him by turning up at his apartment one day, however, and he was genuinely glad to see me. After showing me around his lavishly decorated apartment, and feeding me from his overstuffed refrigerator, he filled me in on what the rest of the family was up to, which only made me more homesick than I already was. He told me all the things he was up to, and then we turned to my problems. Instead of lecturing me, though, we had a good talk. And what meant so much to me—not like a victory but more as an achievement—was that for the first time Miles was speaking to me as an equal and not just a little brother. I began to listen to his advice.

"Ian," he said, "you might not realize how much Mom and Dad and the rest of us want you to come home. I wish you'd consider it. In fact, Dad's coming in from Cairo this week, and maybe you should talk to him, work something out."

"You know Dad and me," I said. "We get together, we're just going to bump heads. And, in the end he's just going to say 'No deals.'"

"Ian, just leave the old man to me."

So Miles negotiated a deal with Dad, and within a day or two I was on a plane bound for Heathrow. The deal was simple. Basically, I agreed to go back to London and finish high school, and Dad agreed not to give me any more of his shit. I got a whole new wardrobe of expensive clothes, and my more than healthy allowance was fully reinstated. I could use the family car, and even keep my hair long. All I had to promise was terrific grades in school.

I was back in London less than a week when I received in the mail from Beirut several newspaper clippings that claimed an "international gang of car thieves" had been apprehended and thrown in jail. In the Arabic papers Mustafa Bamyeh, John Wybro, and Freddie Nassar were named, and there was mention of a "ringleader that escaped the country." Through sources of my own, I learned that they had all been rounded up and beaten until they confessed to having been responsible for *all* the car stealing that had gone on in Beirut for the previous year. Under interrogation, they'd given the names of everyone else in the gang, mine included. I realized how lucky I was to have gotten out when I did. Otherwise I would have been stuck behind bars with the others. As it was, I never saw John Wybro again.

The best part of being in England this time was being reunited with the family, although with Miles in Beirut, Lennie at Vassar, and Dad who knows where, the family consisted of Mom and Stewart. Stewart and I had the summer together before he went off to school at Millfield, a posh English private school, and we spent a lot of it going to concerts and clubs. Without realizing it, within two days of each other, we saw two bands that had more influence over our lives than we could have ever imagined. They were both three-piece bands, and they both had the most amazing drummers. The bands were Cream and The Jimi Hendrix Experience.

My new school, known as Davies, Laing & Dick Tutorial, was an expensive "cram college" where rich folks sent their family fuckups to pass the O-level exams (the British equivalent of an American high-school diploma) that they'd failed to pass in their normal schools. It had very small classes and it gave a lot of individual attention. Most of the boys were wimpy, but the girls were high-society debutantes, many of them quite pretty, and the whole social scene was a far cry from the working-man's life I had led in Ilford. This was tea parties, cricket games, Wimbledon and Ascot, and all the finery of upper-class society in England.

I actually enjoyed being back in school, and for a while I was doing very well. But then, unfortunately, I met a girl named Rita, and that was my undoing. Rita was distraction enough, but the problem was her father, who happened to be the famous race-car driver Sir Lawrence Pomeroy, and author of the book *The Design and Behavior of the Modern Race Car*. He gave me an autographed copy, and it got me interested in driving race cars. It might have stopped there, but he then made arrangements for me to join the world champion Jim Russell's racing school, where I began to race on weekends. We started out in Formula III cars, smaller and lighter than Formula I cars that you see in Grand Prix, but still very fast. The deal was, as I understood it, if you did well in his class, you had the opportunity to get on the team. With my experience gained from racing stolen cars in Beirut, I figured I stood a chance.

Sometimes you can win and still lose. Halfway through the course we had a race between all the students, and I won by a couple of laps. Unfortunately I could think of nothing but racing cars after that, and my grades went down the tubes. When I took my final O-level exams back in London my grades were so bad on the tests that Dad hit the roof. We had a huge fight and Dad said he'd had enough, and this time he really was sending me to a military academy. He declared our little deal null and void, and said I could forget about the racing cars. I said "If the deal's off, then I'm out of here." I threw a bunch of my stuff in a small bag, pocketed my passport, and stormed out of the house.

I was so mad I forgot to bring a raincoat, and it was pouring out. In minutes I was drenched. I took a hike up to the top of Primrose Hill nearby, and sat on a bench there for hours in the rain, wondering what to do. From where I sat, I could look back down on our building, and as it grew dark I watched the lights come on in the apartment. I could see shapes moving around in front of the TV in the living room, and I could see my mom puttering around in the kitchen, preparing the family dinner. They looked so warm and dry, and I was so cold and wet.

I'd really blown it this time, I knew. I had it all, and here I was back out on the street. What the hell was wrong with me? If only I had lived up to my end of the bargain . . . I began to consider my situation, and I couldn't see any hope whatever in it. I had run out of all the options in sight, and burned all my bridges behind me. Winter was fast approaching, and the thought of going back to work on the building sites was just too depressing. Going back to Beirut was certainly not an option; not only was I on the most-wanted list, but now the whole Middle East was engulfed in war with Israel.

I realized that my predicament was all of my own doing, and that I had screwed up big-time this time. But I was determined to find my own solution to the problem, because to go along with Dad's program would be to accept defeat and admit to being a failure. I wasn't quite ready to admit that yet. I still had to prove that I could make it on my own, especially now that I'd turned eighteen.

I was still thinking about what to do when the rain stopped, and I crashed out for the night on the park bench, still soaking wet. Early that next morning, on September 19, 1967, I went down to the American Embassy in London and joined the U.S. Army.

CHAPTER 8

BOOT CAMP

Jodie's got your girl and gone ... sound off!
—TRADITIONAL BOOT CAMP SONG

RIGHT AWAY, I realized I'd made a monstrous mistake. From the moment I first set foot on American soil, at Fort Dix, New Jersey, and for eight weeks after that, I was harassed, shouted at, beat up and abused, woken up at ungodly hours, run all day, kept up all night, drilled, marched, low-crawled, and made to do every form of miserable exercise. All in the freezing cold. And on top of that, there were foot-and-wall-locker inspections, guard duty, KP duty, boiler-room duty, fire-watch, and all kinds of other forms of harassment. Basically, boot camp sucks.

The whole concept of basic training is first to break you down, then build you back up as a soldier. "We don't want individuals on the battlefield. We want men!" they told us our first day, and by then we were so intimidated it made sense. First, the "Green Machine" methodically strips you of your individuality, robs you of the things that make you different from everyone else. Then it begins to reprogram you to follow orders, to function as a unit in a fighting team. So the first thing they do is cut off your hair. They line you up, and one by one they shave your head. When they're done, you look in the mirror and I swear you never saw anything so ugly in your whole life. Just to add insult to injury, the guy who cut mine off, this great big ugly dude, looked at me and said "Sheeeyit! If my dog looked like that, I'd shave his ass and teach him to walk backwards."

Next they confiscated my "civies," and issued me with a whole new set of clothes: olive-drab shirts and baggy trousers, called "fatigues," which I took to mean "clothes that don't fit," itchy wool socks, green boxer shorts, and combat boots that were way too big. I got a helmet that weighed a ton, a gas mask, a field jacket, a collapsible shovel, a compass, a canteen, and an M-14 rifle. Then they gave me a number and a nickname. My number was RA10893974, and my nickname, unfortunately, was "the limey." Like an idiot, I showed up my first day in my finest English tweed suit, and with that and my English accent, I was always singled out for every shitty assignment. What made that ironic was I could see that growing up overseas had given me an appreciation of being American that I wouldn't have had if I'd actually grown up in the States.

At first, I decided I wasn't going to take any shit from anyone. At eighteen, I thought I was pretty tough, but the team of sergeants and corporals who took charge of us had apparently seen tougher. I quickly learned that rebellion has no place in the army. Smartasses like me were grist for the noncoms' mill. Back in school, as the class clown I paid the penalty, if caught, and considered it a small price for popularity. In the army, however, they don't just punish the individual. The whole platoon pays the price. Keep on fucking up, and pretty soon you're a candidate to be guests of honor at what were called "blanket parties": after lights are out, the guys in the barracks cover you with blankets and beat you senseless. These parties generally bring about what's known as an "attitude adjustment."

I wised up before anyone threw a party for me, however, and I soon learned to get with the program. Despite the bullshit, parts of basic training were actually *fun*! I learned how to defend myself in hand-to-hand combat, how to apply first aid, how to survive in the jungle, how to throw a grenade, and how to fire a wide variety of weapons, including the M-14 rifle and the M-60 machine gun, on both of which I qualified expert. It occurred to me that all these things might be of more use to me back on the block in the real world than anything I learned at school.

By the end of basic training I had learned to stretch the limits. On the long marches, when I wanted to give up, the noncoms drove me on, proving that I *had* the strength—I only had to find it. In the end, I had to agree that the army had "made a man" of me, whatever that means. As part of the ritual, the graduates all discarded the nicknames the sergeants had bestowed upon us, and we all chose our own. Don't ask me why, but I chose "the King," only I wrote it in French just to add a touch of class, so it came out as "Le Roi." I printed it on the front of my helmet in great big red letters. Unfortunately, no one in New Jersey seemed to speak French, not in boot camp anyway, so my name inevitably became Leroy.

After completion of eight weeks of basic training, my new-found army buddies and I got our first weekend pass, and we took it in New York City. The bus dropped us off at Forty-second Street, and that's as far as we got. From there to Times Square the streets were lined with sleazy hotels, whores, and clip joints, what most GIs come to New York to see. For the others, this was their first taste of New York. But for me, it was the first real taste of America.

Well, it was quite a taste. We went bar-hopping and looking for girls. The American Indian in our party, a fine, happy guy when sober, got drunk and thought we could take on every bar bouncer in the Big Apple. Aside from getting our asses kicked, I lost all my money.

On my next weekend pass I went to visit my father's brother, who was living up in Connecticut. Uncle Hunter became my hero. He could do more push-ups with one hand than anyone I knew could do with two. And he'd been an honest-to-God war hero. In the army in World War II, he received a battlefield commission to the rank of major at the Battle of the Bulge, as well as the Silver Star, four Bronze Stars, and a Purple Heart. Then he was a colonel in the Air Force in the Korean War. Uncle Hunter's war stories first put the idea of volunteering to go to Vietnam in my head.

My orders after Basic Training assigned me to Advanced Infantry Training (AIT) at Fort Dix. From there I was sent to Fort Gordon, Georgia, to learn how to be a radio operator. All through training, most of the other guys were trying to get out of going to 'Nam—for

WILD THING

example, one guy got out by wetting his bed every night, and another took to masturbating at all hours of the day. But I *wanted* to go to Vietnam. I hadn't gone entirely gung ho, but what the hell, I was young, and I wanted to see a little action. I also realized that I had another couple of years of army bullshit ahead of me. I didn't want to spend it as a private, and I didn't want to spend it peeling potatoes on a base in Bumfuck, Iowa, or somewhere equally as boring. When I finished training as a radio operator, learning Morse code until I could do it in my sleep, I was sent for four more weeks to advanced training in radio-teletype. Then I was shipped to Oakland, California, to prepare for going to war.

At Oakland we saw veterans returning from the war, and it began to dawn on me that we weren't just kidding around; the whole Vietnam business was *serious*. They told us to forget about all that "spit-and-shine" shit we'd done in basic, since in 'Nam you didn't want to be in the jungle with your boots glowing or your belt buckle flashing. The new boots we were issued had metal plates in the soles to protect us from the *punji* stakes, ingenious little traps set by the Vietcong guerrillas for GIs to step on. They'd dig a hole a foot deep, put bamboo spikes on the bottom, then very carefully cover it all with brush. But first they'd pee on the spikes just to make sure that those who stepped on them would get hepatitis.

We also heard how the VC had a wide variety of similar devices in addition to the ordinary array of booby traps. Besides the inconveniences dreamed up by the enemy, the country itself had tortures of its own to present: spiders, heat, and leeches that clung to us as we went through the rice paddies. Finally, they told us about an affliction known as "the Black Syph." The Black Syph was supposedly an incurable form of venereal disease that made your penis turn black then fall off. Then your testicles swelled up and fell off like acorns from a tree. Eventually, your whole body shriveled up and you died a painful death. According to our trainers, you could only catch it in Vietnam, so if you were unlucky enough to get it, you would be quarantined in-country and never allowed to go home. The whole thing may have been an invention of VC propagandists—or of our own, just to scare us into cautious behavior—but it was as real to us then as AIDS is today.

After a couple of days of filling in forms, sleeping through training films, enduring countless inspections and the usual harassment, and just waiting around, we were given our shipping orders. In the end, I was genuinely anxious to get on with whatever was awaiting us in Vietnam. After all, misery in adventurous circumstances was a hell of a lot better than misery in the confines of extreme boredom.

CHAPTER 9

Incoming!

Gimme an F . . . Gimme a U . . . Gimme a C . . .
—Country Joe and the Fish

I ARRIVED in Vietnam when things weren't looking too groovy for our side. The well-known "Tet Offensive of 1968" caught us over-confident Americans by surprise, and the war had taken on a whole new dimension. Somehow, without our intelligence services being able to keep up with them, the VC had stockpiled masses of weapons and ammunition, and had mobilized more than a hundred thousand troops. With forces far beyond even our most pessimistic estimates, they massively attacked cities and towns throughout the country, even succeeding, briefly, in capturing the American Embassy in Saigon.

Later in the year they launched another offensive, this time directed at our troop concentrations and bases instead of civilian targets and Vietnamese installations. It was a big mistake. In the process we nearly wiped them out. Though we lost nearly fifteen thousand men—more than we had lost in all previous years of the war combined—more than sixty thousand enemy soldiers were killed the year I was there. Sixty thousand to our fifteen thousand, not too groovy for their side either. And meanwhile, war had never been declared by Congress.

As we flew into Vietnam we didn't know all this, nor did we have any idea of the scope and significance of the day-to-day fighting. Moreover, our brains were so deadened by more than eighteen hours of flying over nothing but deep ocean that when we got our first sight of land there was a mixture of boos and cheers, mostly boos. The flight in was a trip in every sense of the word. Like everyone else on the airplane, I had one hell of a hangover. I had gotten drunk, slept it off, gotten drunk, slept it off, and gotten drunk again. Now I was sobering up fast. We all were.

All but two of the other GIs on the airplane were complete strangers to me, and I felt like a kid on his first day at a new school, not knowing what to expect. The airplane was a regular passenger plane (TWA or United, I forget which) and not the form of transportation to war I had envisioned. I had a window seat, and I hogged the view. I could see land, but when the land came between the plane and the sun, the land just disappeared. I thought I was hallucinating. Like a mirage, the land would shimmer in the sun, be there one minute and be gone the next. I soon caught on to what it was. On the delta, the land was under a foot of water, covering the rice paddies. Yet even as we began to descend, far past the delta and on to drier land, you still could see plenty of water. Thousands of tiny lakes dotted the landscape, which struck me as strange because with all the lakes and water, the earth was dry and barren. The few trees to be seen were leafless. This, I learned much later, was due to the "Agent Orange" that General Westmoreland had concentrated on the area, in attempts to devastate all of the Ho Chi Minh Trail north of Saigon to Cambodia.

Our landing in Vietnam was the scariest flying experience I have ever had in all my years of flying. The airplane seemed to fall from the sky, as we literally dropped into Vietnam. When the pilot came over the PA to apologize, saying he was diving to avoid being shot at, we didn't know if he was joking, but nobody thought it was funny. And by now I could clearly see from my window that the thousands of tiny lakes I'd seen earlier were actually bomb craters filled with water from the monsoon rains. The craters were everywhere, making it appear that we were landing on the moon. This wasn't at all like arriving for the first day at a new school; more like your first day in hell.

While we waited for the troop trucks to pick us up on the runway, we watched the choppers buzzing around like bees at the far ends of the runways, lazily laying blankets of fire into the trees past the cleared area. Like a Fourth of July fireworks display, their mini-guns buzzed and burped and spat out red tracers showing where the lead was going. Once or twice, a single tracer came back up at the chopper. Then all the choppers would zoom in on that mark and return fire with an endless stream of bullets and rockets, pounding the whole area to a pulp. And despite all the hatred for the enemy that had been brainwashed into me, I couldn't help but admire the poor little bastard who had the balls to take his few shots, hoping to bring down an enemy bird and be a hero for his cause and country.

From Bien Hoa we were loaded on to buses and taken in convoy the short distance to the massive Long Binh base camp. At Long Binh you couldn't tell there was a war going on. It could have been Florida, if not for the horrible and ever-present smell of burning shit in the air. There were manicured gardens, concrete sidewalks, paved roads, a mall-sized PX, a Post Exchange tax-free shopping area, movie theaters, several bars, and even a bowling alley. The GIs on permanent duty at Long Binh wore fatigues with starched creases and had their boots spit-shined. Nobody even carried weapons, except the MPs.

We spent the first part of our first day filling out forms and taking tests (an exercise they called "in-processing") and wondering what was to become of us. As soon as I had some free time I went to one of the bars to ponder what I had gotten myself into, by then realizing that the worst thing about the army is that you never know what's going on. You ask other GIs what's going on and *they* don't know. I learned awfully fast, however, that any GI who's been in the army five minutes longer that you is an expert. And if he's been in 'Nam longer that you by even a day, he can tell you all about it. So, it wasn't long before I found someone to pump for information. Long Binh was the first stop for many of the GIs coming into Vietnam, but it was also the last stop on the way out, and there was clearly a shitload of "short-timers" in the bar that were going back to the world. From their faces, mainly their eyes, you could easily distinguish them from the GIs who'd just come in. One of the short-timers sitting next to me at the bar turned to me and said, "I'm going to kill the motherfucker."

I thought that was an unusual way to start a conversation, so I tried not to touch it. I pretended I didn't hear him. "I'm going to frag the sonofabitch!" he said.

He was right in my face by this time, so I asked him "Anyone I know?"

"The fat bastard that runs this place. See these boots?" he asked, as he put his crusty boots on the table. "They've taken me from Da Nang to Nha Trang. Through the rice paddies and through the jungle. I've stepped in more water-buffalo shit than you could fill a lake with! I've squashed snakes with these boots! And they ain't never seen no goddamn boot polish the whole fuckin' year I'm here. Three hundred and sixty-five motherfuckin' days in this rat-infested toilet, puttin' my sorry ass up for auction, then I come down here to this candy-ass place and some fuckin' lifer's makin' me shine my goddamn boots."

"Well," I said, humoring him, "maybe he objected to the buffalo shit and the squashed snakes. They might have a problem with that back in the States."

"Back in the States?" Now he was looking at me like *I* was a piece of shit. "You mean, back in the world! I'll be damned! You must be an FNG."

"What's an FNG?"

"Fuckin' new guy. Shit, mothahfuckah, you must still be pissin' Stateside water," he said. "Hell, I better not have no problem back in the world. Say, is it true they're throwing eggs n'shit at us, the folks back home? I heard that. A bunch of draft-dodging faggots are throwing tomatoes n'shit at us when we get off the plane. Is that true?"

"I think somebody in San Francisco threw an egg and it hit all the papers," I said. "I wouldn't worry about it too much." I was trying not to be too patronizing since the guy was obviously dangerous.

"I'll blow those motherfuckers away too," he said. He didn't know what he was saying, but he no doubt meant it.

"What can I tell you?"

"Jack shit, man. When I die I know I'm going to heaven. I've already been through hell." Then he took off telling me about it, and once he started there was no stopping him. I didn't try. He'd really been through a lot. As hard as it was to believe much of what he said, I generally knew when a man was bullshitting and this guy wasn't. When the bar closed and he got up to go, he gave me some good advice. "Just make sure you don't get stationed with the Big Red One."

"Do I get a choice?"

"Fuck no."

"What's a Big Red One, dare I ask?"

"Man, you are one dumb sonofabitch. The Big Red One is the First Infantry Division, only the baddest outfit in the whole damn army! They've been the baddest since World War One. They were the first division to go overseas, land in France, meet the enemy, and enter Germany. In World War Two the Big Red One was the first to land in Africa, and it was the Big Red One that stormed Omaha Beach on D day. The First Infantry Division was first to arrive in Vietnam. And, over here," he said, "the Big Red One is the army's answer to the marines."

"The answer to what question?"

"Who can kill the most gooks, I guess," he said, "or die trying."

My orders came the next day, assigning me, of course, to the First Infantry Division, the Big Red One. I was ordered to report to an artillery battalion at a base camp in a place called Di An (pronounced "Zee On"). I found Di An on this huge map over the bar in the enlisted men's club, and when I saw that it was only ten "klicks" (kilometers) north of Saigon, I assumed this meant that it was safely behind our lines. I was wrong. There were no "lines" in 'Nam.

Along with several other GIs with the same orders, I was given a rendezvous point where I would catch a convoy to Di An. It was at that moment that I realized I was in deep shit. All the other guys were riflemen and mortar gunners, so I had a feeling I was going to the boondocks.

As usual, I was getting as much information as I could from every-body around me, few of whom knew any more than I did. But I

WILD THING

learned that the convoy was going up Highway 13, with Di An just a stop on the way. I also learned that Highway 13, going up through the infamous Iron Triangle and on to Cambodia, was otherwise known as the Ho Chi Minh Trail. That was Big Red One country.

For the trip to Di An, we were loaded onto a two-and-a-half-ton truck, a modified deuce-and-a-half with sandbags on the floor and piled up the sides. The canvas covering over the back made it as hot as an oven, but, as usual in the army, after loading ourselves onto the trucks we sat for nearly a hour, baking. Eventually, the driver from one of the lead vehicles came back and told us we were waiting for our escort, a group of ARVN (Army of the Republic of Vietnam) soldiers in four personnel carriers and two tanks, to get their shit together.

"Damn gooks won't get a move on. They say it's getting too late, that we should go in the morning." I asked him why he referred to them as "gooks," since I'd only heard the term in reference to the enemy. The Vietnamese troops he was talking about were on our side.

"Hell, they're all the same," he said. " 'Bout the only difference is, the chickenshit ARVNs are afraid of the dark. That's how you can tell 'em apart from the VC. Turn out the lights and see who freaks out."

"Fuck that shit," said another of the drivers. "I wouldn't be turning out the light with no VC around. No way, Jack! Muthafucka be gone or you be dead when the light come back on."

It was obvious they had more respect for the enemy than they had for the South Vietnamese we were supposed to support. And, I must admit, my first view of the ARVN troops left me definitely underwhelmed. They looked ridiculous. Their U.S.-issue helmets were too large for their heads, and they were carrying M-14s almost as big as they were. In contrast to the American troops, in fatigues a few sizes too big, the Vietnamese soldiers wore their fatigues skintight, making their outfits look like they were made for a GI Joe doll. It also accentuated the fact that none of their other gear fit. And they were *over* supplied, having all the gear the U.S. Army could possibly give them: three or four canteens per soldier, collapsible shovels, smoke grenades, hand grenades, walkie-talkies, and ammunition belts. Whenever the ARVN soldier moved he made an incredible racket as his gear and helmet rattled around.

"I don't like it," the driver said. "While we're sitting here playing with ourselves, Victor Charlie's got all the time in the world to lay a trap for us. Man, I'm too short for this shit!" That was another thing I learned in Vietnam. Anyone who's been there longer than you is too short for this shit. There were too many stories about guys getting killed on their last days of duty.

I asked him if he wasn't just nervous. I said, "Anyway, I thought we were supposed to have this place under control."

"Where've you been, man?" He looked at me for the first time. "Oh, I see, " he said. "An FNG."

"Yeah. I'm still pissing Stateside water."

"You guys are bad luck. But I'll tell you this, boy. We got control of nothin' anymore. It used to be we had control daytimes, then the VC took over at night. Since this Tet shit started the motherfuckers been fuckin' with us any damn time they want."

The convoy eventually began to roll. Leaving the huge compound at Long Binh was like leaving a Hollywood set. Past the gates you come into the real world, and it doesn't look so good. All the buildings and even the police stations are covered with wire mesh, and the ARVN troops are behind thick barbed-wire and sandbag enclosures dotted along the road and on the bridges.

Past the outskirts of town, the paved road ran out and turned to dirt, and the view I had from the back of the truck was of a thick, impenetrable dust cloud. The roads were of a red clay that turned to fine powder when the lead vehicle went over it, and with my truck toward the rear of the convoy, and me at the rear of the truck, I could hardly see or breathe.

I was seriously considering my own personal predicament, and I was truly miserable. It was really coming home to me. What the hell had I got myself into? I had joined up imagining myself to be a fixed-wing pilot soaring across the sky in Europe, and here I was a grunt going down a dirt highway in a deuce-and-a-half. I kept trying to tell myself that things could be worse, but then I remembered I *volunteered* for this shit. That got me really depressed. But then right in the middle of a huge government-owned rubber plantation, not far from one of our biggest military bases in the world and only a mile or so past an ARVN base camp, and in broad daylight, Charlie decided to make things a lot worse.

There was a loud explosion at the front of our column as the lead vehicle, one of the South Vietnamese APCs (Armored Personnel Carriers), went over a land mine. It then careened into the dirt embankment and blocked the whole convoy. Then the VC started shooting at us from somewhere in the dense wall of rubber trees. For an interminable microsecond I just sat there looking foolish, not having the slightest idea how to react, and so did all the others, until bullets started tearing holes in the canvas. Then we got out real fast.

After scrambling out of the truck, I did exactly what they told us *not* to do back in training, jumping straight into the ditch at the side of the road. I couldn't help but dive for where the embankment provided some cover. To hell with the booby traps and *punji* stakes! Mind you, almost everybody else did the same thing on one side of the road or the other, though some dived under the trucks.

Once in the ditch there was fuck all I could do but listen as bullets whistled through the air above my head and thudded into the dirt around me. I was totally unarmed and completely helpless. I had no idea what was going on or what I was supposed to do. I just kept my ass real low and kissed the ground. There was a pop-pop-pop coming from somewhere in the jungle, and then again from somewhere else, but never from the same place twice, making it hard to tell how many snipers there were. It seemed to take forever for the ARVN troops to return fire, and open up with the 50-caliber machine guns which were mounted on the APCs. The gunner on the APC nearest me stayed down in his hole and only popped up every now and again to spray off a few rounds before he jumped down again. All his shots were wasted into the treetops.

From where I was, there didn't seem to be anyone in charge. Some guy kept shouting "What's going on?" And nobody answered him. Guys were calling for medics. One of our guys who was riding shotgun on the deuce-and-a-half was firing his M-16, but he just held it up over his head and pulled the trigger. He couldn't possibly have hit anything. His eyes were closed.

Then abruptly all went quiet, like popcorn that's finished popping. There was absolute silence for a whole minute. Strange, but the silence was actually *loud!* Then suddenly these incredible helicopters came swooping in overhead, tearing up the foliage with their mini-guns and spewing out rockets that crashed into the rubber trees. The Cobra looks like a shark in flight, and was painted with shark's teeth on the nose to enhance the effect. It can fly at over 200 mph and it carries seventy-six rockets. Its mini-guns virtually rain lead; one sixty-second burst puts out enough rounds to cover every square foot of a football field. Every time I saw one, I said, "Man, I'm glad I'm not Charlie."

The cavalry had arrived. The VC bushwhackers knew they were coming, though, and that's the reason they'd gone quiet and fled. I was astounded at the speed of our response to the enemy ambush. All through training I had been less than impressed with the American army, but here, I was just blown away! The Cobras were followed immediately by more choppers that came in spewing American troops and then flew off with the wounded. Within minutes the place was crawling with GIs, and it was like being on a movie set. I was waiting for someone to yell "Cut! Print!"

Some American army tanks arrived (sporting human skulls over the headlamps, all bleached white by the sun), and one of them bulldozed the wreckage of the lead truck off the road. In no time we were loaded back in the trucks, and the convoy was rolling again, like nothing had ever happened.

CHAPTER 10

WHERE WERE YOU IN '68?

War! . . . What is it good for? Absolutely nothin'! . . . Say it again.
—EDWIN STARR

THE U.S. FIRST Infantry Division was banned from Saigon after clearing the Vietcong out, mostly in hand-to-hand combat, following numerous complaints alleging brutality, debauchery, and other forms of behavior typical of invading armies. We now occupied an area stretching along the Ho Chi Minh Trail up Highway 13 from Saigon to Cambodia. Our primary mission was to find the enemy and disrupt his supply lines, thus preventing the flow of arms and supplies from reaching Saigon.

We were living in forts on the edge of the so-called Iron Triangle, an area of sixty square miles bordered by the Saigon River on the southwest, the Thi Tinh River on the east, and the Than Dien forestry reserve to the north. For a variety of reasons, we had to assume that all the inhabitants of this area were VC or VC sympathizers. In any case, the area was no garden spot, cut up as it was by marshes, swamps, open rice paddies, a densely packed secondary forest, and a jungle barely penetrated by a few oxcart roads and foot trails. Yet, despite these inhospitable natural features, the Iron Triangle was a human anthill having a life support system of tunnels, bunker complexes, concealed storage rooms, and booby-trapped trails.

My posting, Di An, was one of many fortified firebases crisscrossing the Vietnamese countryside, each one having a fire pattern that allowed it to cover bases on either side, each of which protected bases on its flanks. It was a dusty, desolate base camp smack in the middle of a huge rubber plantation, rows of tents and tin-roofed hootches surrounded by sandbags, and with its barbed-wire perimeter and standing guard towers, it closely resembled a World War II concentration camp.

The reception center where they put us for the first night was a far cry from the reception center in Long Binh, but it wasn't so bad considering how far out in the boondocks we were. At least we had bunks, blankets, and a roof over our heads. The first night was intense, but I was too excited to be scared. All night long our big guns blasted away in a steady rhythm that bore into our brains like the maddening drip of a water tap, only a thousand times louder. No lights were on in the camp, but the camp was occasionally lit with the eerie light from flares that floated down on small parachutes, sent up every so often by our mortars. Our choppers were buzzing around outside our perimeter, over the rubber plantation, spraying their targets with tracers, which gave the unearthly effect of some sort of alien ray-gun. We sat on top of the sandbag bunkers and watched in awe the pyrotechnics of war. To me, it was like watching a sci-fi movie.

I was exhilarated, yet confused. And mad as hell. The VC might not have been shooting at me personally, but I took it so. Still, I was relieved that I'd seen some action, though slightly embarrassed at my role in it—which was nothing. I resolved that if there was a next time I'd be more prepared, and the first to take action. I wanted to write home about what happened, but then I decided not to. I would only worry my parents. Instead I wrote how wonderful everything was. I guess I was contributing to the big lie, and I still had no idea of what was yet to come.

In the morning I received new orders assigning me to an artillery battery, the First Battalion, Seventh Artillery, and, together with a similarly assigned FNG named John Miles, I walked over to their position on the perimeter of the base camp. After reporting for duty there, we were both sent over to the Third Battalion/Seventeenth Infantry for "in-country OJT."

OJT, which stands for On the Job Training, was a new concept at the time, and it was supposedly developed to fill the gaps in our Stateside training and to correct problems arising from the fact that we had been trained mostly for conventional warfare. It was like boot camp all over again, but a refinement of basic combat training applied to the specific battle situations in Vietnam. Only this time it wasn't on the training field, but out in the jungle. To us, however, it soon became all too clear that the army had sent hundreds of thousands of men over to 'Nam without the proper structure to deal with the huge influx. Soldiers were arriving faster than officers or equipment, and OJT was just a way of dealing with it. The OJT unit at Di An was made up almost entirely of newcomers whose orders sent them to stations that didn't yet exist or weren't ready for them, and so they were stuck with us, some for a few days, some for weeks, and some even for months.

As one of them, I was sent to a makeshift unit housed in a row of huge tents between the helipad and the perimeter. The makeshift nature of the arrangement was accentuated by a commanding officer in the form of a short-timer lieutenant, a combat veteran who looked the part but who was just counting the days until he could get back to his shoe store, his soda fountain, or whatever it was he commanded in civilian life. Also, there were five or six other GIs who looked as though they didn't know where they were, why they were there, or what, in general, was going on around them. On the other hand, the noncoms were all gung-ho lifers who felt it their duty to make us as miserable as possible. Minutes after we arrived, they took us straight out into the rubber plantation and put us to patrolling the perimeter, circling the camp through the dense foliage of the jungle, while holding down the three-man listening posts out in the bush at night.

Back in basic, we joked that whatever they trained you for you'd never do. If you were trained as a cook, when you got to your station you'd end up as a supply clerk or maybe a mechanic. Besides, the instructors at AIT (Advanced Infantry Training) warned us that by the time we saw action most of our training would have become obsolete or irrelevant. So it was that the Morse code, which I spent so many weeks learning back in basic, was never used in 'Nam. Teletypes were said to be nonexistent there. Therefore I was duly warned and fully prepared for the likelihood that I would, at best, be stuck with my primary MOS (Military Operational Specialty) and end up carrying a radio.

But for the army, even that made too much sense. OJT already had more radio operators than it could possibly use, and, with two of the other guys I'd come over with, we made a surplus of three. So instead of radios they gave the three of us M-60 machine guns that were so heavy they seemed to pull our arms out of their sockets. Then, when we weren't on patrol duty, we spent hours on the range and in the bush until we qualified expert in a variety of different weapons, including the M-16 (I already had my expert badge on the M-60, as well as the M-14 from basic), pistol, bayonet, and hand grenade. Also, we were taught "quick-kill": they threw up plates for us to shoot at and we learned to fire at them without even aiming, using only our reflexes, until we were hitting them most of the time. The plates were gradually reduced in size until, in the end, we were shooting at, and hitting, small discs slightly larger than silver dollars. In no time at all I could hit a disc with a single shot fired from the hip. I learned later that this was a useful skill because in jungle warfare there was often no time for careful aim. Targets popped up too near at hand and moved too fast.

The heat in 'Nam was intense, and the humidity unbearable. Our clothes were always soaking wet with sweat, even though the fatigues were specially designed with material that dried in minutes. We took salt tablets to make up for the body salt we lost in perspiration. Dry land was covered with voracious army ants, scorpions, and assorted snakes. The water in the canals and rice paddies was muddy, leech-infested, and smelled of buffalo shit. Despite the fact that we were always in or around water, we were constantly thirsty, so we carried two canteens. In the mornings we were rationed to a helmet full of water, from which we were to brush our teeth, clean ourselves, shave, and wash our socks and so on, preferably in that order.

Our fighting gear started out heavy and soon weighed a ton, and it was invariably awkward to carry. Our helmets were so heavy around our necks that it seemed as though they were about to break them, and they rattled to fuck until we figured out how to tape them up. Much of the time we were suffering from dehydration from all the sweating, and maybe also from the diarrhea that most of us had.

During my first week in 'Nam I got the flu pretty bad, but I went out "humping the boondocks" anyway since I was too macho to admit I was sick. I figured that since I grew up overseas I should be immune to things that affected the others, but no one had bothered to tell the Vietnamese flu bug. Then I got diarrhea so bad I practically lived with my pants down, and for a while they took me off patrol. As some kind of twisted revenge, I was then assigned the "shit detail." Burning shit was without question the absolute most disgusting and degrading experience in my whole life. You drag out these half-drum tanks full of everybody's collected crap, pour kerosene on it, and burn it, then you take what's left and shovel it into a hole and bury it.

After a few days I was glad to return to the field, although I was still sick. I was weak as a baby, and carrying the M-60 was a bitch. We spent that week patrolling through the area around Di An, looking for an enemy whose whole strategy was built on his skill at hiding from us. It was a cat-and-mouse game, but which side was the cat and which was the mouse wasn't always clear. At one point we came to a small stream, and one by one we ran down the bank, jumped the stream, then ran up the other side. When it was my turn, I ran down the bank, jumped across the stream, then fainted, falling spread-eagle into the mud bank on the other side. They had to dig me out.

After that they gave me a radio. I'm not sure it was an improvement. I was given an AN/PRC-10 (we called it a Prick 10) backpack radio, as well as an M-14 rifle. I was glad to be doing a job I was trained for, but I soon realized that carrying the radio was one of the worst jobs anyone could get. It so happened that radio operators had one of the highest combat mortality rates of all. For one thing, the antenna sticks up in the air like an arrow, directing the enemy to where you are. For another, the enemy knew only too well that without a radio we couldn't call back to the base camps for artillery,

117

air cover, or reinforcements. For this reason, the radio man was often the VC snipers' first target.*

They taught us how to look for booby traps, *punji* stakes, and trip grenades, and sometimes we had to learn the hard way. Every morning there'd be new traps in areas we'd been through the day before. And of course we set traps of our own before we came in at night. Anyway, after trudging through the bush for hours, seeing absolutely no sign of the enemy, most of our searches turned up absolutely nothing. Then suddenly we'd be sniped at or ambushed, and all hell would break loose around us. Then Charlie would just disappear. It seemed that the last thing he wanted to do was actually engage us in combat. His strategy was one of harassment, baiting, and deception all for the purpose of luring us away from his supply lines.

Two or three snipers could hold up a whole platoon for hours. Naturally, those that were caught alive weren't shown too much pity. They were really in deep shit. The ARVNs would line them up and ask them questions, and when an interrogator didn't like the answer, he'd knife the prisoner in the gut and move to the next poor sonofabitch. Our own interrogators used methods that were not only more subtle but more scientific, and only slightly less brutal (remember, our training had included large doses of brainwashing to make us see the VC enemy as subhuman, worthy of no more than hostile contempt).

One method, "walking the plank," took advantage of the VC's fear of helicopters that existed for obvious reasons: the only time a VC saw one of these devils it was either spewing troops, raining rockets, or spitting lead. Moreover, a chopper up close is pretty scary to anybody, with those whirling blades going around inches above your head, and the intense shrieking and whine of the engine. So, the hapless VC prisoner is loaded into the chopper and taken way up into the air. Then he's brought to the doorway of the chopper and

---

* The officers in charge, especially the green second lieutenants, actually had it worst of all. Statistics would probably show that the average life span of an infantry second lieutenant in Vietnam in 1968 was not very long. As a result, when we were in the field we were taught to be careful not to identify them to the enemy. Of course, if there was a gung-ho officer that was out to get everybody killed, you'd salute him at every opportunity.

questioned. If he is uncooperative, he's blindfolded and threatened with being thrown out. He mentally examines his two options, and sometimes bravely chooses to die rather than talk. Meanwhile, unknown to the prisoner, the chopper has slowly dropped back down to only a few feet off the ground. If he continues to hold his tongue, the interrogator shoves him out of the copter, and in the second or two before he hits the ground his mind snaps. Having already exhausted his courage and resolve, having given his life for his secrets, he now has no option left but to talk.

There were certainly times I was afraid in 'Nam, but more often I was bored. Months of boredom, moments of hell. Armed men can be dangerous when they're too bored. One time, while waiting for a decision to cross a bridge over the Saigon River, a couple of LURPS (Long Range Reconnaissance Patrol) were smoking pot, and they started placing bets on just whatever popped into their minds—for example, "I'll bet I could shoot the horn off that water buffalo over there." Another guy pointed to one of the many sampans working their way down the river, and said "Shit, I can shoot a moving sampan."

"Shoot," said another guy, a crazy motherfucker called Ed Ryan, "I can shit in one."

The bet was on, and everyone wondered how in the hell he was going to do it. Ed calmly walked about halfway out onto the bridge, about where the sampans were passing under, then he waited until a sampan got directly under him. Just as the sampan reached the bridge, Ed fired off half a clip across its bow. The poor Vietnamese driving the sampan started back-rowing like crazy. But as furiously as he was back-pedaling, the river current kept him from going anywhere, and Ed calmly pulled down his pants, took careful aim, then dropped a large load of shit into the sampan.

Boredom was our worst enemy. Especially when it got to the noncoms. We were returning to the base camp one uneventful day when one of the gung-ho lieutenants decided he wanted to attack an old abandoned village we'd been through about eight times that week already. So we got all pumped up, and we went charging across this

WILD THING

field, firing all the way, until we got to the village. Just like in the movies, I threw myself up against the wall of a straw hut, then I pulled the pin out of a grenade (unlike in the movies, we used our hands, not our teeth) and threw it through a window into the hut. I threw my back up against the wall, and waited. When the grenade went off, the concussion through the flimsy wall blew me up in the air and halfway across the street. The guys were laughing so hard they couldn't come to help me.

As we were leaving the village, one of the point men stepped on a trip-wire that set off a land mine further back in the column. The point man was spared, but one of the sergeants, a weathered veteran with only a few weeks left of Vietnam duty, was blown to smithereens. We knew him only a short time, but we had all benefited from his experience. And now he was dead. The poor FNG that stepped on the wire kept saying over and over, "Why him? Why not me?" He was devastated.

Finally, one of the other veterans came to him and said, "Look, pal. It's not your fault. You were lucky." Then he added: "I'd rather be lucky than good any day."

BASE CAMP VIETNAM

Damn you masters of war . . .
BOB DYLAN

WHEN SOUTH VIETNAMESE president Nguyen Van Thieu declared the Tet Offensive a complete failure and U.S. Army chiefs announced that the Tet counteroffensive was over, they forgot to tell the VC. Around Di An, the war went on. Ground attacks on the perimeter were becoming a rarity, but there was constant sniping, and every few days we had mortar and rocket attacks. We had two siren signals—one steady blast for incoming overhead, and a wailing up and down for ground attack.

Di An, however, was gradually developing into headquarters for the First Infantry Division, and as such, it was a relatively safe place to be. We had the help of the Second Battalion, Sixteenth Infantry, and the First and Second Battalions of the Eighteenth Infantry, and later the Air Cavalry. On our flank was a battalion of Korean troops (ROKs), who were the best security of all.

The artillery unit to which I was assigned, for some reason known as "Pheons," was made up of about five hundred men. We were assigned to support the First Infantry Division's Second Brigade. We towed 105mm howitzers at first, but soon we got the more powerful 155s. These were used to fire protection for other base camps in the chain, but we also had mortar batteries to fire protection for ourselves.

The way it worked, our forward observers (FOs) would go out with the infantry and send back information and coordinates for the "big boys" (artillery) to fire at. To everyone's frustration, all coordinates had to be cleared first through the local Vietnamese government, which we all knew (or assumed) to be heavily infiltrated by VC. Many times our guys would find the enemy, meet resistance, and call in artillery, yet clearance to fire would be denied. Whenever the enemy resisted instead of disappearing, it meant we'd found a large ammo dump or something major. The provincial chief would claim he had ARVN troops in the area that might get caught in the middle, when we knew there wasn't a single ARVN within miles of the combat zone. This was usually the case.

But this didn't mean the guns weren't kept busy. We often ignored the clearances and fired anyway, and much of the fire was H&I. H&I (for Harassment and Interdiction) was where we randomly bombarded places around the countryside where we suspected Charlie might be. At the time, that was a lot of places. Our guns were almost never silent.

The company area of the Seventeenth Artillery, in fact the whole Di An base camp, was a rough affair when I got there but they were starting to paint the rocks white. Already there were signs of entrenchment, or permanence. Hootches like ours, with corrugated-tin roofs, concrete floors, and mosquito-mesh walls were being built to replace all the tents, and a large airfield was being built to accommodate the arrival of the Air Cav. The roads were dust or mud, depending on the season, but soon they began to lay down proper roads, and by the end of my year they were paved. A large mess hall was under construction across from where we built our hootches. It was obvious the Big Red One planned for us to be here for quite some time.

The radio team to which I was assigned was composed of four operators and a team chief, all of them short-timers. The team chief, a Sergeant Floyd Gartley, had only a few weeks left, and to say that he didn't give a shit anymore would be a major understatement.

Floyd didn't give "a flying fuck." That was his favorite expression. Ask him anything, and he'd say "I don't give a flying fuck" or "I'm too short for this shit." That sentiment was held by pretty much the whole company.

The radio team was part of the commo team that was headed by a sergeant major who was not only short, but also due for retirement. He didn't give a flying fuck either. Just so long as we didn't do anything that might cost him his stripes, he was happy to let us do whatever we wanted. He was a professional, and he kept things pretty tight as far as the work we did, but he never harassed us about the length of our hair, our uniforms, or the rest of the military rigmarole.

Aside from manning the radios and receiving and relaying messages from the field, we also had another function. To my surprise we had two radio teletype rigs mounted on the backs of two three-quarter-ton trucks and which were therefore, mobile, and theoretically could be sent to the field. But, thanks to Sergeant Gartley, we never had more than one truck working, never more than one teletype machine, and never the two together. That way the teletypes were never field ready, so no lunatic lieutenant could get the silly notion to try them out in the jungle.

I began to get homesick. Mail call became the most important time of the day, and I waited for my name to be called each day like a child waiting for Santa Claus at Christmas. The joy of receiving a letter, or better yet a care package, was immeasurable, but so was the disappointment at not hearing your name called. Letters were read over and over, and carried with you wherever you went, and, on rainy patrols or in muddy foxholes, kept drier than even your ammo.

My family and friends would write to me with news from home, and it was my only form of communication with the outside world. Fiona McRobert wrote to me often from England, and since I came over without leaving a girlfriend behind to dream of, she became my surrogate sweetheart. I put up her photo in my bunker alongside the pictures the other men had of their girls back home, and soon, in my mind, we were lovers again.

Our surroundings were as different from the world I knew back home as it was possible for them to be—no flash cars, no dates on a Saturday night, no cruising for burgers down the strip. The friends I made were close, close because we lived together and covered each others' ass, but yet they were so different from me in interests and background that I shied of being *too* close. All of us talked about our lives back in the real world, but usually in terms that were at least partly fantasy. Maybe that's why so many of us were disappointed when we got back. After all, for all practical purposes, reality was right there, right then.

The most glaring reality was the absence of any privacy, any individual existence at all except that each of us dealt with this group existence in his own way. Some guys freaked out and, one way or another, went off the deep end. Others just resigned themselves to whatever happened. I learned how to be both "we" and "I" by being at the same time a participant and an observer. Come to think of it, I loved it—not all the time, but enough to have seen me through it all, and to have mostly fond memories as I think of Vietnam.

Not long after I got there most of the guys I'd gotten to know reached their DEROS (Date Eligible for Return from Overseas) and were rotated home, and a bunch of new guys came in. Assigned to my radio team was Ron Jaragosky, a huge, imposing guy who looked like a mean-ass killer but who turned out to be a peace-loving hippie from Haight-Ashbury, and another Californian named Nakahira. They worked in commo with me, pulling shifts on the radios and teletypes. Ron was generally a pleasant fellow, but despite his peace signs and hippie beads he'd kick your ass in a minute if you accidently knocked over the framed picture of his girlfriend he kept in our bunker. He'd proved himself in combat during his OJT, and came to commo a corporal. Nakahira was a karate expert who spent his time alternating between brushing his teeth and breaking cinder blocks with his bare hands.

They had us working eight-hour shifts right around the clock. Since we handled messages classified as Confidential, Secret, and Top Secret, we were able to close off our area with barbed wire and make it off-limits to absolutely everyone, including officers. This allowed us to sit in our bunker ("the pit") and do anything we wanted. Nobody could fuck with us. We did let in our friends, of course, and we'd even have some pretty wild parties, drinking beer, smoking pot, even opium, and listening to reel-to-reel tapes. Jimi Hendrix, Janis Joplin (with Big Brother & and the Holding Company), and The Doors were our favorites. Ron Jaragosky and John Miles had guitars, and the rest of us would bang on tin cans or anything else we could find. One time we recorded a bunch of our favorite songs and we called ourselves Stark Naked and the Car Thieves. The tape had all sounds of 'Nam, helicopters flying by overhead, gunfire from the perimeter, and it ended with incoming mortar nearby, and then the sirens.

Somehow we managed to have fun in 'Nam. We had an officer, I'll call him Lieutenant Cohen, who was into trading things with the other base camps, and one day he came back from Saigon with a bunch of movies. He then got the bright idea to build a theater so we could show them. So we went to work, a grateful change from filling sandbags, and we built this huge barnlike building, then painted one wall white for the screen. We even had a special balcony for the projector (also scrounged up by Lieutenant Cohen) that was large enough to accommodate those of us who had contributed to the building of the theater, a sort of VIP section.

So when the theater was finished, we invited everybody over to watch our first showing, a movie called *The Green Berets* starring John Wayne. The place was packed with GIs by the time we ran the first reel. It might be interesting to note that the Green Berets were none too popular with the boys in the Big Red One, since we considered them to be nothing more than government hype, but when the scene came up on the screen where the gooks came over the wire, one of the GIs in the audience stood up and started shooting at the screen. Soon enough, everybody joined in, and before we came to the end of the movie, the screen, one whole wall, was completely demolished.

We kicked Charlie's ass in '68. By the end of the year there were no more ground attacks on the base camp, and even the snipers ceased to harass the perimeter guards. During the day it was relatively safe and worry-free. After dark it was a different story. When the sun set,

WILD THING

the country reverted to Victor Charlie, and every night he reminded us of the fact. As soon as the sun went down we waited, and soon the concert would begin. First there was a whistle, then a crash, and then caa-RUMP! Then the sirens that signaled incoming shells would begin to wail. Then more crashes and caa-rumps, and the answering sound of our own heavy artillery. From the perimeter we could hear the drum roll of small arms firing away into the dark at nothing in particular. One time a rocket found the ammo dump and all hell broke loose. Another time our shithouse was hit, causing quite a stink. But more often than not the rockets fell harmlessly away from the intended target, and our casualties were few.

By Christmas, the war died down almost completely around Di An, and the mortar and rocket attacks diminished considerably. In the end there was only one lone VC out there each night. At dusk he came, lobbed in his one rocket, then went home to bed. Every evening we sent out patrols to find him, but we never did. He began to earn our respect, although his aim was lousy. We gave the little bastard a nickname—"the Phantom," or something like that. We had to admire a little ninety-pound gook who would hand-carry a fifty-pound rocket all the way down the Ho Chi Minh Trail, mostly at night, through all the snakes and leeches, past all our troops and traps and technology, just to get that one shot at us. He probably never even got to fire the damn thing. After all that, he'd just hand it over to someone else, then off he'd go, back up the trail to get another one. The guy that actually fired it probably worked on our base camp during the day so he could measure off the targets.

CHAPTER 12

DEAR JOHN

We've gotta get out of this place, if it's the last thing we ever do.

—THE ANIMALS

ON THE BASE CAMP, the war was a bore. Every day, marked off on our calendars one by one so that we'd always know precisely how "short" we were, we spent hours building up the base camp and erecting sandbag bunkers. The tin-roofed hootches we slept in were completely surrounded by ammo boxes filled with laterite, with sandbag bunkers at each end. The mess hall, the CO's office, the commo hut, supply tent, even the shithouse were in a bunker. The only thing not in a bunker was the shower, which never had water and was used only infrequently anyway.

The war had become a simple matter of avoiding getting hit by the odd rocket. Our unit wasn't going into the field much anymore. When they weren't putting us to work on some kind of manual labor, most of our time was now spent pulling eight-hour shifts in the command bunker, or in our commo bunker on the radio teletypes. We sat in a bunker listening to a small speaker we'd wired up to the truck-mounted radios and waiting for the signal that told us to fire them up so as to receive an incoming message, or occasionally to send one out.

You might say I was crazy to begin with but, anyway, I began to behave like one of those gung-ho kids you see in the movies. I was always volunteering for action duty whenever I could, although there really wasn't much action anymore. Guard duty on the perimeter was really my only source of action, and even that had become a dead source. The VC just weren't coming to the party at the perimeter anymore.

But being gung ho was only part of it; there was at least *some* method in my madness. All the other guys were draftees, two-year men, but when they were sent home after a year in Vietnam, they were almost always discharged. The high cost of restationing and reoutfitting returning veterans with no place to send them made the army adopt a policy of discharging those with only a few months left. As a volunteer, I had another year or more to go and I didn't want to spend it peeling potatoes. As I saw it, the only way to avoid the military's horseshit was to get some stripes. But there was a problem. It was virtually impossible to make sergeant as a three-year man unless I reenlisted first. But in 'Nam, where rules were often bent, it was possible to get "battlefield stripes." So, mindlessly, I stepped forward for every shitty assignment.

Our boss in commo, Lieutenant Cohen, was the officer whose recommendation I would need. But soon after the episode with the movie theater, we rarely saw him. I thought that was rather strange, although the officers had their own compound, and we never saw much of them anyway. I began to watch him to learn his schedule, hoping to take every opportunity to be around the command bunker whenever he was. He always came in on specific days. I also noticed that those were the days we got out supply and demand reports. These told where everything was going, and where there were shortages. I had a friend over at the motor pool check the requisition sheets for Lieutenant Cohen's jeep. Sure enough, his destinations were places mentioned in the reports. It was easy to guess what he was up to. He was into the black market.

I *was* only guessing at the time, but it seemed obvious that he was trading goods between the various outposts and base camps, and also with the South Vietnamese. He had figured out from the info on the teletype reports how to make the most of the shortages in one place and the glut in others. The army tends to send ice to the Eskimos and coals to Newcastle. Generators were going to places that had plenty of electricity, and refrigerators to places that had none. If the brass back in Bien Hoa were short of jeeps, Lieutenant Cohen would solve the problem. He'd pick up generators in Ben Cat and trade them for refrigerators in An Loc, then trade those back to Ben Cat for some jeeps. Then he'd trade those to the officers in Bien Hoa for God knows what. Since it was all Government Issue to begin with, it was easy for him to come out ahead in each transaction, and still look like a Robin Hood to his "clients." In the end, from what I could gather, he had a fairly large commercial empire, with warehouses full of goods, everything from mopeds for the Vietnamese to TVs for the GIs.

This was the sort of situation a young man brought up in Lebanon would recognize, along with an instant understanding of how to make the most of it. I went to Lieutenant Cohen and announced that I wanted a job as his bodyguard, riding shotgun on his trips. It was a job he was glad to give me.

Anything was better than sitting around on the base camp, and every trip with Lieutenant Cohen was an adventure. I got to see sides to the war that were out of reach to all but a few officers and soldiers in Vietnam. We went all over the III Corp area, visiting the most remote firebases and the biggest. On one trip into Long Binh, which, by this time, had become even more like being back in the States, I was thrown into an MP brig for most of a day (until Lieutenant Cohen found me and rescued me), for failing to salute an officer, something we were not even allowed to do in the boonies. On a trip to the Twenty-fifth Infantry in Cu Chi, we saw the tunnels that were found to be stretching for miles, surrounding the base camp, and even under the base camp itself. We saw places in our own area I hadn't known about, First Infantry firebases up in the black hills near Tay Ninh and remote outposts in the Iron Triangle, some with only a handful of Americans and ARVN troops. We went up Highway 13 to the base camp in Quan Loi near the "fishhook" of Cambodia, and got stuck there one time when the North Vietnamese tried to overrun the place.

◆◆◆

WILD THING

The big problem was that Lieutenant Cohen was one brave sonofabitch. His balls must have been the size of grapefruits. He took chances I never would have taken on my own. He'd tell me about some great deal he had going, right in the middle of the shit, and ask me if I thought we should go for it. But I was out to impress him, so I couldn't exactly be chicken. We tried to latch onto a convoy most times, but Lieutenant Cohen would frequently take us off on our own. He didn't mind going to places where we shouldn't have been—for example, free-fire zones on roads that were classified "off-limits—unfriendly."

Lieutenant Cohen usually did all the driving, with me riding shotgun. There was one time he ran the jeep off the road when we thought we saw an ambush ahead, banging himself up pretty bad. I had to take over to get us out of there. That was one time I was glad of my Jim Russell Racing School training. Otherwise I rode shotgun and kept my eyes peeled and my M-16 rifle ready, even when we were in the villages where we were inevitably surrounded by hordes of curious or begging kids. Especially then, since we'd been warned that kids often planted hand grenades or satchel charges. I could believe it, but actually I was more worried about them grabbing the tool box or the gas tank off the back of the jeep. What was I going to do then? Shoot them?

I wanted to impress the lieutenant but he would never let me in on his clandestine transactions. When we got to our various destinations, Lieutenant Cohen would leave me in the jeep or drop me off at the enlisted men's club if there was one. I'd never been a drinker, but out of sheer boredom I started putting away some beers, even in the villages where it was rumored that the VC would piss in it, hoping to give us hepatitis. As a matter of fact, I was slightly inebriated when I volunteered for a particularly dodgy assignment, one that even Cohen was loathe to undertake, but I was going for my stripes.

The lieutenant had some paperwork that had to be delivered to a firebase up near Quan Loi, which was under threat of attack at the time, and he was needed elsewhere. I convinced him he should let me handle the delivery while he took care of his other business. I decided to impress on him that I had "leadership qualities," so I convinced him to let me bring some of the other guys from commo, whom I referred to as "my men." And my men? Ron Jaragosky came along for the fun of it, but the only way the others would agree to volunteer for such a mission was by my promising to let them stop off at the local whorehouse on the way back.

Ron (Jag) Jaragosky, John Chupa, Blake, and I drove up to where Lieutenant Cohen was doing business. We delivered the papers without incident, but on the way back the guys made me live up to my promise. We made a detour into a village outside Di An that we knew had a "massage parlor." It was in a rundown shack on the outskirts of the village, and it only had two girls, but that worked out all right since we couldn't leave the jeep parked outside. The area was off-limits to the Big Red One, so we went in turns, two at a time. Jag and I were unlucky on the coin toss and got to go last. Nobody likes "sloppy seconds," but with a prostitute I suppose that's all there is anyway.

So Jag and I drove around for a while until it was time to trade places with Blake and Chupa. Inside the brothel we had to flip another coin to decide who got the good-looking girl, and who got the dog. The good-looking one really was incredibly beautiful, like a little porcelain china doll. She didn't look more than sixteen, though it was impossible to tell with Vietnamese girls. The other girl was really ugly, fat as a cow and surely pushing fifty. As Jag so politely put it, "She looks like someone set fire to her face, and put it out with an ice pick," and "What did she do, French-kiss a locomotive goin' ninety?!" Needless to say, I lost the coin toss.

They spoke a kind of GI pidgin English, a mixture of Vietnamese and GI talk, French and American slang, and you had to figure it out in order to negotiate with the Mamasan about the price. Mamasan wanted five dollars for each girl, and we were only offering a couple of bucks.

"Fi' dollah, fi' dollah. You bang babysan long time. She make you beaucoup dinky-dow."

"We must be dinky-dow to come here in the first place. We'll give you two dollars and a pack of Marlboros."

"No way. You numbah ten GI! You horny. Babysan boom-boom outasite, numbah one blowjob. She cherry."

WILD THING

"How could she be cherry? Our friends were just in here."

"You friend, faggot! She cherry! Fi' dollah." We finally cut a deal, then went to our separate rooms.

Anyway, I wouldn't have the chance. We were interrupted by a loud crackle coming from a two-way radio right outside the house. Mamasan came running in screaming "MP come! MP come!" Jag and I were running around trying to get our pants on and our shit together, and to find a place to hide at the same time. Mamasan showed us to a secret hiding place, but it was too small for two large Americans, even for one. Jag ran to the back window of the house and leaped out, and I was right behind him. We took off down the yard and dove into a chicken coop at the bottom of the garden. But the chickens made one hell of a racket, and the smell was overpowering. Covered in chickenshit, we ran out of there and headed across the rice paddy to the rubber trees on the other side. Halfway across the paddy Jag tripped over a dike and his rifle went barrel first into the thick mud.

We made it to the tree line and stopped to look back at the whorehouse. Apparently we'd made it without the MPs seeing us, because they went into the house and stayed there for a very long time. It became obvious they were getting some pussy for themselves. As we watched helplessly from across the rice paddy, we saw Chupa and Blake go by the house in the jeep, then high-tail it out of there. Obviously they thought we'd been caught by the MPs. It was starting to get dangerously dark when the MPs finally sauntered out, mounted their jeep, and rode off. But no sooner had we started back across the rice paddy when out of the rubber trees down the road on the other side of the house came six or seven men in black pajamas carrying rifles, headed straight for the whorehouse.

"Oh, shit!" I said, "is that who I think it is?"

"You're damn right, Leroy. That's Victor Charlie all right."

"You think they saw us?"

"I don't think so. It looks like they were waiting for the MPs to leave. They're probably going to collect their taxes from Mamasan."

"Well, Mamasan knows we're here." The VC were walking casually down the lane, confident that all the Americans were back on their base camps, and I had the lead man clearly in my sights when Jag stopped me from pulling the trigger. "Hold it," he said. "My rifle's jammed. Let's see what happens before we take on a whole squad of those motherfuckers."

They went into the house, and then they came out to the chicken coop, with their rifles at the ready. It appeared that Mamasan had indeed blown the whistle on us. When they started fanning out across the rice paddy, I opened up on them, emptied a full clip, then we took off into the forest and kept running. We didn't stop until we came to an oxcart path which we followed in the general direction of Di An. We didn't want to use the road for fear of mines, but we also didn't know how long it would take for the VC to come after us, so we decided to take our chances.

By now it was nearly dark. Sometimes when we stopped to listen, we thought we could hear the sound of men coming behind us. Ahead of us, we heard the sound of an approaching motor scooter. Without a word we jumped into the bushes, me on one side and Jag on the other. Before long, a Vietnamese man in black pajamas came puttering down the road in our direction. As he came near, we jumped out waving our hands, shouting "Dung lai, dung lai!" (Stop!), but he couldn't stop, and he and his bike went careening off into the ditch. Before he could dust himself off, we grabbed his scooter and high-tailed it out of there.

We headed back the way the man came from, hoping it would lead to the main road to Di An, but instead it grew smaller and smaller until it turned into nothing more than a narrow path. Eventually we were forced to abandon the scooter and continue on foot. The path came to a point where it split into several trails, each going a different direction. We chose one that led into the rubber plantation, knowing that Di An was somewhere in the middle of it, and we followed it into the jungle. The moon was full, but it was still impossible to see anything under the trees, and the path was extremely hard to follow. We were slowed down by having to check for booby traps, either the enemy's or our own. We had to negotiate our way carefully around every branch crossing our path for fear of *punji* traps. We knew it was foolish to stay on the trail, but we didn't have much choice under the circumstances.

The trail eventually came to a large clearing, on the other side of which were rows of barbed wire and then guard towers and bunkers. To our dismay we saw that it was the ROK (Korean) base camp that adjoined our own. This was bad news. We feared the Koreans almost as much as the enemy. Unhindered by some of the restraints that Americans were held under, the Korean forces had a reputation, and our admiration, for a policy of shooting first and asking questions later. Approaching their perimeter at night didn't seem like a good idea.

The ROKs would rake the jungle every few minutes with their searchlights, and with sporadic bursts of machine gun fire every ten minutes or so. We soon decided that they weren't shooting at us personally, to coin a phrase from the old man, but this didn't make us feel any better. We decided to go back to the split in the trail, and try an alternative path. This time, after hours of painstakingly working our way along the path, we came out on the outside perimeter of our own base camp.

We were still in a jam, however. If we tried to approach the perimeter there still was a chance one of our guys might panic and blow us away. And if we made it, there still would be a big stink and we'd have a lot of explaining to do as to how we got into the predicament in the first place. Jag didn't care but I did. I didn't want to be court-martialed and lose any chance of getting my stripes. I suggested that we wait until daylight and try to get in without attracting attention to ourselves.

"Leroy, in case you forgot your basic training, there are one hundred and thirty-three kinds of snake in Vietnam. One hundred and thirty of them are poisonous. Then there are the scorpions, the leeches, the tarantulas. Not to mention unfriendly natives. We're probably sitting in the Phantom's favorite spot, for Chrissakes. I'm not staying out here longer than I have to, not for a New York minute."

"Jag," I pleaded, "if we go in now they'll throw the book at us."

"So fucking what?" he replied. "We are already in a world of shit. What are they gonna do, send us to 'Nam?"

"They'll charge us both with AWOL," I said. "In case you forgot your basic, that stands for absent without leave. They'll bust us down to buck privates."

"I could give a flying fuck. They can bust me right out of this man's army, and see if I care."

"They'll extend our tours for sure." I knew that would work. Nobody I knew in Vietnam wanted to go home more than Jag.

So finally he agreed, and we spent the night in the rubber trees, watching our perimeter in the moonlight, from Charlie's side of the fence. Every so often our mortars sent up flares to light the perimeter so we could see everything clear as day, yet still be invisible behind the trees. In the morning we made our way back to the road, flagged down a water truck, and hitched a ride through the gates. Chupa and Blake were sure surprised to see us. They figured we were locked behind bars in the stockade, or worse, prisoners of the Vietcong tax man. Meanwhile, some good came of our escapade; on some pretense we were able to report the location of the trails to our patrols. Ambushes were set and within a week or so the Phantom was caught. It could be coincidence, but Ron and I figured the man on the motorbike had indeed been none other than—the Phantom.

In any case, all my attempts to impress the lieutenant were wasted on him. It seems he had his own agenda. As his illicit empire grew to be more than a small base camp like Di An could handle, he asked for a transfer to Saigon and got it, a very unusual occurrence. Without warning, Lieutenant Cohen was gone.

As we went into the new year, 1969, we weren't all that worried about another Tet attack. Our intelligence reports told us that the Vietcong were pretty much wiped out from the last one. And from the huge body counts that were being reported no one could imagine the enemy mustering much of an effort. By coming into the open in 1968 the Communists, for the first time, foolishly gave us an opportunity to utilize our superior firepower and technology, and we very nearly annihilated them entirely.

Our bombing and patrolling of the Ho Chi Minh Trail had cut the flow of supplies to Saigon almost completely, and we were no longer finding any large caches of ammo or supplies. During November and December, contact with the enemy had virtually ceased. The truth was that the Vietcong *were* planning another all-out attack. The difference was that in 1969 the targets were to be the U.S. forces and

WILD THING

base camps instead of the civil targets of Tet '68. But the intelligence we were getting gave us no inkling of it.

Even so, the brass weren't going to take any chances, and for weeks before the Chinese New Year we were all on alert and pulling extra shifts on guard duty. The artillery and mortar teams were working around the clock, and the guns were melting their barrels. Coordinates would come in over the teletypes for H&I, which meant we were guessing where Charlie might be and firing at that spot without warning. I don't know what good it was doing, but it was so loud and so constant it was driving us all crazy.

I now had only a few months left so I was getting *really* short, too short for this shit. Things were generally pretty tense when Jag and I were assigned to a mission up in Quan Loi, but fortunately we encountered no action. When we got back from the field we were given a few days off before going back on shift. So, I was hanging around with the grunts over at Dracula Company when the medic came into our bunker and asked if anyone wanted to do some LSD.

As short as I was, I didn't give a flying fuck, and I was curious to see what acid was all about. We all wanted to know what the hippies back in the real world were getting off on, and we figured we could take anything those pussies could. None of us could imagine a bad trip being as bad as some of the shit we'd been going through. I took a tab of orange paisley and dropped it, as did most of the other guys.

For half an hour or so, nothing happened. Everybody was bumming out, saying we'd been ripped off. Just then, the VC started shelling the base camp. Not the odd rocket here and there, but a barrage of them all over the camp. All of a sudden the steady signal on the sirens went off, signaling that we were under ground attack. That meant the enemy were coming over the wire. And just then, the acid started kicking in.

We were rounded up and taken to the perimeter. We'd been drilled in the event of a ground attack, but this time people were running everywhere, and somebody was shouting that Charlie was on the base camp, that he'd gotten some sappers through the wire. The next thing I remember is that I was in a bunker on the perimeter tripping my brains out with a couple of other guys that were in the same fix. I can't tell you how many of the enemy we killed coming over the wire, or if we killed any at all, because when the flares pumped up by the mortar teams came down they made the shadows move, and we were shooting everything that moved. I thought there were hundreds of them. A lieutenant came into our bunker and ordered some of us to follow him. I do remember we laughed our asses off in his face because he said "Half of you men come with me!" There were three of us.

I've had to rely on others to reenact what went on that night, and for a while thereafter. The events, as I try to recall them, had no rhyme or reason, and I still have dreams of things I can't place in time. From what I gather, a preplanned counterattack was put into effect, and anyone on the base that wasn't tied to an essential duty was rounded up to take part. We were put into platoons and sent to strategic positions on the base camp, while some were sent out to circle the wire and try to trap Charlie against the perimeter. I just followed orders, and somehow got roped in with the wrong unit, carrying an M-16. Next thing I knew, we were going over the wire and off the base camp. The lieutenant, one I'd never seen before, didn't know where we were either, because he gave the wrong co-ordinates over the radio. I heard it, but I thought I was tripping. There was a firefight off to our flank. One of our choppers came by pumping rounds from his mini-guns, coming down very close to our position, and one of our guys freaked out, and started shooting back. I'm sure he was thinking that the chopper was a Martian spaceship. Well, all hell broke loose. That must have cleared my brain a little bit, enough to make me get on the radio and call off the chopper. The radio man was dead.

I must have done *something* right in Vietnam. I was awarded the Bronze Star Medal, the Good Conduct Medal, four campaign medals, the National Defense Service Medal, the Vietnam Service Medal, the Republic of Vietnam Commendation Medal, and a VBC with palm (I never have figured out what that is). But none of this had anything to do with my eventual promotion. Casualties were so high that year, I was promoted to sergeant at the age of nineteen. I was told at the presentation that I was the youngest soldier ever to make sergeant. Maybe it was true, maybe it wasn't, but since the rules

WILD THING

were new, and since the average age of a grunt in 'Nam was so much lower than in other wars (nineteen, as opposed to twenty-seven in World War II), it was at least possible.

I still had to go before a board and pass a review of officers to convince them I could handle the stripes. I had to answer a bunch of technical questions about the equipment, and know my MOS inside and out. I had to know military history, how to give orders, chain of command, drill and ceremony, and how to clean an M-16 blindfolded. My Bronze Star helped, but the hardest part of all was to convince them that I was just like them: a lifer.

This achievement, it seemed to me, was a first in a long life of fucking up, an achievement I could call entirely my own. It hadn't been given to me, it hadn't been bought. I had fought for it, damn it. And somehow, once I pinned on the three chevrons, I took on a certain feeling of pride as well as a sense of responsibility. I felt like I had to prove myself worthy of them.

Every day, I got up earlier than the others to get my shit together, and I learned to love those early mornings in 'Nam, the only part of the day that was bearable from the heat and moisture. Learning to get by on very little sleep is probably the best thing I got out of the whole experience.

I spent my last month in Vietnam trying to make the most of it, even as short as I was. I was careful not to let the stripes go to my head, and I avoided most confrontations with the other men, but still I tried to make improvements to our work area. I scrounged some PSP (large metal plates) and laid it down under the trucks so they didn't sink into the mud during the monsoon season. I had the guys build a bunker around the gas cans that we used for the generators, then I had them build a bunker around the generator. Nobody cheered when I decided to get both rigs and both trucks working all at the same time.

As it came time for me to go, I was almost sorry to leave. I had come to know this place—I had built some of it with my bare hands, for Chrissakes! It had, in a very real way, become home, and my friends were here. I felt like I had people who *needed* me. And something else: it occurred to me that I had nothing to go home for anyway. Fortunately, it also occurred to me that maybe Vietnam had gotten to me as it had to others I knew, and that maybe I wasn't thinking straight.

About a week before my DEROS, I was sitting around the commo bunker and I got this bright idea for using the clear plastic that the artillery shells came wrapped in. I went over to the mortar placements and rounded up all the sheets of the stuff that were being thrown out when the ammo boxes were opened. Then I nailed them up around the windows of our commo bunker in the compound. The idea was to keep out the dust, but they also looked great, and they gave the place a touch of class, just like they were real windows. But they also kept out the air, and the place became as hot as an oven. I was taking the stuff down when Buck Private Blake came to the security gate and asked if he could have some of the plastic.

Blake was a real war casualty, and half brain-dead at the best of times. When you've been in combat a lot, you get the "thousand-yard stare"; Blake's stare went for miles. You'd think he was high on drugs all the time, and maybe he was. He walked around the place like a zombie. I asked him what he was going to do with the stuff.

"All I know is that I was told to get some body bags. We're out of body bags, so they sent me to see if we could use some of that plastic you got. Is there any left?"

"You can have it all. But what's going on? Who's it for?"

"John-boy," said Blake.

"Bullshit, you fuckin' space cadet. John Miles? No fucking way! The guy was a walking lucky charm!"

"Well, he's real lucky now. At least he won't be putting up with this shit no more." Blake was serious. His own life was a living hell. It was rumored that there were some people that were so screwed up by the war the government wasn't letting them go home, and Blake was at the top of the list.

John Miles had arrived in Vietnam the same time as me, and he was due to go home the following week. I couldn't believe he was dead. I asked Blake, "How did they get him?"

"They didn't," he said, disgusted with me for even suggesting it. "Damn, Leroy! You know ain't no motherfuckin' Charlie gonna get John-boy. Fuck no. It took a woman to get John-boy."

I ran over to the hootch where John Miles' blood-soaked body was sprawled across his bunk. The whole top of his head was missing. His brain was dripping in blobs from the ceiling, where nine or ten new holes in the tin were letting the rain in. John had sat down on his bunk, put the barrel of his M-16 under his chin, flipped it to fully automatic, and leaned on the trigger.

There was a letter that was found on the bunk by John-boy's body. It went something like this:

Dear John,

> *I'm so glad you're finally coming home, I know it's been pure hell for you. I will miss getting your letters and writing to you, but I think now is the time I need to tell you the truth. I didn't want to make things worse for you by telling you before, but now I must.*
>
> *When you left for Vietnam, I spent as much time with your best friend Jody as I could, since he reminded me of you. I cried on his shoulder endlessly. He was so understanding, and we fell in love. We got married in August and moved to Canada where Jody can try to change his identity and avoid the draft. About the money you've been sending every month that we were saving for our wedding. I did save it for you. Honestly I did, all the way up until two months ago when Jody got this great idea to open an antique shop. He said we could double your money. Unfortunately there wasn't enough money to keep it going and we closed down last week. I'm afraid everything has gone down the drain.*
>
> *Jody hasn't been feeling that well lately anyway, so we decided it was better that he didn't have to work. I'm working at the day-care center so we can afford to buy his food and beer.*
>
> *Oh, by the way, I hope you'll be happy for me, I'm pregnant!*

> *Love,*
> *Mary Jane Rottencrotch*

CHAPTER 13

BROKE, BUSTED, DISGUSTED

I was in the right place . . . but it must have been the wrong time.

—DR. JOHN

SOMEONE FAMOUS SAID, "That's war. There is no glory in it." If war is a mind-blowing experience, so is coming home from one. I had been afraid to come to Vietnam, but now, in a strange kind of way, I was afraid to leave. I was all emotions at once: fear—since it was almost a known fact that you were going to be zapped on your last day in 'Nam; elation—I was going home, bro, back to the World!; sorrow—for leaving my close friends behind; guilt, for the same thing. And so many reasons to stay; hell, I was just getting good at it!

But, after a year in Vietnam (plus a whole extra day spent as a victim of harassment in Long Binh on the way out, because my boots weren't shined and my hair was too long), I said good-bye to my buddies, turned in my M-16, and boarded the "di-di bird" for home. From Bien Hoa I flew on army transport to Okinawa, Japan, and then to Hawaii, where we had a one-hour layover before continuing on to the mainland on a United flight.

In Honolulu I tried to buy something at the trinket shop at the airport, but the girl behind the counter refused to serve me, and she called me "a baby murderer." "Are you crazy?" I said. I felt as though I had been hit in the back of the head with a baseball bat. With all the killing in Vietnam, I never felt like "murdering" anyone, but for a moment I wanted to murder this stupid, ignorant girl.

Then at Oakland Air Force Base there was a crowd of people waiting for us, not with flowers and ticker tape, but with eggs and tomatoes. It was a large group of hippie college students protesting our involvement in Vietnam. The guy next to me on the bus to the base was a young medic who had lost an arm. He told me he would give his other arm just to see those yellow bastards rot in hell.

After several hours of debriefing at Oakland, I caught a military flight to the East Coast, which stopped four times along the way and took more than twelve hours. Then there was a whole day of waiting at McGuire Air Force Base to take a seven-hour flight home to England. The whole trip took eighty hours through fifteen time zones. By the time I arrived in England I was a walking basket case.

So, after a further train ride from Mildenhall Air Base into London, and a bus ride or two across town, I arrived at the family house at 21 Marlborough Place, in St. John's Wood, a complete physical wreck. I was so excited at being home I was going out of my mind, yet when I got there, no one was home. I didn't have keys, but the door was open so I went in. Someone threw a switch and the lights went on all over the house. "Surprise!" Miles had decided to throw me a welcome-home party, and invited all his friends. I could have killed him. Instead, I burst out crying. And then, everyone broke down and wept.

My next assignment was to Fort Lee, Virginia, just outside of Washington, D.C. For a Vietnam vet, it was an assignment from hell. Because of its proximity to the Pentagon, Fort Lee was a spit-and-polish camp used as a showcase for visiting dignitaries and heads of state. As a result, even the NCOs like myself were forced to submit to twice-daily white-glove foot-and-wall locker inspections, mandatory early morning reveille, endless hours of drill and ceremony practice, and even more hours of pointless parading around the parking lot. Our hair had to be short, shorter than you could pinch.

Our boots and belt buckles had to be so shiny you could shave in them. After coming from Vietnam, this bullshit was particularly hard to take.

I was first given a desk job, as a colonel's orderly or some title like that. It was regarded as a cushy assignment since it got me out of most of the parading around, but I wasn't cut out for the ass-kissing required for the job. It lasted only a few weeks. After that they made me a drill instructor. I was given the task of training the troops being mobilized for riot control during the upcoming May Day Peace March on Washington.

This put me in an awkward situation. The antiwar protesters, needless to say, were "pinkos," and "draft-dodging cowards" in the eyes of most of the other soldiers and officers at Fort Lee, few of whom had even been to Vietnam themselves. Their hatred for protesters in America was at least on a par with their hatred for the enemy in Vietnam. So here I was training troops with drawn bayonets, and some of us in charge were issued live ammunition, presumably to use on American citizens. I didn't agree with that at all. War is one thing. I bought the concept of fighting for a people's freedom, but surely that included people's right to protest. In any case, I couldn't see what the Army was doing engaging in civil matters.

But I was still a soldier, and had to do as I was ordered. So, I was stationed as sergeant of the guard at the Arlington National Cemetery during the protest, and got caught wearing a peace badge that was buttoned onto my uniform by a pretty young protester. I nearly got busted down to private, and only got out of it by explaining to the officer who spotted it that the girl had slipped it on me while I was feeling her up, not that I'd put it there myself.

Things went from bad to worse after that. Whereas I was expected to support the war in Vietnam, I was seriously beginning to question it. I had come to see that while American intentions were noble and good, as a nation we lacked the resolve to get the job done, and therefore further loss of lives was senseless. The more I voiced my opinions, the more I alienated my fellow NCOs.

I didn't fit in with them anyway. All the other NCOs at Fort Lee were career soldiers, known as "lifers." I was all too obviously counting the days when I could put as much space as possible between

WILD THING

myself and the army. They were just as obviously watching me in hopes they could find an excuse to bust me. This sort of situation can make a man paranoid, and paranoia, I've found, is at its worst when it's compounded by boredom. After all the excitement in Vietnam, now I was bored to distraction.

In retrospect, I may have been losing my mind. I became a loner. I was not allowed to fraternize with the troops of lower rank, and I had no friends among my peers. I had my own room in the barracks, and I kept to myself a lot. I bought a BSA 650 cc motorcycle for transportation, which was not exactly a social vehicle. This was an extremely traumatic time in my life. Vietnam haunted me and I went through a great deal of mental turmoil. Regardless of how I felt about the war, I still felt responsible for my men, the friends I'd left behind. I felt guilt for all the ones that never made it back alive. Grim images of death kept me up at night. I found it difficult to go off base into town, where I'd see young ladies alone on the street, or in the park, and feel remorse that they might be someone who had lost a lover or brother or husband, perhaps one of the brave men I had known. I'd see happy couples too, and hate them for their selfish happiness.

One weekend in July, on the date *Apollo 11* landed on the moon, I took a trip to Virginia Beach to try and unwind, but it did me no good. The place was overrun with sailors on the prowl for one-night stands, and college kids trying to get drunk and invariably succeeding. As I watched the televised broadcast of the first men to walk on the moon, I had an overwhelming feeling that there had to be something to life more meaningful than what I was doing. In this state of mind, perhaps not fit to make any kind of rational decision, I returned to Fort Lee and volunteered for another tour of duty in Vietnam. I had only seven months of service left and a full year was required for a transfer, so I also reenlisted in the army for an extra five months.

With my orders to return to Vietnam, I got a month's leave in advance, a courtesy they extend to suckers like myself who might not last out their tour in Vietnam. Naturally, I took mine in London where I thought I could get in a maximum of partying. I was wrong. It turned out that practically all of my friends had jobs or were otherwise occupied, so I ended up moping around 21 Marlborough Place, even more bored than I'd been back at Fort Lee.

One Thursday morning, January 29, 1970, to be precise, I decided to pay a visit to my old girlfriend, Fiona McRobert, out in Ilford. I should mention that whenever conversation in 'Nam went toward "girlfriends," as they often did, for lack of having a real girlfriend to brag about I used Fiona as my "girl back home" and I often fantasized about her as such, even though it had been a long time since we had anything going. When I called her she was excited to hear from me, but I was more excited than she was. We arranged to meet during her lunch hour that very day.

But when I went to the old man for the keys to the car, he said "no way." Instead, he reminded me that I was banned from driving the family car, dating back to before I ran off to join the army. All the shit I'd taken to prove myself, and he was still treating me like a juvenile delinquent! I was shattered. I was angry at the power he still had to put me down. But I was still determined to go see Fiona. I gave a long, dramatic, tearful speech about how if I was responsible enough to fight for my country, surely I was responsible enough to drive the family car. That worked, and was the only respect I ever got for my military service.

I was more than an hour late when I arrived in Ilford, by which time Fiona had gone back to work. I called her and she was pissed off, having spent her lunch hour standing on a corner, but she agreed to meet me after work. I decided to stick around Ilford to see her even though it gave me only half an hour before I would have to head back to London. I had promised to have the car back by a certain time, and one thing was for sure—I was going to keep my word to the old man. Otherwise I'd be banned from driving the family car for life, and with all due respect to Fiona, nothing could be worse than that.

To kill the time, I went looking for my old mate, Eddie Coltham. I went to his house, the same one I had lodged in years before, but his mother said he wasn't home. She directed me to the house of one of his mates, saying, "You can't miss it. There's a big psychedelic poster in the window."

I found it easily enough, but Eddie wasn't there. "He's not here

145 WILD THING

just now," said the long-haired bloke who came to the door. "But we expect him back any minute. You're welcome to come in and have a cup'a tea if you want to wait, mate."

I went into the front room and sat down with two other hippie blokes who were there, while the person who answered the door went into the kitchen to make tea. Just then . . . Bang! Bang! Bang! The front door came off the hinges, and in barged eight plainclothes policemen from Scotland Yard. "We've a search warrant to search the premises for illegal drugs. Don't anybody move!"

For half an hour they searched us, and all over the room, but they couldn't find anything. Then a few more cops arrived, and they came back into the front room and began to search all over again. This time they miraculously came up with packets of hashish everywhere, including underneath where I had been sitting, and behind the pillow on the couch, and even in the pockets of my jacket. One cop reached into my coat pocket and brought out a packet of something wrapped in tin foil. I'd never seen it before.

"Is this yours?" he asked.

"Not unless it's a Cadbury's chocolate," I said, trying to put the conversation on a friendlier footing.

"Oh dear, oh dear, oh *dear!*" he said. "A bleedin' Yank!" He went through my pockets and when he saw my military papers assigning me to Vietnam his eyes bugged out and his moronic face lit up like he'd won the Irish sweepstakes. "Oy, oy, oy!" he exclaimed. "We've got ourselves a deserter from the United States Army!"

From my life of misadventure, I recognize Deep Shit when I see it, and this was it. I had a five-day beard, I was dressed in clothes that made me look like a weekend hippie, I had on a Carnaby Street shirt that was just the sort of thing an American soldier on the run would cover himself with, and I was confronted by a gaggle of sadists with a combined IQ approximating room temperature.

The four of us were arrested and charged with possession of an illegal substance, specifically cannabis resin (hashish), and off to the paddy wagon we went. Even as I was being thrown into the back of a black maria I still didn't realize the mess I was in. I kept thinking that everything would be straightened out down at the police station, and I'd soon be on my merry way. My main concern was getting Dad's car back on time. I pleaded with the coppers to drive it back to the station rather than leave it in that dodgy neighborhood, and to my delight, they said okay. But none of them wanted to take the responsibility, so they insisted I drive.

If I thought I was going to get off easy, at the Ilford Police Station I received a rude awakening. Without so much as a chance to relate my story, I was booked, stripped down to my shorts, and searched, then I was given a blanket but no pillow, and thrown in the slammer. When the jailer turned the key to my door, and said "See you in the mo'nin', cobber," it finally hit me. I was in jail. Again! Only this time it would take more than a kindly old lady to get me out of trouble.

The next afternoon I was brought before the Magistrates Court, where three magistrates decided that the charges against me were serious enough, and the evidence to support them strong enough, for my case to go on to a proper jury trial. That trial was set for four months later, and I was returned to my cell.

On Monday someone in the embassy said he'd check my credentials with the Pentagon and get back to me as soon as possible, but it wasn't until Wednesday that some MPs in a khaki-colored Ford sedan picked me up to take me to the U.S. Army Base in Ruislip. There I was put in the brig, which was nothing more than a converted shipping container with holes cut in the metal walls for windows, which were welded over with iron bars. I don't recall exactly how long I was held there, but it was weeks before I was able to talk to the army captain in charge of handling legal problems between the British authorities and U.S. military personnel, since he was stationed in Germany. He was sympathetic, surprisingly, but not very encouraging. I saw from the medals on his uniform that he had been to Vietnam. I pleaded with him to let me go since I had only a few days of leave remaining before I was due to return to the war.

"Soldier," he said, "I'd say you were between a rock and a hard cock."

"Sir?"

"According to our agreement with the British Government," he said, "I can't let you leave the country until your case has gone to court. That won't be for several months, so you may not be going back to 'Nam at all. That's the good news.

"The bad news is you're facing a very long time behind bars. Up to ten years from the Brits. If they find you guilty, then you'll be court-martialed. That could get you another ten, maybe more. Failure to report to a combat duty is a cunt-hair shy of desertion, and drugs is no defense. Get the picture, troop?"

"Affirmative, sir," I said. "So what do you think my chances are of getting a fair trial?"

"From what I understand," said the captain, "you've got eight highly respected limey bobbies from Scotland Yard who will swear in court they caught you with your hand in the cookie jar. According to their testimony you were in the company of known drug dealers and you were allegedly in possession of eight grams of cannabis resin. That is a lot of cannabis resin. Sergeant, you're definitely up Shit Creek without a paddle."

My case did not come up for several months. On my day in court I came looking as good as I could. I was spit-and-polish personified. My hair was trimmed, my face shaved, and my shoes were so spit-shined I had to wear shades. I wore a freshly starched dress uniform, and I pinned all my medals on my chest. Not taking any chances, I even pinned on a few Girl Scout badges I stole from my sister, Lennie.

I gained some confidence from the fact that my dad was able to get me a top-notch barrister, a bona fide Queen's Counselor, which as the name implies means that he was one of a select few to give legal counseling to the Queen of England. But under the British system the barrister is kept one step removed from the defendant, so I never even got to meet him before the trial. I could see he was a heavy-weight when he came in the courtroom, with his white wig on and everything, and the court had to rise like for a judge. I, for one, was impressed.

My spirits were soon brought back down to earth. In the first few minutes of the trial it became evident that Eddie's friends were indeed heavy-duty dealers. All of them had been "inside" a number of times, and two of them were still on parole. As far as the cops were concerned, I was cut from the same cloth; guilt by association. Their testimony nailed me along with the others.

By the time my QC went to work, I had already been made to look guilty as hell. The cops even had me saying things like "All this for a few puffs?" and "This will ruin my army career." That was a laugh. So my QC started to question them one by one.

Queen's Counselor:	"You say in your testimony that the room was dark, the curtains drawn, the smell of incense in the air?"
Copper:	"That is correct, M'Lord."
Queen's Counselor:	"Did it seem to you that, shall we call it a 'pot party' was in progress?"
Copper:	"Yes, M'Lord, I would say that, yes."
Queen's Counselor:	"And would you say that my client was an active participant in this pot party?"
Copper:	"Yes, that would be my guess."
Queen's Counselor:	"And I assume that my client, being under the influence of some kind of mind-altering drug, was slurring his speech, stumbling about, that sort of thing. Like someone intoxicated, or on drugs?"
Copper:	"Yes, that's quite an accurate picture, I'd say."

Then he called the next copper, and got him to corroborate the first copper's story, and embellish it even more, and the same with the next copper after that. I kept wanting to shout "Objection!" to my own counselor's questions. I couldn't believe it! My QC was making it easy for them. I remember thinking: "First I'm framed! Now I'm fucked!" My QC was on their side.

After he called all eight coppers, the QC recalled the first one, reminding him that he was still under oath. He asked him how he had gotten back to the police station after the arrest. The copper actually forgot, as did I. His notes on the incident ended with the arrest. He had to be reminded that they had let me drive my father's car to the jailhouse.

"Would you please tell the court," the QC said to him, "how a responsible officer of the law could allow a prisoner to drive through the streets of London during evening rush hour, the streets teeming with British subjects, in a car full of Her Majesty's finest police officers, if the driver of the vehicle was in the state you have described so explicitly as being under the influence of intoxicating substances?"

The first officer realized he'd made a mistake, and began back-pedaling. He suddenly wasn't quite sure it was me who had said those things, and he didn't actually *see* me with drugs. The QC even got him to refute a part of his testimony. The next officer, who'd been coerced into corroborating the first officer's story, was also re-called, and now he was faced with perjury. One by one the cops fell apart, their story unraveled, leaving more than a shadow of doubt as to my guilt. The jury only took a few minutes to deliver a verdict. I was declared "not guilty." One of the other three men got off with me, but the other two went to trial a week later. They each received a seven-year jail term.

◆◆◆

By now I only had a few months of service left, so my orders for a second tour of Vietnam were rescinded and my file in Personnel was marked "Temporary Assignments Only." Since no one had any con-structive ideas on how to make use of me on a temporary basis, I was first assigned to a lonely outpost called Burtonwood Army Depot, up in the north of England. BAD was a communications station con-nected to an RAF air base in Lancashire, situated halfway between Liverpool and Manchester, and for some reason almost everyone there was civilian. My job was switchboard operator—not *too* bad, since all the other switchboard operators were girls, and my boss was a dear old lady who felt sorry for me, and who let me make frequent long-weekend excursions to London. Though BAD was classified as a "hardship post," it was heaven to me. I was only too glad to be free, and I enjoyed that summer as I'd never enjoyed it before.

I was in the United States Army, but I was living like a limey again. I rented a small room in Warrington, the nearest town, which I shared with three girls and a baby. Once again, I was putting shil-lings in the meter for electricity, and living off baked beans on toast, two channels on the television, and down to the pub for a pint in the evenings. With the back pay that I received for the time I was in jail or waiting for trial, I bought my first car, an English Ford Popular, four on the floor. With a steep downhill grade and a stiff tailwind it could go nearly forty miles an hour, but it ran forever on a gallon of gas. I eventually traded that car for an equally worthless piece of junk, a beat-up old Sunbeam Alpine sports car that I really grew attached to. The driver's door wouldn't open, but the passenger door worked fine, and it cut my drive time to London in half.

Of course, living it up in England was too good to last. In October 1970, the same week that both Janis Joplin and Jimi Hendrix died, I received orders stationing me in Germany, where I'd be forced to serve the five extra months I'd reenlisted to go back to 'Nam. I was transferred to snowy Coleman Barracks, a dreary army outpost guarding a stockade near Mannheim, Germany. I protested the extra five months on the grounds that my orders to go to 'Nam were rescinded and therefore my reenlistment should be too, but it did no good. I showed up in Germany as ordered, but I refused to wear my uniform. By this time I was so fed up with the military and so eager to get out that I didn't care what they did to me. I wore snakeskin boots to the first formation on the morning of my arrival, and from then on I was christened "Snake" by the men.

I should have been busted down to private, but instead luck was with me. I was marched into the company commander's office where I was threatened with serious punishment, but instead I discovered the opportunity to cut a deal which not only got me off the hook, it virtually got me out of the army. It so happened that my orders to fill the team's chief slot on the commo team screwed up the company commander's plan to fill the slot with an ass-kissing lifer corporal who'd just re-upped. I therefore suggested we strike a bargain. I would allow them to have their slot, putting their man in my position, and in return they would forget I exist. The CO agreed. After that I moved off the base, wore civilian clothes, and only had to come in once a month for my paycheck. It amounted to a five-month's paid vacation.

After three years and five months in the United States Army, Sergeant Copeland, RA10893974, packed his belongings into a duffel bag and caught a military flight to the United States. On a cold and windy day in January 1971, he was honorably discharged, getting out where he came in, at Fort Dix, New Jersey.

Now Ian Copeland, civilian, was faced with the big question, yet again. What to do with his life?

WILD THING

CHAPTER 14

LONG-HAIRED HIPPIE, FINALLY

If you're going to San Francisco . . .
—SCOTT MCKENZIE

WHEN I WAS discharged from the U.S. Army I had no more idea of what I wanted to do with my life than I had going in, and nothing you do in the army prepares you for the shock of getting out. One minute you're clothed, fed, housed, and told what to do; the next you're out on the street to fend for yourself.

Facing the real world can be frightening for anyone. For me it was a real predicament. Most of the other ex-GIs returned to their home-towns to pick up the pieces from where they'd left off. From where I'd left off it didn't seem worth it. I had nothing going for me back home in London. I knew that as an American it would be impossible to find work. In any case, I wasn't keen on the idea of moving in with the folks, so I had no place to go.

I took the easy route. I decided to go where the wind blows. I would take the opportunity of my unemployment to check out America and simply enjoy being a civilian for a while. My plan, if you can call it that, was to travel across America looking up friends I'd made in the army, as well as those I knew from Beirut. Wherever

I could I would work, but I could last for a while on the small amount of money that I'd saved. Realizing that the first thing I needed was transportation, I returned to Fort Lee, Virginia, and reclaimed my motorcycle left in storage.

For the next few months I spent my days and nights laboriously putting the bike back together on the floor of my sister's apartment in Washington D.C. I had stripped it completely, down to the very nuts and bolts, and packed the many parts in grease, so putting it back together meant turning Lennie's living room into a garage, with bike parts spread all over the place. But Lennie put up with it, no doubt willing to pay the price for an opportunity to use me as a case history for her thesis; it so happened she was working for the District of Columbia dealing with deprived children in some sort of social project, while working on an M.A. thesis for Georgetown University on juvenile delinquency. She might have been better advised to do one on Post-Traumatic Syndrome, though this was not yet a recognized ailment at the time.

By now my feelings for the war in Vietnam had changed dramatically. As I walked the streets of our capitol city, watching the politicians pass by in their stretch limos, I couldn't ignore the fact that their decisions were costing human lives. I knew they made those decisions to win votes, not necessarily to do the right thing, and I sensed that the American public was slowly losing its stomach for war. My experience had shown me that we were quite capable of winning the war, as we virtually did in 1968, but only if we were determined to do so, and that required a resolve that was being eroded every day. Like everyone else, I couldn't help but be affected by the gory television images of the continuing carnage in 'Nam.

I decided to take part in a protest march being organized by a new and loosely formed organization calling itself "Vietnam Veterans Against the War." On April 18, 1971, I threw my lot in with a thousand other veterans who came from all over America, and for five days we protested the war in Vietnam. We called it "Operation Dewey Canyon III," after two operations in 'Nam involving the invasion of Laos, and we staged an "invasion" of Washington, D.C., "a limited incursion into the country of Congress." The Nixon administration put up a fight. First they tried to block us from marching into Arlington Cemetery, where we wished to pay tribute to our fallen friends. Then the Justice Department outlawed us from camping on the Mall in front of the Capitol. The Supreme Court ruled that we couldn't sleep on the Mall, but we took a vote and decided to defy the ruling, and set up camp there anyway. The next morning we heard on the news that the police were ordered to clear us out of there, and at dawn we prepared ourselves to repel them as best we could. Having been on the other side of the fence, I was only too aware of the hatred men in uniform were capable of toward protesters, so I was prepared for the worst. But to our surprise and joy, the police disobeyed orders from the Justice Department, the equivalent of a mutiny, and refused to confront the veterans. To us, that was a major moral victory. I can tell you, many of the guys on that Mall were in desperate need of that.

As a final act of protest, on Friday, April 23, we all marched up the steps of the Capitol, where we were stopped by a barrier. One by one we hurled the medals we'd won in Vietnam over the barrier at the Capitol building, each of us making some kind of speech, impassioned plea, or simply cussing out the "establishment" before discarding our precious medals. For many of us, myself included, it was one of the most moving moments of our lives. As it turned out, it was the turning point in our nation's protest movement. For the first time the protesters could not be simply dismissed as draft-dodgers, Commies, or cowards. These were American soldiers, men who had been there and fought for their country. When they said the war was wrong, middle America and the real "silent majority" began to feel free at least to question the war without feeling unpatriotic.

With that off my chest, and with my bike put together, I said good-bye to sister Lennie early one morning and took off for Beaver Falls, a sleepy little steel town in the mountains of Pennsylvania. There I hooked up with Ray Dicicio, an old army buddy from Germany. He managed to get me a job in the steel mill where he'd worked before going into the army. The work was hard for me, but harder for Ray, since he had to start at the bottom of the ladder again, and friends of his that had not served in the forces—guys that once worked under him—were now foremen, his bosses. Still, everything was going fine, at least for a while. We worked during the day, then in the evenings we lived like hippies in a Furry Freak Brothers comic. We grew our hair long, and threw away our razors.

WILD THING

I couldn't see my future in it, but it was enough just to be out of the army.

One day we went for a swim at a favorite place on the river where there was a rusty old crane hanging out over the water from an unused loading dock, which we used to swing out over the river and fly hundreds of feet into the air before plunging into the water. We took some old inner tubes, tied a case of beer onto one of them, and drifted downstream with the river, soaking up the suds and the sun. And that day Ray told me he was going to California. He dropped the bomb casually, just as though he was only announcing how he intended to spend the evening, and, just as casually, he explained that some of his *"paisanos"* were in business in San Francisco and in need of "soldiers."

"We just got out of the army, and you still want to play soldiers?" I asked. But Ray had made up his mind. With his girlfriend, Elaine, his plan was to hitchhike west in search of a better life. Of course, this meant that I would have to think again about what to do myself. "Come with us to California," Ray said, but I didn't give it much serious thought.

A few days later, I was sitting in a diner when I overheard a conversation in the next booth. Some guy was talking about how bad he wished he had a bike like the one parked out front, meaning mine. I got to talking with him and found out that all his friends had bought motorcycles and he was stuck riding around in a beat-up Cadillac. We left the diner together and I had a look at his Cadillac. It had a dented front wing that was repaired but not painted, but other than that there was nothing wrong with the car. Inside it was cherry. It had a fancy radio with a push-button antenna, power seats, power mirrors, cruise control, three cigarette lighters, and even a lever to move the steering wheel aside to give you room to get in, so as not to wrinkle your tuxedo. Just joking, I suggested we trade. To my astonishment he grabbed at the idea and agreed to make the swap! We traded pink slips right there on the sidewalk. I then drove straight over to Ray's house. I burst in on him and Elaine right in the middle of having sex, and dragged them out half-naked to show them the car.

"What you are looking at," I said, surprising even myself, "is your ride to California."

Miles, meanwhile, was living at 21 Marlborough Place, our family home in London. Instead of dealing with rich Saudi sheiks and wealthy Arabs, however, as my father had intended, Miles was beginning to become involved in the music business.

While still studying for his thesis at the University of Beirut, he had become involved with organizing the decorations for a college ball, and in the process had met a band of English musicians called Rupert's People who were performing at the dance. Miles had been experimenting with the psychedelic effects of black lights, and so he came up with an idea to paint the band's girlfriends with Day-Glo paint and have them dance on the side of the stage while the band performed. It was a hit, and the band adopted it into their show from then on. Several months later Miles bumped into the band again, only this time it was on the streets of London.

Rupert's People were invited over to the family house in St. John's Wood, a posh neighborhood. Over tea they explained to Miles that they were on the verge of breaking up due to hard times, in part because their manager had absconded with all the money from their shows in Beirut. No doubt thinking Miles was a rich American, they jokingly asked him to manage them. To their surprise, Miles said yes.

Miles, however, was not a rich American. He was still in charge of the family fortunes (whatever that was), but Dad was not exactly ecstatic about the idea of Miles sinking money into a rock-and-roll band. Nor was he too happy about the noise from the basement, which Miles had converted into a rehearsal studio. It soon became obvious that the band would have to play to earn some pay. Miles's first job, therefore, was to find them some work.

He began by looking through the back section of the *Melody Maker* and *Sounds* to see where all the other bands were playing, then he'd call the clubs up and try to convince them to book his band. It was not something he enjoyed. Early in the experience, he was approached by a chap called Ricky Roach (his real name, as far as I know) who offered to sell Miles his contact book, a complete list of phone numbers for all the clubs, colleges, and promoters. Miles was skeptical, so Ricky agreed, for an extra tenner a week, to demonstrate the book's value by booking some shows himself.

Ricky Roach picked up the telephone, and in a few minutes he was filling Miles's datesheets. He seemed to be a wizard on the phone, and able to get put right through to all sorts of people whom Miles hadn't been able to reach. Miles's booking worries were over. He bought the book, and kept Ricky Roach on for an extra week.

In the middle of the second week, Miles got a phone call from one of the guys in the band saying that something was seriously wrong. They had driven all day to the first of Rick's bookings, and when they got there the club said they'd never heard of the group, and they'd certainly never booked it.

"Are you sure you're at the right place?"

"Miles, there's only one club in the whole bloody town of Cleethorpes."

When confronted with the problem the next morning, Ricky threw a shit fit! He got on the phone and tore somebody a whole new asshole. He was shouting and carrying on for twenty minutes. When he finally got off the phone, he explained to Miles that the guy at the club in Cleethorpes was drunk or something, and he'd rebooked the date for next week for more money.

The next night Miles got another phone call from the band's lead guitar player announcing that there was "something fishy going on." The band was at the address on the contract, but there wasn't a club there. There *had been* a club, but it had closed ten years or so earlier, to be replaced by a porno theater.

In the morning, Ricky put on a first-class dramatic performance. He was even more angry than he had been the time before. He snatched the telephone off its cradle, dialed a number, and went into spasms of fury at whoever was on the end of the line. Miles snatched the phone away from him in time to hear from the other end of the line: "We're sorry, the number you have dialed is no longer in service . . . Please check the number and try again. . . . We're sorry, ..." Ricky Roach was a first-class con artist.

Miles then went back to booking his own dates. Rupert's People enjoyed a short-lived success (their single "Reflections of Charles Brown" made it to 34 on the British charts), but they were a good learning experience. Well-intentioned and hard-working as the band members were, with a good-looking lead singer but only average musical talent, they soon became frustrated as the many more talented bands passed them by, and one by one they quit to find "real" jobs. First, Ray, the bass player, left to become an architectural draftsman, then Steve Brendel, the drummer, quit for a job as office boy at Apple Records, where he could hobnob with The Beatles. (Once, while home on leave from the army, I went over there to visit him, and nearly knocked Ringo on his ass as I came out of the elevator.)

Shortly before Rupert's People's final demise, however, Miles was impressed at one of their shows by the opening act, a three-piece band from Torquay called Empty Vessels. He approached them backstage to compliment them, only to be told that they too were breaking up, due to the illness of their guitar player, Glenn Turner. Miles then offered the remaining members, Glenn's brother Martin Turner and drummer Steve Upton, the use of the basement at 21 Marlborough Place to audition for a new guitarist. After auditioning thirty or forty guitarists, however, they couldn't decide between two of the best of them, and Miles suggested they take them both. So Andy "Snap" Powell and Ted Turner (no relation to Martin) were both hired, and the band was renamed Wishbone Ash.

As the first band to use two lead guitarists, Wishbone Ash got a lot of press and media attention, and their self-titled first album was a fairly big hit in England. Their second album, titled *Pilgrimage*, was also well received, but the third one, *Argus*, was a monster, and it began to sell well in America too. By this time, Miles had placed his bands with a small-time but well-known booking agent in London, a prematurely gray-haired young hustler called John Sherry, and together they formed an agency with a large roster of artists. It was called JSE, (for John Sherry Enterprises), though Miles was the only one to put any money into it.

Wishbone Ash was eventually booked for a tour of America, set up by a booking agent in New York, and Miles came over with them for their first tour.

◆◆◆

WILD THING

Ray, Elaine, and I took our time crossing the States, stopping to stay with friends along the way, and taking in places of interest like the Grand Canyon, following Route 66 just because we liked the Rolling Stones song. By the time we reached California we were broke. We ended up in the hills around the San Francisco Bay, a place called Castro Valley, where we found out that Ray's *"paisanos"* were dealing dope. They didn't want soldiers, they wanted bodyguards, and fools to run their drugs for them.

It was not long before my social security checks ran out. Along with a hundred thousand other out-of-work veterans, I was facing a desperate situation. No work, and no future. I was willing to do anything, any menial task or manual labor, but there was nothing to be had. To get a job as a waiter at a restaurant, for instance, you had to know the owner intimately, and even dishwashing jobs had waiting lists. I once answered an ad for a job with a singing telegram company, and I was beat to it by twenty other guys.

I also answered an ad in a newspaper calling for Vietnam vets to volunteer as mercenaries in the Congo, to show you how desperate I was. I was all set for my audition at their recruiting station when Miles called me from Los Angeles.

"Do you have a driver's license?" he asked. I did.

"I need you to come down here to L.A. right away," said Miles. It never occurred to him that I might be doing something important. "I've got a job for you," he said.

"Mannah from heaven, Miles. What kind of a job?"

"Tour manager," he said.

"What's a tour manager?"

"A glorified roadie, basically," he replied. "You take care of the band, drive them around, and when I'm not there, you pick up the money at the shows and pay for hotels, that sort of thing."

"Sounds good to me," said I. "Long as I don't have to wipe their asses."

"You do!" he said. "These are musicians, these are stars. In order to be a star, you have to be treated like one. But," he continued, "here's the main reason I called you. Anyone can drive a car, but I need you for a special reason. It concerns Ted Turner, the lead guitarist." Miles then told me in painful detail about how Ted had disappeared for two days or more, just before their important showcase debut at the famous Whisky a Go Go in Los Angeles. Apparently, he'd run into some weirdo Jesus freak who took him out to the desert and turned him on to mescaline for the first time, and Ted showed up at the Whisky, still tripping, with only minutes to spare before going on stage. Miles was convinced the show was a disaster, and now he wanted me to help him keep Ted away from strange drugs, and especially Jesus freaks.

"Ted's guitar hero is Peter Green," said Miles, "and he was led astray by Jesus freaks. I don't want to see Ted follow in his footsteps. As far as drugs are concerned, I know Ted's going to smoke pot. I can't stop it, I've tried. I want you to hang out with him and keep him away from people pushing the harder stuff."

Within a few hours I was in my Cadillac driving merrily down the Pacific Coast Highway on my way to L.A. One minute I'm bumming spare change for food and contemplating war in the Congo, and the next I'm touring around the country with a rock-and-roll band. From absolute rock bottom, I had miraculously been swept to the top of the world.

Having seen America as a poor drifter, now I was treated to the best of everything. In every city, each local promoter would go out of his way to impress the band with his hospitality and with his influence, and we were given first-class treatment all the way, from the minute we came to town to the moment we departed. In New Orleans, for instance, where the band was particularly popular, the promoter, a young entrepreneur named Don Fox, hired a brass band to meet us at the airport, and had limos take us around to all the highlights of the city, including the best of the nightclubs, where we were treated like visiting royalty.

Wishbone Ash wasn't exactly a monstrous touring attraction, at least not in the terms I would come to realize years later, but they were definitely on their way up, and to me in my world at the time, they were most happening. As the tour progressed, their album began to take off, and from week to week the band's popularity grew in each town. At the beginning of the tour we would consider ourselves lucky to get an interview with the local radio stations, and by mid-tour they were begging for the band to come on. Our itinerary for the last half of the tour was constantly changing as our agent upgraded our bookings and improved upon the level of acts we were supporting. By the end of the tour we were playing in stadiums with some of the biggest acts of the time, such as Kansas, Joe Walsh, and The Guess Who.

In those days a band's status was judged according to the number of groupies they drew, and Wishbone drew quite a few. Groupies were serious business then. Frank Zappa popularized them in song on an album in the late sixties, and by the early seventies they were a phenomenon. Backstage in Chicago we were fortunate enough to meet the famous Cynthia Plaster Caster and her band of horny broads, a bunch of young students from the University of Illinois who had dedicated their lives to making a collection of plaster-cast molds—of the aroused penises of rock stars. Among their collection were those of Jimi Hendrix, the Young Rascals' lead singer Eddie Brigati, MC5 guitarist Wayne Kramer, and some of the members (no pun intended) of The Who, the Jeff Beck Group, and Buffalo Springfield. So for the guys in Wishbone Ash it was considered an honor to be asked to contribute to the collection. In Little Rock, Arkansas, we were met by a very aggressive groupie named Connie, whose determination was to blow every member of the band *and* crew of every substantial band that came to town, as well as anyone else even remotely associated with them. Her trick of the trade was to get backstage first and give a blowjob to the guy in charge of the band's dressing room, on the condition he would keep all the other groupies away. And then there was the infamous Suzy Creamcheese, I think it was in Houston, who covered her clients in cream cheese, then carefully licked it all off.

Not all of the groupies were so hardcore. Most were just innocent young girls enamored by the glamour of rock and roll, and it amazed me what power it had over them. I never could quite figure it out, and perhaps I was just jealous of the guys in the band, but I always felt sad for the groupies. I never found them attractive. Well . . . almost never.

The tour took us to every major city in the U.S. and Canada, mostly dates supporting major headliners, but quite often they did some headlining themselves. For a general apprenticeship in the pop world, I couldn't have landed in a better place. I could see and meet backstage many of the bands I'd been listening to from the bunkers in 'Nam, and in a funny way, backstage and in the dressing rooms I fell into the same kind of camaraderie that existed there. Not to belabor the point, my tour with Wishbone Ash ended just as abruptly as my tour in Vietnam. I was just getting into it when they came to their last show in New York City and then flew back to London, leaving me stranded on the East Coast. I was without wheels, since I'd left my Cadillac parked in the garage at the Sunset Marquis Hotel in L.A.* Not that I would have known where to go from New York if I did have a ride. Once again I faced the big question: "What the hell do I do now?"

I hung around New York City for nearly a week before deciding. My taste of the music biz had been enough to whet my appetite for more, and for the first time in my life I felt like I had some idea of what direction I wanted to go in. I figured if I was to get into the business, a good place to start would be to talk it over with Miles. So, with what little money I'd saved, I bought a one-way plane ticket back to Blighty.

---

* The Cadillac, a 1962 Fleetwood, was picked up by Stewart and it served him well while he was at college in San Diego.

WILD THING

CHAPTER 15

007—English Agent

If it doesn't come naturally, leave it.
—Al Stewart

The two questions I'm most often asked are "How did you get into the music business?" and "What made you decide to become an agent?" The third is "Are The Police ever going to reform?"

The first one is easy. I got lucky. I got a phone call from my older brother, Miles, and my only qualification was that I happened to have a driver's license.

The second question deserves more serious consideration. Of all the positions within the music business, clearly the top of the ladder is the musician, the person who makes the music. I love music with a passion, but I have little or no talent to make it myself. When I was a teenager I had a part of my finger amputated and that put an early end to my guitar playing, which was pretty dismal anyway. I had trouble keeping a steady beat, which meant leaving the drumming to my younger brother, Stewart. I love to sing, but my best friends tell me to shut up when I do, and even my father, who was a brilliant trumpet player in his youth, told me I was tone deaf. What's worse, I suffer from mike fright. I can face a crowd of people with no problem, but put a microphone in front of me and I freeze. So much for being a performer.

On the business side, most of the key positions require expensive training or start-up money to begin. These days it's the lawyers that are making all the money, and I never officially finished high school, never mind college. Publishers and record companies are required to pay advances to artists for their songs, and most managers have to finance the bands in their early days. Money was something I didn't have. Therefore, my only choice was to start out as an apprentice in one field or another and work my way up. It was almost by chance that I chose to become an agent.

Most agents I know in America started out as buyers for a club or a college, and from there they get a job in the mailroom of a major agency, an apprentice's job from hell if ever there was one. My story was slightly different, if for no other reason than the fact that I started out in England.

Things were a mess back in those days, and in my eyes that was the beauty of it. In the early seventies the music industry in England was only just beginning to recognize itself as a "real business," when in fact music was already Britain's number one export. Just as my father described the early days of the CIA, when operatives were mavericks and a law unto themselves, the music business was run by novices, and the rules of play were not yet written. Rock stars were born every week, it seemed, and with them new managers, promoters, and agents. The best part of it was that in this game anyone could play, if only you could find a seat at the table.

I landed in London with only the determination that I wanted to be in the music business, but as to how to go about it, I really didn't have a clue. That, of course, is the hard part of getting into any profession. Where to start? I had less than a hundred dollars in my pocket and zero prospects for a job. Brother Miles had stumbled into becoming the manager of a British pop band when a desperate Rupert's People mistook him for a rich American; with my long hair and unshaven face, and dressed in my faded jeans and combat fatigue jacket, it was certain that nobody was going to mistake me for one. I was next to destitute.

Miles, on the other hand, was doing amazingly well. Wishbone Ash had become a major record-seller and touring attraction in Europe, and their success enabled Miles to expand his management operation. Rupert's People broke up, but John Tout, the keyboard player, soon joined another band and brought them to Miles. The band was called Renaissance, and it featured an extremely gifted singer named Annie Haslam who became one of the premier female singers in Britain at the time, and soon thereafter in the United States. Miles then took on the Climax Blues Band, four talented lads from the small town of Stafford in the north of England who played a hybrid of American rock and roll and blues, and a Scottish pop group called Glencoe, both of which were receiving good press and showing great promise. Unfortunately for me, however, none of his bands were in need of tour managers at the time, and my American driver's license, which got me my job with Wishbone Ash in America, wasn't much help to me here.

After a month or so in London, residing at 21 Marlborough Place with the family, I began to grow more and more despondent. Had I made a drastic mistake in coming home to England? Was England really my home? Did I even have a home? My buddies had returned to America from Vietnam to find it nearly impossible to get a decent job, or any job at all, and so had I. Here, I couldn't even get a work permit. I couldn't collect social security. Since I was broke, I spent most of my time sitting around the house in St. Johns Wood. My father seemed to relish the fact that I was back under his wing, and I couldn't stand that. That, more than anything, finally motivated me to get off my ass and get a job and a place of my own.

A few weeks before Christmas of 1971 I was visited by Ahmed Mamlouk, alias "Blondie," my old friend from Beirut of The Nomads fame, who'd since become a political refugee and immigrated to the United States. Having not seen each other for many years, we talked and laughed over old times and filled each other in on all that had happened to us since. I told him of my desire to get into the music business, something that was not lost on Blondie, who had been forced to give up playing drums and become a fashion photographer instead. Blondie stayed at the house for a couple of days, and one night my father came home from a cocktail party slightly inebriated. He began to lecture me about finding a career. Convinced that we were all wasting our time with the music business, and perhaps blaming Blondie for instigating it, he pointed to Blondie and

167   WILD THING

said to me: "What do you want to do, Saaarge, you want to end up like this bum?" I was so humiliated the argument led to tears, and this was a major turning point for me. The idea of getting into the music business became an obsession.

I put a call in to John Sherry, the booking agent for Miles's bands. Sherry was an important figure in the music business, so I felt nervous asking him for help. But, aside from Miles, he was the only person I knew to turn to. I was hoping he could introduce me to the managers of his bands so that they might consider me for employment. John Sherry agreed to meet with me, but he was not to be the bearer of good news. All of his bands were already over-staffed and the line for jobs was long. Tour managers were a dime a dozen. In fact, his advice was that I start out like everyone else in the business, either as a musician, which I knew was out of the question, or as a roadie, humping equipment in and out of clubs. But, as I sat in his office watching his booking agents work, another idea occurred to me. I could be a booker. It didn't look to be all that difficult.

By utilizing all of the powers of persuasion at my command (basically by not taking no for an answer), I was able to talk him into letting me try out as a rookie booker at John Sherry Enterprises, where I was squeezed into a room with four other agents, all talking on the phones at once. It was made clear to me from day one, however, that my blood relation to Miles would not mean a thing if I couldn't cut the mustard. Actually, the family connection may have worked against me. To start with, my weekly salary was five pounds sterling, or about twelve dollars.

But it was a start, and not bad considering I barely knew what an agent was. The four other bookers at JSE were: Dick Jordan, already an aging hippie; John Fenton, who had the general appearance of a Carnaby Street boutique salesperson; Alan Reeves, a London East-ender who'd sell his mother if he got the right price, provided he was paid in cash so that he could avoid being taxed on the transaction; and Ed Bicknell, a handsome young dude in a velvet suit with bell-bottoms and a funny Yorkshire accent, whom John had given the title "Booking Department Head and Chief Booker."

It was from Ed Bicknell that I learned the ropes. His rap was as smooth as that velvet suit he wore, and he made booking shows look unbelievably easy. As I sat and watched him that first morning, he'd simply get someone on the line, a buyer for a club or a college, and chat with them like an old friend, and before he'd hung up the phone he'd have made at least one booking, sometimes several.

He had an irreverent sense of humor, and a personality all of his own. "Hello, sweaty knickers," he'd say, to some young social sec obviously of the female persuasion, "What can I do you for today?" Ed was such a charmer. He had all of his clients, both male and female, eating out of his hand. What I didn't realize was that Ed was showing me up. Most of the people Ed talked to that day *were* old friends, and many of the sales he made had been set up already. "What dreary bands can I book for you today?" he'd say, nonchalantly. He'd already booked them beforehand.

I soon learned that it's a long and painful process an agent goes through to sell a booking on a band, even for a popular one. Simply put, the agent must fill the band's datesheet with live engagements, and in order to do that he must convince the promoter (the buyer) to risk putting a band on in his particular venue, and pay too much for the privilege. He must then convince the band (or the band's manager) that it's worthwhile to play there, for a fee that management always considers to be too little. Into the whole process comes a lot of bickering over costs, billing, ticket prices, playing times, who else can be on the show, how it's going to be promoted, etc., and then checking stage sizes, power requirements, lighting specifications, security arrangements, backstage facilities, and so on, just to make sure the band can even do the show in the first place. Each band has its own set of requirements, and these vary from tour to tour, sometimes mid-tour. So, by selecting shows that had already been through this process, Ed had made a very difficult and time-consuming job seem simple.

I was thrown in the deep end right from the start. For my first day on the phones, Ed gave me the job of filling the Roy Young Band's datesheet, while failing to tell me that the band was dead or dying. They were, in all fairness, a great band, but they'd been playing the blues around the country for years, and had "overplayed the market," having played so many times in each place that nobody came anymore. I couldn't *give* the band away, yet I was told not to take less than three hundred quid a show. The Roy Young Band was never

WILD THING

worth three hundred quid, even in their heyday, and they never even had a heyday.

So when I got on the phone, I didn't find the going as easy as Ed had made it seem. I phoned every social secretary listed in the Students' Union handbook, and I got not a single bite. I called all the clubs that advertised in *Melody Maker*, and all the promoters we had on file. Most of them wouldn't even take my phone call, and that was frustrating enough. But then when I did get through, and still nobody was interested, I was thoroughly deflated. Even those polite enough to ask laughed at the price I was asking for the Roy Young Band. The experience would have completely destroyed my confidence had I not caught on to the fact that Ed was only giving me the "new boy" treatment.

But when I did catch on, having nothing to lose, I began to use each of my telephone calls to develop my presentation. I experimented with every possible kind of approach. I tried to imitate Ed and the others as best as I could, but since they were all such characters it was nearly impossible. In the end I gave it the good old all-American hard sell. To someone who sounded even vaguely interested I'd declare, "Holy shit! Today's your lucky day! I'll tell you what I'm going to do. Today, and only today, I'm giving Roy Young away for *free;* or at least half price. That's right, you heard me, half price, only *three hundred quid!*" Or, "Buy Roy Young now, and I'll give him to you for the same price next time when his new record comes out!" New record? He should live so long!

The other agents at JSE were appalled at my uncouth behavior, and none too impressed with my salesmanship. To make me even more unpopular, in between phone calls I took out my frustrations by beating on my desk with a huge mason's hammer I'd found lying around the mail room. This seemed to make the others exceedingly nervous. I rankled them even further when, in my "new boy" eagerness, I called colleges that the other agents had already been working on, ones that were out of bounds to me. That was the final straw. By the end of my first day all the other agents revolted. En masse they went to John Sherry and complained that it had taken me only a few hours what normally took a dud agent at least a week to screw up.

Ed was the only one with a sense of humor. He told me years later that he had given John Sherry an ultimatum. "I overheard Ian this afternoon," he said back then, "trying to book a date in Edinburgh the day after a booking in Land's End. As any fool can tell you, these are at opposite ends of the country and quite impossible to travel overnight. So I suggest you either get rid of him," he said, "or get him a map."

The next day, however, I actually succeeded in making a booking. This, after being told not to even expect a booking in my first week. I was over the moon. I was so proud of my achievement that I strutted around and made a big deal of it, and gloated to the other agents. I ignored their knowing advice not to get too excited, and put it down to sour grapes on their side.

Sure enough, the next day my first booking fell out. I had succeeded in sweet-talking a college social secretary into booking the Roy Young Band, but the events committee at her school overruled her. My confidence was crushed. As well as banging my hammer, I took to throwing darts at the cork-covered wall right behind Ed's head.

In truth, I very much wanted Ed to like me. I had enormous respect for him. As an agent, he was my idol, and I was in absolute awe of his genius. He was the hottest agent in town, and he had more exclusive accounts for booking shows at colleges than any other agent in Britain. The volume of bookings he made for JSE far exceeded those of all the other agents in the office put together, and no other agent in London could touch him.

Fortunately, before I drove him into a near nervous breakdown, some of my bookings stayed in, and concerts I'd set up for the Roy Young Band actually played. I was given a raise, to a whopping fifteen quid (forty dollars) a week, and Ed set about systematically to teach me the fundamentals of booking. He showed me that if you could convince yourself, in all honesty, that nuns needed condoms, you could sell them condoms.

He also taught me how to make the most of the fact that I was the only "Yank" calling up buyers all over Britain. This fact, it happened, *did* impress most of the buyers, especially the young social secretaries at colleges, since they probably figured I was a big-timer from New York or L.A. on a sabbatical to Britain. Like Ed, I managed to make a lot of personal friends at the colleges and universities, and ultimately built up a strong clientele of those who did all their booking through me.

I should explain that in Britain at that time, agents served a dual purpose, representing a roster of bands while also representing the venues. Promoters at clubs and colleges would settle on a favorite agent, and through him book all their events during the year, whether or not the bands they wanted were on that particular agent's list. The agent would then shop around at all the other agencies to make up a composite list of bands from which the buyer could choose. So although most agencies had a roster of acts to attract business, most of the bookings were done through the agents that controlled the venue, and commissions were split with them. Because of this, the most powerful agents were the ones with the venues, not the ones with the acts. It was still a relatively new concept for agents to concentrate solely on filling a specific band's datesheet.

But times were changing, and my early training with the Roy Young Band was to prove very useful to me in the mid-seventies. I naturally began to concentrate on booking Miles's bands, and making sure that his new bands found enough work to survive without taxing his resources too much. The practice of dealing through other agents for certain venues, generally accepted though it was, got in my way when I wanted to fill a datesheet on a particular band. I couldn't expect other agents to do my selling for me, and some of the new bands had to be sold the old-fashioned way. So, I decided to break the rules; I took to calling all the promoters, even ones I knew were booked exclusively by other agencies. It didn't win me any new friends—in fact, it caused quite a stir—but I filled my datesheets and kept my bands happy.

It so happened that one of Miles's many schemes inadvertently put the nail on the coffin of the old system of booking in Britain. When he found it difficult to get press on some of his bands, he simply determined to start his own magazine. He hired Doreen Boyd,* a competent and intelligent lady who'd been a secretary to

---

* Doreen Boyd works for Miles to this day, thus holding the distinction of being the longest-lasting Copeland employee. She now runs the fan clubs for The Police, Sting, Animal Logic, Jools Holland, Squeeze, and others, and she handles merchandising for several of the bands on Miles's record label, IRS.

some publishing tycoon, as a front for his clandestine operation, and, on the floor of our family living room at Marlborough Place, the two of them put together the new magazine. It was full of reviews of Miles's bands, written by Miles himself, but there were also reviews of other bands just to give the magazine an appearance of impartiality and authenticity.

Miles sent his publication, a monthly called *College Event*, to all the promoters and college social secretaries, and soon it became their bible. In it were all the various agency rosters, listing all the bands and their prices, and information on whom to call. For the first time, a college social secretary new on the job could immediately find the agent responsible for any particular group, and could then call that agent directly for a booking. After a while, agents who had the acts started getting enough direct calls to keep them happy, and they became reluctant to split their commissions. Soon enough, if you wanted an act, you had to call the agency who had exclusive representation of that act. The emphasis at the agencies, therefore, shifted from the salesmen who were good at selling the acts to the ones who were good at signing them.

One of my most devoted clients, a big spender named John Giddings, social secretary at Exeter University—being both astute and ambitious—soon began to shop around for bands on his own and I was out of a client. Next to go was Martin Hopewell, my buyer from Reading University, and behind him Paul King from Brunel University.* I came to realize that representing artists rather than buyers was where it's at.

I got lucky with my very first signing. While in the studio visiting a band we represented, another band was rehearsing across the hall, a blue-eyed soul band called Ace (featuring Paul Carrack, who years later joined Squeeze). They were working on a soulful original song called "How Long" that I overheard and absolutely loved. After spending some time talking with them, and listening to more of their catchy music, I asked them to let me represent them as their agent, and since no one else had asked, they agreed. I then went back to the office and proceeded to put together a long run of dates in pubs all over the country, the idea being to headline them whenever possi-

---

* Giddings, Hopewell, and King all became successful agents.

WILD THING

ble, so they would thereby receive bigger billing in all the advertise-
ments. Though the shows were all small, when you looked in the gig
guides of the music trade papers, *Melody Maker, Sounds,* and the *New
Musical Express,* Ace was all over them, and it gave the impression
they were a big band. Not long after I signed them to JSE, Ace released "How Long" as their first single, on an obscure record label
called Anchor Records, and to everyone's surprise, it hit the charts
and climbed all the way to number one.

I couldn't believe my good fortune. Even Ed Bicknell was proud
of me. Now, all of a sudden, my phone was ringing off the hook, and
nearly all my calls were incoming instead of outgoing. I quickly
learned the difference between the position you're in when people
are calling you to buy an act, and when you're calling them to sell.
As offers started to pour in from all over the country, and all over
Europe, I was suddenly able to be more discriminating about venues
for the bands to play, and more demanding in what to expect when
they got there. With sometimes several offers for the same date, I
began to scrutinize the venue's hall facilities, PA systems, and the
state of their dressing rooms.

By their own talents as a live band, and through the careful and
clever guidance of their manager, Tony Dimetriadis,* Ace proved to
be the only band to come out of the "pub rock" circuit successfully,
recording three albums for Anchor Records; all of the other pub rock
bands broke up after one or two. As it turned out, "How Long" was
to be Ace's only major hit record, but for my first signing it was a
damn good start, and it proved I had "ears." Needless to say, in this
business, it helps to have ears.

My second signing was yet another stroke of luck, a classic case of
being in the right place at the right time. Wishbone Ash was playing
an unannounced show at a club in Hampstead, and I'd gone to help
the guys carry in their equipment. Another group of musicians were
on stage winding up their rehearsal, having rented the club during
the day for that purpose, and one of the guys was a friend of mine,
the ex-guitar player from Glencoe. Apparently they had never done
a live show, but they were fantastic. Though they were all white

---

* Tony Dimetriadis moved to America in the late seventies, where he settled
in Los Angeles. He currently manages Tom Petty & the Heartbreakers and a
number of other major artists.

boys from Scotland, they had as much soul as any of the black soul bands from America that were popular at the time. We got to talking, and they asked if I'd be interested in helping them find work.

"What do you call yourselves?" I asked.

"We don't have a name for the band yet," said my friend Onnie McIntyre. "We've only been playing together a wee few weeks."

I said, "Well, how would you describe yourselves?"

"I ca' nay say," he replied. After giving it some thought, he said: "I suppose we're just an average white band."

The Average White Band they became, and soon they managed to get a record deal with MCA Records, and though their first album was only moderately well received, mostly through their growing reputation as a great live band I was soon able to build the band up on the concert circuits of Europe and Great Britain. Their second album, containing the hit single "Pick Up the Pieces," was a smash hit, and made them the first band I worked with to have an album go to number one in the European and American charts simultaneously.

As the Average White Band's records began to hit the charts in America and overseas, I was faced with a brand-new challenge. I had learned an awful lot about booking shows in Europe, but now I was confronted with booking the rest of the world. I knew that to book dates in America I would need to find an American agent, but none of those I talked to were interested, at least not at first. It might have been easier, at the time, to sell snow to an Eskimo. Nobody in America wanted to hear about an all-white soul band from Scotland. When their record went into the U.S. charts, however, it became a different story entirely.

At this stage of the game I was still poor by anyone's standards. I'd been given a raise or two at JSE, but considering how low my salary was at the start, even when I doubled my pay it was still a paltry sum and I could barely afford to eat. I couldn't bear the thought of living off my parents, and even going home for meals meant suffering through endless lectures from the old man. I was young and idealistic, and he was a seasoned man of the world, and he took great pleasure in ridiculing my points of view. No matter what position I took, Dad would take the opposite view, and we would argue endlessly.

WILD THING

I lived for a long time in a windowless unfinished attic in a house at the bottom of Muswell Hill. To get to it I had to climb a rickety old aluminum ladder, and I shared the bathroom and a small filthy kitchen with the people that lived below, about ten or eleven people, mostly Irish laborers. They were constantly drunk, almost always fighting, and they cooked things like boiled cabbage that smelled dreadful and stank up my attic room so bad I could hardly breathe. In the winter it was so cold that no amount of blankets could keep me warm, and in the summer the heat was stifling beyond imagination. There was, however, one good thing about it. The cat-sized rats that were in abundance downstairs never seemed to bother to visit me.

When the Average White Band took off in America it was not long before they moved there, setting up their base in Westport, Connecticut, about an hour's drive north of New York City. Their road crew had occupied a pad in London on Reddington Road, a marvelous two-bedroom apartment with a large deck and a fabulous view overlooking the lush greens of Hampstead Heath. When they vacated it I moved in, and although there was rent to pay it wasn't much because it was an illegal rental or something, and the crew had been in there for ages. The little old lady that owned it lived downstairs in her own apartment and though she was constantly complaining about the noise and threatening to throw me out, she couldn't tell one long-hair from another and never knew they'd moved out.

To pay the rent I ended up sharing it with an eager English chap named Luke O'Reilly, the product of posh British "public" schools, who had been the resident limey DJ on station WMMR in Philadelphia before returning to England where he ended up working as a tour manager for Miles, handling the Climax Blues Band. Luke's time at the radio station gave him a knowledge of what would get played in America, and in that regard he was a man who truly had "ears." One evening he dragged me down to a local Hampstead bistro to check out a starving English folk singer called Al Stewart. Luke wanted to manage him, but he could only do so if I agreed to represent him as the agent and find him work, since Luke couldn't finance him otherwise. Al Stewart was broke. I didn't realize how broke until he finished his dinner, grabbed his acoustic guitar, and started singing to the diners in the bistro. He was literally singing for his supper.

I thoroughly enjoyed his performance, but I informed Luke that I had no idea what to do with a folk artist, since they were usually handled by folk agents, and folk music just wasn't my thing. Yet, Luke kept raving about this guy and begging me to come with him to one of his ''bona fide'' gigs. I finally agreed, if only to get the persistent Luke off my back, and we drove to where he was performing at Southampton University, where, as it happened, I had just been the week before to see a band I handled called Vinegar Joe (featuring a young Robert Palmer and Elkie Brooks). Al's show was sold out, I noted, while Vinegar Joe's show had not been. This impressed me. One thing was for sure, Al's fans were devoted. During his intense performance, you could have heard a pin drop. Al's show was superb, and when I turned to Luke to tell him I thought so, barely above a whisper, the nearly two hundred people in the audience turned around and went ''SSSSSHHHHH!''

After the show, we went backstage to congratulate him, and Al said to me: ''Luke tells me you're going to be my agent, is that true?''

''Well, ...'' I hesitated, not because I didn't appreciate his music or his show, but because I still didn't know what I could do for him. Just then, someone from the college entertainment committee came into the dressing room to settle up and pay Al for his performance. I was amazed to see that he was getting only a hundred quid, when I had gotten five times as much for Vinegar Joe a week earlier (and though they drew far fewer people to their show, the college was happy enough to pay it). I found the social secretary I usually did business with, and I asked him why the difference? He explained that Al was booked by the college folk club, who usually put shows in the school cafeteria, and only got the use of the big hall once or twice a year. Every time Al played at the college he did sellout business, but the folk club had a smaller budget, so they were used to paying low money for their functions. And the folk artists were used to accepting. They never questioned it.

When I went to work as Al's agent the next day, I made a ton of telephone calls and found that this was the case all over the country. Al had been selling out at the large halls in the various colleges, but, like all folk artists, he had a folk agent who booked him with mainly

WILD THING

folk promoters, and poor Al was singing for his supper as a result. Simply by calling the promoters I customarily dealt with at the colleges, by the end of the week I had ten bookings at five hundred quid, four or five at seven-fifty, and one, at Leeds University, for an astounding thousand pounds. In less than a few weeks, a happy Al Stewart moved from minimal wages to lots more money. He used the extra money I found to put a real group together for the first time, and to cover studio expenses for recording his next album, *The Year of the Cat*, the first platinum album (for sales in excess of 1 million copies) to go on my wall. It would ultimately sell more than 5 million copies worldwide.

Over the course of the next few years I proceeded to sign more unknown bands and build them up, and occasionally to sign acts that were already established, most notably the guitarist Jeff Beck. He was already a venerable guitar giant in England at the time, and I signed him simply by agreeing to fill the datesheet for another band managed by his manager, a straitlaced English gentleman named Earnest Chapman. The band, a funky little three-piece, was called UPP, and they happened to be incredible. Jeff Beck had befriended them and he produced and played all over their first album, which actually worked against them, since everyone expected him to show up at their club shows. This meant they did good business, at least for a while, but inevitably the band was faced with playing mainly to disappointed Jeff Beck fans. Shy and reclusive, Jeff had a hard time showing up at his own shows, much less somebody else's.

When he did show up, he didn't always play. I once was asked by Earnest Chapman to book a show for him at the Marquee, a popular showcase club on Wardour Street in London where many of the great bands in Britain got their start. Jeff, I was told, felt like doing it, even though he was much too big an artist to play there. On the night of his scheduled performance there was a line for tickets that stretched the entire length of Wardour Street, then went around the corner and halfway down Oxford Street. They waited for hours to get in. Jeff Beck came walking down the street, guitar case in hand, right past all his adoring fans, oblivious to all their greetings and words of encouragement, walked into the club, and after less than ten minutes, walked out of the club, back up the street, right past all his fans, and never came back. Don't ask me why. I never did find out.

Jeff Beck was one of the few artists I've represented over the years that I never got to know well. As with Morrissey many years later, I almost never dealt with him directly, but always through management or a spokesperson. Both artistes shared a deep mistrust of anyone associated with the business end of their art, and both left it for others to deal with, which meant that my relationship with them was always somewhat precarious. If the manager gets fired, the agent is often the next to go. The new guy in charge wants to change everything, if only for the sake of something to do, and since record companies advance money to the artists, and therefore have watertight contracts, it's usually the agent that gets the shaft. As it turned out, Earnest Chapman held on to Jeff Beck for the next ten years or more, and manages him to this day. I held on to him until I moved to America, at which time I passed him on to an agent named Phil Banfield, but more about that later. Morrissey, on the other hand, went through at least six different managers after the time I started to represent him, back when he was with The Smiths and later on his own. I'm almost proud to say it wasn't until the seventh that I was fired.

Crammed into the offices at JSE, life at the agency was not unlike that of a sweatshop. Yet though it was nothing but hard work, still it was fun, perhaps the most fun I've ever had as an agent. Every single day presented a whole host of new and exciting challenges, as well as an endless parade of problems to overcome. I had a phone in each ear all day long, and then I was going to shows every night, seeing the bands play, or looking for new bands to sign. Signing them wasn't always easy. Holding on to them after you signed them wasn't always easy either. The competition from the other agencies was intense, and if you let up for a minute, or turned your back on one of your clients, some other agent was in there in a heartbeat, bending your client's ear.

WILD THING

An agent must be part salesman, part politician, part baby-sitter, and sometimes whipping boy; when anything goes wrong, the agent's bound to be blamed for it. The job is a stressful one, and the personnel at JSE went through quite a few changes, some for better, some for worse.

Chief booker Ed Bicknell, tired of making a fortune for John Sherry, split from JSE to form his own agency, in partnership with a hot new social-sec-turned-agent called Rod Macsween, but eventually went into management.* John Fenton, too quiet and inhibited a gentleman to make a great agent, quit to become a rock concert promoter in his home town, St. Albans, but unfortunately lost his ass on several stiff shows in a row, and ended up as a salesman at a boutique in remote Bognor Regis. Hippie Dick Jordan, who had been a club booker before being an agent, moved over to head up Miles's newly formed record label, BTM Records. Not everyone is cut out for this kind of work.

After four grueling years as an agent as JSE, after most of the others had left and gone their own way, I was made a junior partner and the agency became Sherry Copeland Artists (SCA). My weekly salary was raised to a hundred pounds sterling, which still wasn't much (about two hundred fifty dollars), but I considered it to be an astronomical amount. I thought I was living on top of the world. Realizing a lifelong dream, I bought an old 3.2-liter Jaguar at an auction that would almost never start without a push and drank gas so fast I could only afford to drive it on special occasions. I also bought an oversized waterbed, a hip thing to do at the time, that nearly caved in the floor of my bedroom when I filled it, and I added a no-longer-trendy velvet bell-bottom suit to my wardrobe. About this time Luke O'Reilly started having some success with Al Stewart, and we began to throw loud music parties at Reddington Road that soon became

---

* In the 1980s, Ed Bicknell discovered Dire Straits, becoming one of the most successful managers in the business. Rod Macsween joined forces with Barry Dickens, another powerhouse agent, to form International Talent Booking, which currently represents many of the biggest touring acts in Europe.

the talk of the town, if only because we provided plenty of free booze.

It was about this time that I met Marianne Faithfull, a beautiful blond singer and actress with whom I fell madly in love. She was known for her hit single "As Tears Go By," her rendition of a song supposedly written for her by Mick Jagger and originally performed by The Rolling Stones. But she was mostly famous for being Mick Jagger's outrageous girlfriend. Who hasn't heard the story of the narcotics squad raiding a Rolling Stones' "orgy" in London and finding Mick going down on Marianne, and her with a Mars chocolate bar stuck in her vagina? It was a story she claimed to be a fabrication of the British tabloids, but nevertheless, it made her a folk hero to the rebellious youth in Britain at the time.

A few days before meeting her, I saw her starring in the movie *Girl on a Motorcycle*, and I was starstruck from the moment I laid eyes on her. To meet her in person was a complete surprise.

She walked into my office looking for someone else. Someone, she openly explained, that she could "smoke a spliff" with while doing business elsewhere in the building. I apologized for being the wrong person. "But you're in the right place," I said.

So began our affair. Marianne had faded somewhat from the public spotlight since ending her affair with Mick Jagger years before, but now she had recorded a wonderful song called "Wrong Road Again" and she was poised for a comeback. I thought so, anyway. Unfortunately for me she had no band and no plans to tour, so there wasn't much I could do to help. Marianne made me her boyfriend and manager anyway.

Marianne had class, in every sense of the word, despite her reputation. Her family was of royal blood, and she exuded an air of confidence that came with the territory. At times she was strong willed and outspoken, at others she was coy and demure, and she always kept me guessing. She had a wild temper, but her sense of humor rarely left her. One time, she came into the office and I told her that I had gotten an acting part for her.

"Fabulous, dahling," she said, yawning. "What is it?"

"It's a commercial for Mars Bars," I joked.

Marianne was not amused. She flew completely off the handle.

181

She stormed out of the office, cursing me all the way. But just before slamming the door, she turned and yelled:

"Anyway, it was a Milky Way!"

As for our romance, it was short-lived and mostly one-sided. Marianne has since made it public or I wouldn't mention it, but she was having serious drug problems at the time, more serious than even I realized. I still smoked pot, a habit that remained from my time in Vietnam, but she had a thirst for much harder drugs. Her addiction caused problems in our relationship, and nearly led to disaster. One summer afternoon we had sex in her apartment off Regent's Park, and afterward she ran a hot bath. Then she shot up some heroin in the bathroom while I napped, and passed out in the bathtub with the water still running. By chance I awoke and went to the bathroom to find her before she drowned. She had locked the door so I had to remove it from its hinges in order to get in. By this time her head was underwater.

"I don't want to be famous for being the one to find you dead," I told her, but I was so infatuated with her I persisted with our relationship, such as it was. We dated for a while longer, going to see bands together, and taking weekend trips in the countryside to visit her dear patrician mother. I tried to steer her away from hard drugs, but my attempts were futile and eventually they drove us apart. It so happened Marianne's best friend was a low-life lady who sponged off her unashamedly, and managed to do so, it seemed to me, by keeping her drugged out of her head. This woman perceived me to be a major threat to her free-loading lifestyle, and rightly so. If I had my way, I'd have banned her from the planet.

Marianne and I drifted apart before the summer was over, I'm sad to say, but ten years later we would come together again; she with a monster hit album called *Broken English,* and I as her agent in North America. More recently, I would read her published autobiography only to find myself referred to collectively as one of her many lovers in those days, in a chapter titled "The Lost Years" no less. I would also find, to my horror, that I was not the only one to have fished her out of a bathtub to save her life.

◆◆◆

Meanwhile, Miles was always a constant source of bands, and even Stewart came into the picture. Stewart was going to college in California, at U.C. Berkeley, playing drums for various local bands. When he came home that summer Miles put him to work as the manager of an embryonic group called Cat Iron. Cat Iron was the result of Miles's decision to put together a band that would be willing to play out some of his crazier notions, shamelessly willing to do things that no self-respecting group of musos like Wishbone Ash would ever think of doing. He wanted them to be inventively outrageous.

These were the days when extravaganza was the name of the game, glam rock was in its heyday, and bands who'd do anything to grab at success outdid each other in expressing extremes. Record companies, fat from profits, encouraged the trend and were *giving* money away. Miles, always full of wild and outrageous ideas, went to Ben Nesbitt at Sovereign Records and came away with approval on a budget to make Cat Iron England's answer to Alice Cooper, one of the most elaborate stage productions of the day.

To bankroll the adventurous project further, Miles, John Sherry, and Ben Nesbitt (whose publishing company owned the rights to Bob Dylan's songs, among others) roped in additional financial backing from some prominent personalities that had nothing to do with the business, but who were sold on the idea by Miles's sheer enthusiasm. Two Worlds Artist Management (the name acknowledging the worlds of difference between Miles and John, two long-haired rock-and-roll entrepreneurs, and the others, who were all straight businessmen) was formed, with Lord Goodman (lawyer for Britain's Prime Minister Edward Heath, as well as for the leader of the opposition party), John and Ray Bolting (the famous film producers), and Sir Max Rayne (London's largest property developer). They started out representing three acts: Vinegar Joe, Flash (featuring Yes guitarist Pete Banks), and, of course, Cat Iron.

The band was made up of Mick Jacques and Glenn Turner (the brother of Wishbone Ash's Martin Turner, who had been in Empty Vessels, and who had since recovered from his illness) on guitar, Kim Turner (Martin and Glenn's younger brother) on drums, and Tony Brinsley (nobody's brother) on bass. Kim was only fifteen years old, and Stewart, who was only nineteen, was put out on the road with Cat Iron mainly to baby-sit Kim.

We claimed Stewart had a Ph.D. in music, and he was put on Cat Iron's payroll as a highly paid "Musical Director." A small fortune in new equipment, amps, and instruments was spent, and each member of the band was given a generous allowance to improve his wardrobe. Since it was maintained that "stardom" was a state of mind, their living accommodations were also upgraded. They moved from modest squats in Finsbury Park to fancy apartments in more fashionable Swiss Cottage and Knightsbridge. (Stewart was himself earning enough to move in with me in Hampstead, after Luke O'Reilly left for America permanently with Al Stewart.) No expense was spared on the band, no gimmick overlooked. For example, Miles and Stewart arranged for Kim Turner, age fifteen, as I said, to marry an eighty-three year-old woman. They got as far as Vidal Sassoon's, where Kim had his hair multicolored for the wedding (publicity) shots, but when Kim's mother spotted the pictures in *The Sun*, she descended on Marlborough Place, took Kim by the ear, and frog-marched him home.

Three roadies, two trucks, PA, lights, smoke bombs, and special effects didn't quite make it The Who, but it was insane for a band that was only earning fifty quid a night. Cat Iron was the first band to use a smoke machine, but it was a crude version that used oil to make the vapor, and as a result, after every show everything and everyone was covered in oil. Stewart organized an elaborate stage show, and even managed to work his way into the act. During their set, he would suddenly burst onto the stage dressed in a police uniform as if he was busting the place. He'd grab the microphone to disrupt the show, then suddenly the lights would go off, strobe lights would come on, Kim would then leap over the drum kit and grab Stewart, and the rest of the band would pull an enormous fake penis out of Stewart's pants while Kim cut it off with oversized shears.

Cat Iron proved to be nothing more than an exercise in how to spend other people's money, and that could only last for so long. By the end of the summer, the financial backers pulled out and the band split up. But at least Stewart gained some valuable experience, and the following summer Miles put him to work again, this time as tour manager for his new signing, Joan Armatrading. After that tour was over (he and Joan got along fine, except that after each show they wound up chasing the same girls), Stewart decided he ought to complete his education formally, so he went back to college in California.

While Miles, Stewart, and I were each involved in our own projects, quite often we would put our heads together and come up with a common solution to all our problems. Sometimes we didn't even plan it, it just happened. Such was the case when we all got involved with a band in England called Curved Air that was once a major attraction but who'd split up at the height of their popularity. Since I now had a "folkie" act, in Al Stewart, I was expected to find a folk artist for the support slot of his tour, and who could be better than the superb singer from this recently defunct rock-and-roll band who'd since gone solo? Her name was Sonja Kristina, and I met her by chance through my neighbor at Reddington Road. It so happened that two other ex-members of Curved Air were in Al Stewart's band, the keyboard player, Francis Monkman, and the drummer, Florian Pilkington-Miksa.

As if to illustrate further how things can happen by synchronicity, Miles, at roughly the same time, had just spotted Darryl Way, who'd played violin with Curved Air and had since moved on to a group of his own called Darryl Way's Wolf. Miles had received a tape from Darryl, but he was not impressed with the band. He did like Darryl's playing, however, and he said to him: "I see possibilities in you personally, but your band sucks."

The next day, Darryl called Miles and informed him that he had fired his band and wanted to know what to do next. "I just did what you told me, Miles," he said. He'd said the magic words. Miles judges those around him on a scale of one to ten, depending on the extent to which they turn the orchestrating of their lives over to him. Within a week, Darryl was living in the basement of our house at 21 Marlborough Place, and he began to put together a new band with Miles as its manager.

Stewart, whenever he was home from college, spent most of his time at Marlborough Place, down in the basement rehearsal studio. In between all the other bands that were using the place, including the new version of Darryl Way's Wolf, he'd dazzle the other musicians by sitting in on jamming sessions and doing some really fine drumming. It occurred to Darryl that with Stewart as his drummer he would have a bit of career insurance, and Stewart, when asked, was glad to take a summer gig in the band. They decided to rename it "Stark Naked and the Car Thieves," borrowing the name of my bunker band in Vietnam.

But with all of the ex-members of Curved Air floating around our offices, and all of them hurting for money, it was inevitable that Miles and I would think of putting them back together again. All of them needed the cash that could be generated by a tour and a subsequent live album, and although they had broken up because they hated each other, it soon became obvious that a bit of hatchet burying was the only solution to their problems. So Stark Naked and the Car Thieves was shelved, and Curved Air was revived. Stewart, cursing Miles and me both, was forced to give up drumming for a while, and we compensated him as best we could by giving him a job as the group's tour manager.

The Curved Air tour was a huge success. Their concerts sold out all over the country, and over on the Continent as well. In December of 1975, they recorded a live album at Bristol Polytechnic and Cardiff University, and Miles put it out on his new record label, BTM Records. It did remarkably well. As before, they appealed to what was basically a cult following, but it soon became a typical superstar rock-and-roll band, tarted up with the excesses of the day: lots of lights and special equipment and an army of roadies to handle it, staying in fancy hotels and riding around in limos, throwing lavish after-show parties where there was always an abundance of booze and drugs.

Curved Air's success wasn't quite enough to ease the personal differences that persisted in the band, however. Musicians are often known to forsake a position that many would die for over what seem to some like minor problems, and such was the case with Curved Air. Phil Kohn, who was not an original member of Curved Air anyway, remained on bass, but Francis Monkman left the band to rejoin Al Stewart, and Florian Pilkington-Miksa quit since he didn't need the money in the first place. (How could anyone with a name like "Florian Pilkington-Miksa" need money?) Monkman was replaced by a guitarist named Mick Jacques, while Florian was replaced by . . . who else? Stewart Copeland. With the new lineup they set about recording another album, I booked another tour, and before long Stewart began to be recognized, virtually overnight, as one of the top pop drummers in Britain. It deserves mention, however, that the first of the many rave reviews he received in the music trade papers was written, in fact, by himself.

Meanwhile, Sherry Copeland Artists had by now become one of the most successful entertainment agencies in London, with some of the world's biggest touring acts. I was the agent for some of Europe's hottest bands, and I began to sign acts from America, beginning with Country Joe McDonald and the Fish, which was of particular meaning to me since his "Vietnam Rag" had been one of our favorite marching songs in 'Nam.

Miles was also doing phenomenally well, successfully managing Wishbone Ash, Climax Blues Band, Curved Air, Renaissance, Al Stewart (in conjunction with Luke O'Reilly), Caravan, Joan Armatrading, and several other up-and-coming acts. With these groups, backed up by a PA company, an equipment-hire service, several trucks, and some buildings and warehouses to house it all, Miles had become head of one of the most powerful management companies in Britain, where it was unusual for a manager to have more than one or two acts at a time.

Stewart was now gainfully employed with one of the top bands in the country. As a "rock star" he was afforded all the luxuries and accoutrements that go with it, and he was on top of the world. All three Copeland brothers, in fact, were flying high. Little did we know. Our shit was about to hit the fan.

CHAPTER 16

THE CRASH OF '76

I belong to the _____ generation.
—RICHARD HELL AND THE VOIDOIDS

In 1973 the Arabs decided to raise the price of oil, and so set off a chain of events that had a drastic effect on the rest of the world, and especially on Great Britain, which relied almost entirely on petroleum from the Middle East. Within a few years the economy in England was a shambles. In one of many reactions to the financial crisis, the British government decided in 1975 to raise the cost of postage and double the cost of phone calls, and as a result drove our office operating expenses through the roof. Essentially all of our business was done over the phone. If we weren't on it, we weren't working. Each date that we booked for our bands required piles of contracts to be mailed back and forth for signatures from the promoter and the band's manager, and then sent on for filing with the Musician's Union. Virtually overnight, the agency business went from being a profitable proposition to a money-losing operation.

It was just as bad for record companies. Singles and LP records were the preferred choice of the musical consumer in those days, and vinyl, from which records are made, is a petroleum product.

Immediately the cost of making records went sky-high, and profits at record companies went plummeting down. As profits decreased, so did the amount record companies were willing to fork out for the bands. This didn't help the situation for us at the agency either; the result was that the record companies began releasing fewer records, and financing far fewer tours.

To make matters even worse, the guys in the bands continued to live in dream worlds and were oblivious to what was happening to the economy. Record companies were insisting on "hit singles," while the bands were wandering off into art, making "concept" albums with long solos and obscure lyrics. The principle that time is money, especially if you are in a recording studio being charged by the hour, was totally foreign to them. Unfortunately, much of it was to be on Miles's tab.

By a peculiar twist of fate, all of the bands that he managed went into the studios to record at the same time, and all of them took far too long to make their records. Curved Air, for example, spent several months making their record, but when eventually it was finished the record company flat rejected it. The band had no option but to go back into the studio and start all over again, this time with a different producer—more time and more money down the drain. As if to prove that bad luck comes in threes, almost the exact same thing happened with two of Miles's other bands, Caravan and Renaissance.

The crash of '76 could not have come at a worse time for Miles. Wishbone Ash had finally finished their fourth album, which also took ages to make, especially considering it was a "live" album, and so it too was expensive to record. The band spent extra time in the studio, totally rerecording some of the tracks, because the success of this record was critical for them; it was what they desperately needed to elevate them to a higher level. As it was, they were a fairly big band in Britain and Europe, and even in the United States, but they were poised to become a *very* big band if only their record took off. Everyone was pleased with the time and money spent, and everyone thought the record would be a hit. But still the record company balked at spending the money that was needed for promotion. Live albums were still a fairly new concept at the time, and record companies didn't have much faith in their potential to sell records. Peter

Frampton would soon change all that with the phenomenal sales of his multi-platinum live album, but that hadn't happened yet.

Undaunted, Miles came up with a creative idea of his own to promote the album. He decided to put all of his BTM acts together into a big festival package that could tour all over Europe, thus allowing Wishbone Ash prime exposure in the major markets. By stacking the bill with Climax Blues Band, Caravan, and Renaissance, we could break those acts in Europe as well. It was a fantastic idea, and all of the promoters in Europe eagerly agreed to book it. One particularly adventurous promoter in Holland, a young hippie named Cyril Van Den Hemel, advised us to take the plan one step further. He suggested that we move into large stadiums with the package by adding an even bigger act, a clear headliner. By calling the William Morris Agency in America, he'd found that Lou Reed was available. Lou Reed would be perfect. His hit single "Walk on the Wild Side" was a smash all over Europe, and he was a guaranteed ticket-seller. So, through Cyril we booked him to be the headliner of what Miles called the "Startruckin' Tour." The whole idea was a novel concept, and nothing short of brilliant. Unfortunately, it put us *all* out of business.

In the beginning, the Startruckin' Tour seemed to be the hottest promotional scheme in the history of rock and roll, and Miles spared no expense to get it right. Nothing like this had ever been done before, and it was a mammoth undertaking. We booked the package in all the biggest cities of Europe, and spent massive amounts of money on promotion, on hiring trucks to haul around a massive PA system, and on chartering a huge airplane to carry all the bands, with *Startruckin'* painted on the nose. A great deal of effort went into ensuring that this tour, aside from benefiting the bands' careers, would be lots of fun. It was, after all, to be the world's first rock-and-roll circus.

The first sign that the tour might come apart was an eleventh-hour tip-off from God-knows-where informing us that the infamously volatile Lou Reed had fired his manager. The new manager claimed he knew nothing of the tour. After putting in long-distance calls to places all over the world, Miles tracked Lou Reed down in New Zealand. He was connected with Lou's room, only to hear from his boyfriend (named "Rachel") that Lou was indeed ignorant of any proposed tour, and, furthermore, that he would be unable to perform even if he had wanted to.

Miles couldn't accept it. After being told to hold several times while Rachel acted as intermediary to Lou Reed, Miles insisted that he be allowed to talk to the artist himself.

"I'm afraid that's impossible," said Rachel. "He's locked in the bathroom."

"Well, I'll just hold on 'till he comes out," said Miles. "I've got to speak with him."

"You can hold on if you want, but I don't think that's a very good idea," said Rachel, sounding extremely unconcerned. "He's been in there for over three days now."

"But what am I supposed to do?" screamed Miles. "He's already on all the posters and in all of our promotion! The shows are already on sale! He can't pull out now! I've got cables from William Morris confirming everything," said Miles.

"Well, I'm sorry, darling," said the boyfriend, "but you'll just have to get over it. Anyway, he's not with the William Morris Agency anymore."

We never did find out what his problem was. We had enough problems of our own. Though we were tempted to cut our losses and can the whole thing right then and there, Miles felt that he had set his bands up for this, and he wasn't going to let them all down. He would renegotiate terms with the promoters, at whatever cost, and go ahead with the tour. With only a week to go before the first date, Cyril Van Den Hemel managed to line up Ike and Tina Turner, for an exorbitant amount of money, and the tour was rescued with only a few shows lost. Unfortunately, those few shows made a big difference financially, and though the tour went off successfully for the bands, who all benefited greatly by playing to massive crowds, behind the scenes we were scrambling, and the tour scraped through just barely. When the bills came pouring in, it became clear that the tour was a fiscal disaster.

"Cashflow" became the key word in our vocabulary, and the absence of it (the cash, not the word) made the Startruckin' tour a painful experience. Lou Reed's pulling out made the people hired for the tour afraid that they weren't going to get paid, so they wanted their money up front, as did all the bands. In order to pay everyone off, Miles was driven into the poorhouse.

After the Startruckin' Tour, Miles's whole management operation began to slowly fall apart at the seams. In fact, from the moment he began to look a bit shaky financially, all the people who'd been so helpful to him scattered like rats on a sinking ship. He suddenly found out who our real friends were, and there weren't very many. The staff were disappearing for better jobs on a daily basis. The company accountant held Miles up for ransom, then tried to take over management on some of his acts.

By the summer of '77 my situation at the agency was also rapidly deteriorating, partly as a result of Miles's misfortune, but mostly because of my own stupidity. John Sherry, perhaps seeing his meal ticket in trouble, decided he'd better cover his ass. By cleverly convincing me that the agency was in dire straits and about to go under, and that we should sell out before it was too late, he sold Sherry Copeland Artists booking agency to NEMS Enterprises, the famous company that had promoted The Beatles. In the process, I got fucked.

John also convinced me that I should stay in the background while he negotiated the deal because my very presence might suggest to NEMS that his relationship with Miles was in trouble. The end result was that John got a great deal for himself, a fat salary, a percentage of profits, a nice penthouse office, and a flashy company car, a Jaguar XJ6 complete with car phone. Apart from keeping my job, and getting an office of my own, I got jack shit.

When John Sherry sold out the agency to NEMS, I was kept on the payroll, but I had not bothered to insist on a contract with the new company. No longer an owner, I now had to justify my existence purely on the strength of the commissions earned by my bookings, and almost none of my acts were working. Summers were dead months for the agencies in Britain in any case, since there were no college dates to rely on for bookings, so John sold me on the idea I should go to the States as tour manager with Caravan, on *Miles's* payroll. With the way things were going, I was only too glad to get out of there for a while, so I agreed. Little did I know, but my days as an agent in England were numbered.

♦♦♦

Caravan's first U.S. tour was my third as a tour manager in America, and it was to be the most educational. With Wishbone Ash I was simply along for the ride, and we went first-class all the way. The next summer I tour-managed Flash in America, and with Two Worlds Artist Management's open checkbook there was never a problem too difficult. Caravan's tour, on the other hand, should never have happened. Their album entitled *Cunning Stunts*, came out in America and quickly flopped, and so the record company refused to provide the money required for "tour support." Yet Miles was determined to break the band out in the States and he didn't want to give up without a fight, so we came over anyway. With Miles's "cashflow" problems back in Europe, however, we simply didn't have the money to tour with, and had no business even being on the road. In short, Caravan's tour was a classic clusterfuck!

We somehow managed to pull it off with the help of a New Jersey gentleman named Joe Newman, who looked every bit a man from the motor trade. Joe was a pathological hustler. When it came to saving money on the road, he seemed to know every trick in the book and then some. He was a master at pinching pennies, or at stretching them out anyway. For example, he showed me how to get motel room beds for eight people in the band and crew, while only paying for two.

First, he'd locate a suitable motel, the kind where you can park your car right in front of the rooms. Then he'd wait until after the show to check in, when it's late in the evening and only the night clerk's on duty. While the others stayed hidden in the car, Joe and I would go into the receptionist's cabin and each book a single room, specifically requesting that they be way in the back and away from the street. Joe would explain that we needed to sleep late and wanted to be as far as possible from the noise of traffic, but this also meant we were as far as possible from the reception desk. Complaining all the while about how tired we were, really hamming it up about how we were just aching to fall into bed, we'd thank the unsuspecting clerk and go off to our rooms.

Well, as anyone who's had the dubious pleasure of spending a considerable time as a guest at any number of Holiday Inn or Travelodge type hotels can tell you, it so happens that most "single" rooms actually have two beds. So the two rooms we booked actually gave us beds for four. Joe would then mess up these rooms to make them look as if they had been slept in, or else he'd rearrange the knobs on the television sets so as to make them seem broken. Next he'd call the night clerk, who, rather than leave his post, would apologize profusely and ask Joe to come back to the desk for another two rooms. When Joe gets back to the desk, moaning and groaning and laying it on about what a terrible inconvenience it is, the poor clerk is so apologetic he doesn't mind that Joe has left the keys in the rooms. "Don't worry," he says, "the maids will get them in the morning." Now we would have eight beds, having only paid for two.

Joe also had a way of getting rental cars for free. Rental companies, in those days, customarily allowed their customers simply to drop off their cars at special stalls in the airport parking lots, leave the keys in the ignition, and mail in the rental agreement paperwork. When we arrived at an airport, Joe would search the parking lots until he found a car with the keys still in it, and off we'd go with it. Joe had once worked for Hertz, and he knew that it would be days before they matched up the paperwork to discover the car had been missing. The next morning we'd simply drop it off at the airport, and fly off to our next destination.

Airline companies were not safe from Joe's cost-saving methods either. Joe had figured out that their personnel were subject to shift changes also, and by using that to our advantage, he managed to get our backline equipment shipped as excess baggage instead of as freight, which saved us a small fortune. He'd call the airline company at the airport, and in the course of confirming our flights, he'd inquire when the freight handlers changed shifts.

"I got screwed up recently when some of my equipment got lost during a shift change," he'd explain, "and I want to avoid arriving with my equipment when they do." Then, of course, we'd arrive at the airport just as they were about to change over.

The band, Joe, and I would all show up at the ticket counter, along with several extra suitcases, which we'd pay for as excess baggage by weight. Joe would then drive the truck around to the other side of the baggage area and drop off our tons of equipment flight

WILD THING

cases with the receipt stubs for our excess baggage taped onto them. The new shift would assume the old shift had weighed them and wouldn't bother to check before loading them on to the flight.

Joe's way of doing things made life on the road a little hairy at times, but he saved us enough money to make it all possible, allowing the show to go on. In the last few weeks of the Caravan tour, though, it wasn't his kind of know-how that we most needed. I began to arrive at shows to learn that the agent in New York had appropriated all the up-front money, so even with Joe's artful dodging I had a hard time making ends meet. To pay the bills and fly the band home to England at the end of the tour, I spent every bit of cash I had, including my own pay for the whole tour.

I then went to Miles's New York office to settle up the tour accounts, expecting to get paid, or at least get a ticket to London. But by now it was obvious that things were not going well for BTM. Ray Caviano,* the hard-working manager in charge of the New York operation, was entirely straight with me. "We're going bust," he said, "and we'll need any money that comes in just to stay afloat. I'll do my best to cover you, but I'm not going to bullshit you, Ian. You'll be lucky to see a penny."

Ray had been running Miles's New York office for over a year from a corner of Alan Grubman's law offices in Manhattan, and he was not the sort of guy to be worried without reason. Alan Grubman† was Miles's lawyer, so I discussed my precarious predicament with him. I told him I had used up all my cash to make sure the guys in the band got home, and I had left myself in the lurch. If Ray was straight with me, Alan Grubman was even more frank. "Ian," he said. "You're a schmuck."

The best I could do was sit tight and hope. Hope? Anyone with half an eye could see that BTM was sinking fast, and there were no

---

* Caviano resurfaced a year or so later and became the king of the disco scene. He was instrumental in launching K.C. and the Sunshine Band and formed a record label with Warner Bros., which churned out disco hits too numerous to mention. His brother, Bob Caviano, was the agent for Grace Jones.

† Miles was Grubman's first music business client. Alan went on to become the most successful music business lawyer in the world, representing clients such as Sting, Bruce Springsteen, Madonna, Bon Jovi, Michael Jackson, and so on, as well as many of the industry heads.

lifeboats apparent on my side of the ship. While waiting for my plane ticket back to London, I thought I would use the time to investigate the possibility of finding employment as an agent in America, so I started making some phone calls.

Miles had a month left on a leased apartment in Manhattan, a one-bedroom flat down in the basement of a tall building on York Avenue and Eighty-Second Street, next to the river. It was dank, dark, dreary, and depressing, with hordes of cockroaches despite the fact that there wasn't anything for them to eat, much less for me, but it was a place I could stay until the rent was up. I spent a week making appointments with all the major agencies in the city who would bother to see me, including some to whom I'd been selling acts from London. Most of them received me warmly—at least on the face of it.

At the William Morris Agency I met with a young agent I knew named Bob Ringe, who seemed interested in getting me a position with his company. Bob explained, however, that I would be forced to start off in the mail room. It was strict company policy. Everyone in the company had "learned the ropes" by working their way up from the mail room, and it was extremely unusual for an outsider to get in without first going through the indoctrination process. But I felt that my five years as an agent in London might help me start a few rungs up the ladder, so I convinced Bob Ringe to set up a meeting with his boss.

In my naïveté, or sheer conceit, I'd assumed that the agencies in America would be fighting over me, each trying to outbid the others in salary and other inducements. To put it bluntly, I thought I was a pretty hot shit agent. But at William Morris and the other agencies I met with they didn't seem to care about *me*. My track record for signing bands in Britain didn't impress them, not enough anyway. My talents as a booker seemed of even less interest. They all wanted to know about one thing, and one thing only. What acts could I bring with me?

As it was, the acts I'd been sending over from Britain were spread out among a wide range of agencies in America, including the one I was meeting with, so I could hardly make a sales pitch based on how I might retrieve them. Nevertheless, my meeting with Bob Ringe and his boss went well enough for yet another meeting to be set with his boss's superior. I was told to wear a sports jacket for the first meeting, but now I was required to wear a suit and tie. Then more meetings, and more after that. I couldn't help asking how long it would take before we got to the tux. *Somebody* had to be able to make a decision!

To be fair, it was the same everywhere. At the other agencies in New York I saw the same sort of thing. Fuck you, what acts can you bring us? As if this simple criterion were not intimidating enough, the totally sterile appearance of their offices, any one of which could have been at General Motors or IBM, were completely different from the funky but functional rock-and-roll atmosphere of the British agencies. From what I could tell, the American agents were all slotted into vast corporate pecking orders, and they all seemed more concerned with holding on to their positions than they were in advancing the careers of their artists. It's all about money; in both Britain and in America, money is the name of the game. But English agents tend to look for things that are cool to do, and then try to make money out of them. American agents seem to do it the other way around. They look for what will make money, and the mere fact of the money makes it cool—or cool enough for practical purposes.

There was one exception, however, among the American agencies I talked to, but not one in New York. While the others gave me nothing but lip service, I did get an encouraging phone call from an open-minded Southern gentleman named Alex Hodges, who offered me a job with the Paragon Agency, way down south in Macon, Georgia. Paragon was handling virtually all of the major Southern rock bands, like The Charlie Daniels Band, The Allman Brothers Band, Lynyrd Skynyrd, The Outlaws, and Marshall Tucker Band, and they also represented the Climax Blues Band, who were managed by Miles. Alex Hodges seemed to be much more interested in my future potential. He told me he wanted me to help him sign bands from England.

"I don't even have to like 'em," said Hodges. "I only like Southern rock bands, and I don't need someone else to sign Southern rock bands. I want you to sign bands I can't stand."

To be honest, I never gave it much thought. I was flattered by his trust in me, but I just couldn't envision moving from London, England, to Macon, Georgia. My next meeting with the William Morris Agency was not for another week, however, so I was stuck in New York, holed up in Miles's barren apartment, waiting to meet with someone I wasn't at all sure I wanted to work for. It was one of the most depressing weeks of my life. After several days of going into the BTM office and coming out empty-handed, I began to grow more and more despondent. In a city with a population of over seven million, I knew not a single friend. I was in the entertainment capital of the world, but couldn't afford a ticket to a show. I passed by some of the finest restaurants, and yet I was desperate for something to eat.

On one such visit to BTM I noticed a stack of promotional posters that were collecting dust in a corner of the office. Renaissance was at the peak of their popularity in America, and were particularly strong in New York, so on impulse I grabbed a handful of their posters. I packed a few under my arm and walked over to Bloomingdale's department store on Fifty-ninth Street and Lexington.

Taking a position on the sidewalk across the street, I started trying to sell the posters. At first I didn't sell any, and I became demoralized very quickly. Then I realized that I wasn't really putting my whole heart into it. I was embarrassed to be doing what I was doing, and too concerned that someone I knew might see me. Then my stomach growled; I hadn't eaten in days. I said "Fuck 'em!"

"These posters are so cheap they're almost free," I shouted in the manner of a circus barker. I charged across the street to Bloomingdale's and stood in front of one of their revolving doors, accosting people as they exited the building. "That's right, folks, *free,* . . . almost!" Free was enough to catch their interest, but then I had to sell them. "Get one now and save your marriage. *You, sir!* Have you got a steady girlfriend? *No??* Well, if you had one of these rare one-of-a-kind posters on your ceiling above the bed, you'd score every time, sex ga-ron-teed with each poster. Get one now while they're *almost free!* Just two dollars!"

The hungrier I got, the more outrageous I got. "Buy two, one for your bedroom, one for the sauna. Buy three, one for the pool." I put on one hell of a show, and I began to enjoy it, especially when the posters started selling like hotcakes. When I got down to the last three or so I started to shout "Last one! Half price! Just three dollars!" The last three went in no time. To this day, I remember one guy in particular. I raised the price twice right in front of him without even selling one, and he still thought he'd better buy it quick before I raised it again.

I first treated myself to a T-bone steak at Tad's (which I considered a wanton extravagance at the time), then I returned to the BTM office and picked up the rest of the posters, including some Al Stewart posters, and I took a train to Philadelphia where Renaissance and Al Stewart happened to be doing a double-bill at the three-thousand-seat Tower Theater. When I got there I started selling the posters in the lobby of the venue, and they sold as fast as I could count the money. I kept raising the price and still they sold. Eventually, I was getting five dollars each, and the last ones went for six.

Bands in those days weren't selling their posters at concerts, and the ones I'd plucked from the BTM office were meant only for promotion, to be given away free to record stores. If fate would have it, I might well have stumbled upon a new trend in the history of pop exploitation, and gone into the merchandising business to make a fortune. But it was not to be. Luke O'Reilly, my old roommate and good buddy, now extremely successful as Al Stewart's manager, came out to the lobby between bands and caught me selling his posters. To my surprise, and utter dismay, he hit the roof. He was furious, outraged that I was "commercializing" his artist. In a rage, he confiscated all my remaining Al Stewart posters and had me ejected from the venue.

I'd managed to earn just enough to pay for my way back to England, and I was so eager to get home that I canceled my meeting with William Morris and bought myself a ticket.

When I got back to London I still didn't comprehend just how bad things were, and I was in for a real surprise. I walked into my office at NEMS and there was someone sitting at my desk. I thought he was just borrowing my phone. I introduced myself, and asked him who he was. "Hello," he said, "I'm Ian Flooks."*

"Ian. Hey, I like that," I said. "Well, you just go right ahead and finish your call, Flooksy. I'll just go shake the dew off'n my lily, say hello to the gang, and see if I can get somebody here to rustle me up a decent cup of tea."

When I'd done that and came back to my office, Flooks was still sitting there behind my desk, using my phone. I sat down on my couch politely to wait, but when he continued to make calls, and to take incoming calls as well, it finally dawned on me just what was going on. At the same time, it occurred to Flooks that John Sherry hadn't told me. This was no longer my office.

I stormed into John Sherry's office, demanding an explanation, and he was oh-so-apologetic. "I'm ever so sorry," he explained, so cool butter wouldn't melt in his mouth. "I thought you had gotten a job in America."

I had been weaseled out of my job. I wasn't exactly fired, I simply had no office. I was already off the payroll, and although that was supposed to be temporary, John now offered me a salary on a commission basis, knowing full well that most of my bands weren't working at the time.

And soon I was homeless as well. I had been sharing a house in Barnes with Stewart and Sonja Kristina. Now that Curved Air had split up, they were both in the same boat with me, and none of us could afford the rent. The landlord, who just happened to be Curved Air's ex-drummer, Florian Pilkington-Miksa, let us live there virtually rent-free for six months, but then he needed the pad for himself and eventually he turfed us out. At this point Stewart, Sonja, and I were about to be out on the street.

Miles was also having financial difficulties. By now he had lost almost everything. The bills from the Startruckin' Tour just kept coming in, and to live up to his promises to the bands, he had to pay them off or release them from contract. His management company went into liquidation, and the bailiffs came and put a padlock on his

---

* In the eighties Ian Flooks formed his own booking agency called Wasted Talent, becoming one of the most powerful agents in Europe, representing bands such as U2, UB40, Simple Minds, and so on.

WILD THING

BTM offices, after first removing anything of value. When they had gone, he snuck in to rescue what was left, mostly promotional posters, badges, and a funky old typewriter that was better left for dead. All his bands ditched him except the Climax Blues Band, whom he kept loyal by promising to deliver them a hit record within a year. As a final blow, he was forced to move from his plush BTM buildings back into the same dilapidated Dryden Chambers offices he had started in with John Sherry nearly eight years before. To help pay the rent he was forced to sell posters and badges at concerts at night and on weekends.

Even our family house at Marlborough Place was threatened. Mom and Dad had by this time moved to a cottage in the country, but in order to save the house they had to move back into the city and reoccupy Marlborough Place, so that when the bailiffs came Miles could show it was Dad's name on the deed.

Stewart and I were facing the same possibility. But just as the deadline came for us to vacate our lodgings in Barnes, our mischievous father came to the rescue. Dad called me to ask for a favor. He explained that an acquaintance of his, a young American lady named Marcy McDonald, was in some trouble and needed our help. Marcy, who just happened to be Mohammed Ali's publicist, had a magnificent flat in Mayfair that she had loaned temporarily to a friend of hers who then refused to leave. She had been out of the country, Dad explained further, and had allowed the friend, a certain Lady Georgina Campbell, to occupy her apartment while looking for a permanent place to stay. Marcy had accepted a token rent, however, and by British law that meant Lady Georgina was within her rights to stay, and she won it in court. Marcy, desperate to get her apartment back, then went to my father for help.

Dad figured that Marcy might not have the right to get an undesirable tenant out, but there was nothing in the law to stop her from letting more in. If Lady Georgina was unhappy with her new flatmates, well, that was too bad. His somewhat devious plan was for Sonja, Stewart, and me to move in, and to bring over all our "Arab cronies, loud musicians, and hoodlum friends." Essentially, we were to terrorize the poor woman into leaving. As we saw it, at least it was a place to stay while we looked for lodgings of our own. The fun was about to begin.

After several weeks of wild revelry, obscene behavior, extremely loud music, and late-night partying (in the mornings I'd find that the mysterious tenant had left a cup of coffee and an aspirin for me by my bed), Lady Georgina showed no signs of moving out. If anything, it was we who felt uncomfortable. She kept very much to herself in the following weeks, and we rarely saw her, only signs that she had been there. When we did see her, she came with some pretty odd friends of her own, and we finally discovered that she was actually a transvestite, or more correctly a transsexual since she'd had a sex-change operation.

Marcy came by the flat every so often, but she never spent the night for fear of her ex-roommate. It was not long before we realized that Lady Georgina was not the problem. She was the solution. As long as Lady Georgina stayed, so could we. She was only staying because of the battle between them. It had become a *cause célèbre* to her. Marcy eventually threw her hands up at the whole affair, and went back out on the road with Mohammed Ali, leaving us to fend for ourselves.

The unshockable Lady Georgina did move out eventually, and we never heard from Marcy McDonald again. Through my father we heard she had moved back to America, and the Mayfair flat was ours—at least for a while. When the landlord called for the rent, we claimed we'd paid the transvestite, and left him to figure it out. We were only stalling for time. In England, we knew, there's such a thing as "squatter's rights."

The short-term benefit to this whole episode was a rather posh apartment in fashionable Mayfair, but the long-term effect was to change our lives and shape our futures in ways we couldn't possibly have known at the time. And it all began at one of our wild parties, in the autumn of 1976.

It just so happened that a bunch of young punks, who'd formed a band called The Sex Pistols, managed by a cunning young entrepreneur named Malcolm McLaren, took offices on the next floor up from Miles at Dryden Chambers. Because of that, Miles somehow got involved in booking their tour of Europe, a chore for which no

WILD THING

one envied him since no reputable promoters in Europe dared present the outrageous and controversial punk band. Their abrasive singer, Johnny Rotten, had gone on national television in England and was provoked into using a few four letter words, causing such a stir in the press media that the band became famous, or rather infamous, literally overnight. The next day they were on the front page of all the newspapers, including *The Daily Mirror, The Daily Express,* and *The Daily Mail,* as well as the evening papers, *The Evening Standard* and *The Evening Sun,* with headlines that screamed "THE FILTH AND THE FURY!", and "PUNK ROCK GROUP START 4-LETTER TV STORM." They were all over the TV news channels that night as well, and the interviewer that provoked them, Bill Grundy, was suspended for two weeks, causing even more sensation. The next day they were front-page news again, in *The Daily Express* as well as *The Mirror,* who this time gave them the front page *and* the center spread. They were accused of spitting on a picture of the Queen. All of this notoriety was great for The Sex Pistols. In the world of rock and roll, notorious and famous aren't far apart.

They couldn't have gained more press if they'd caused a revolution, and in many ways they did. Their single, "Anarchy in the U.K.," was suddenly the hottest record in England. It was selling so fast the stores couldn't keep it in stock, yet the British public's outcry forced the record company, EMI, to withdraw it. The younger elements of the British public, the kids and teenagers, were curious to hear what all the fuss was about, and began buying up anything they could get their hands on, as long as it was considered "punk." Unfortunately, however, the controversy also led to a strike by the union workers at all the venues in England where the band had been scheduled to play, which caused the cancellation of The Sex Pistols' British tour, and made it extremely difficult for Miles to find them work on the Continent.

It also so happened that Stewart was hanging around Miles's office one day, and he ran into them on the stairs between floors, where there was a queue for the loo shared by both offices. While waiting for a piss, they introduced themselves, and Stewart, thinking they'd be a perfect contribution to our efforts to terrorize poor Lady Georgina Campbell, invited them to one of our wild parties at our Mayfair pad. And he told them to bring all their friends.

So I'm enjoying myself upstairs at our party, in the middle of chatting up some bird, when I'm summoned down to the living room by Al Stewart to sort out a problem. Apparently, there was a battle going on at the turntable over what records to play. To my surprise, I found a fairly large contingency of "punks" at the party who were insisting on playing their own favorite records, much to the dismay of my friends, who were all in their late twenties and wanted to dance to James Brown. My personal concern was to get back upstairs, but in order to stop it from turning into a real fight, I decided instead to play DJ. I agreed to play something for everyone.

"So, what would you like to dance to?" I asked the punks.

"Dance?" (pronounced "dawnse"), "Who wants to dance?" they said, horrified. "Dancing's not cool, man. Get with the times."

What I witnessed whenever I put on their music was something I just couldn't believe. My friends would immediately clear the dance floor, and the punks would get up and go bananas. I'd never seen anything like it. What they did *was* dancing. But it was nothing like our way of doing it, and the music was different too. Our dance was cheek-to-cheek and holding hands, theirs was pogoing up and down and slamming into each other. Our music was love songs, with long melodic guitar riffs and funky rhythms, theirs was anger and angst, expressing the frustrations of their generation. The leather clothes and chains they wore, the spikes in their hair, the safety pins in their cheeks, even their attitude, everything about them was so alien to what we were used to. My friends and I, we were all a bunch of hippies.

But I was fascinated by them, and so was Stewart. I was especially interested when I overheard one of them refer to my friends as "old farts," and one of my friends saying about punk music the same sort of things I had heard from my parents a generation earlier, when they were arguing that Bob Dylan couldn't sing and the Rolling Stones weren't musicians. It made me realize that what I was witnessing was the beginnings of a musical generation gap.

They were unknown then, but many of the punks at the party were members of, or soon to be members of, the punk bands that were springing up in the wake of The Sex Pistols—Billy Idol and his band Generation X, various members of The Damned, Chelsea, the Buzzcocks, Chrissie Hynde, Siouxsie Sue, Jam, The Clash, and the

WILD THING

godfather of punk, Mark Perry, the editor of the punk fanzine *Sniffin'*
Glue. Malcolm McLaren was there with some of The Sex Pistols (not
the infamous Johnny Rotten himself; according to Johnny, Malcolm
never allowed him to go out then, as part of his master plan to create
mystique around the band). The aficionados of the punk scene were
still a relatively tiny group at the time, but all of them hung out
together.

They left behind a 45 record titled "Blank Generation," by a group
called Richard Hell and the Voidoids. We found it on the turntable
the next morning as we were cleaning up the mess. Stewart put it
on, and we listened to it over and over, utterly fascinated by it. It was
so simple. Direct. Raw. Irreverent. Underproduced. No gimmicks, no
tricks, just good old back-to-the-basics, like the beginnings of rock
and roll, only brought up to date. "Blank Generation" is what
opened our eyes, our ears, and our minds to a whole new style of
music.

For the next few months, Miles, Stewart, and I began to frequent the
clubs where the punk bands were playing (mostly dives and dingy
bars we'd never have considered putting our bands into), checking
out the new punk scene. The first show we caught was an electrify-
ing performance by Chelsea at the Rock Garden in London's Covent
Garden, where Gene October proved that under the new rules you
could be a star by simply looking the part. With the punk bands, it
wasn't necessary for musicians to be able to play their instruments,
they just had to have the balls to get up there and pretend to. The
next show we saw was Johnny Thunder and the Heartbreakers, also
at the Rock Garden. In my opinion they were dismal, but there was
still something about them and their music that was exciting. What
struck me most about the punk scene was that the real show was not
always on the stage, but often in the audience. In fact, the punk
scene was so small when it started that some of the earliest fans of
The Sex Pistols became bands themselves, like Siouxsie & The Banshees and The Pretenders.

In September they held a "Punk Festival" at the 100 Club on
Oxford Street, and Stewart and I blagged our way in. As if to illus-

trate the shortage of punk bands at the time, the "festival" lasted only two nights, involving nine bands, and one of them, The Vibrators, wasn't even a punk band. On the first night the bill was Subway Sect, Siouxsie & The Banshees, The Clash, and The Sex Pistols, an amazing bill in retrospect, though they were all relatively unknown at the time. The second night began with a crappy French group whose name I'm not ashamed to admit I forget. Then came The Damned. During their set Sid Vicious from The Sex Pistols threw a beer mug at the stage, but it missed and hit a pillar instead, where it shattered and hit a girl in the face, causing her to be taken to hospital where she was reported to have lost an eye. The show went on with The Damned followed by The Vibrators, and then the most popular of all the punk bands of the day, the Buzzcocks. At this point the audience erupted, going absolutely berserk to the fast songs. Kids at the front started invading the stage, then diving back into the audience before the stage bouncers could get to them. Though there was no more real violence, the 100 Club was forced to ban punk shows, and punk was thereafter banned from most of the clubs in Britain.

Stewart was inspired, to put it mildly, by the raw energy of the punk scene, and he immediately set about forming a punk band of his own. He came up with the name for his band before he even had any musicians. He saw the name on a passing police car, and thought to himself what a great way to get lots of free advertising. He designed The Police logo, then The Police badges, even a Police record sleeve for a record that wasn't made yet.

Next, to find the musicians he put an ad in the music papers and began to audition hostile young musicians in our flat in Mayfair, using Lady Georgina's now-vacant room as a studio. Both of his favorite groups, The Jimi Hendrix Experience and Cream, were three-piece bands, and Stewart had already decided The Police would be too. Guitar, bass, and drums.

He was on the verge of committing to a couple of musicians he was satisfied with, from a band called The Rockets, when he got a phone call from a bass player called Sting. Stewart had seen him perform in Newcastle with a jazz band called Last Exit, and Stewart had been very impressed. Sting was in London to meet with his publisher and was trying to find some way of moving to the capital.

It so happened Stewart's phone number was one of the only London contacts he had.

Stewart assumed that Sting was following up on his backstage invitation to join a band, but he didn't want to scare off his other musicians, so he hastily rounded up a Sicilian friend named Henri Padovani to play guitar, and the two of them went to work frantically putting together a set to impress Sting. It wasn't going to be easy; Henri knew two chords on guitar, and that was about the extent of it.

When Sting first came over to the Mayfair flat I was suitably impressed. He was good-looking, boyish but at the same time manly, and he seemed a nice enough chap, though slightly shy I thought at the time. I didn't realize then that he wasn't like all the others that Stewart had been auditioning in our flat, who'd come in answer to his ad. Sting, in fact, was a real musician, and wasn't at all convinced about the punk ideas Stewart had in mind. He wasn't shy, I now realize, he was just keeping his thoughts to himself. In any case, I could see that Stewart, who obviously saw qualities not quite so apparent to me, was taking great pains to make a good impression on him.

To demonstrate the Copeland clout, Stewart had me get backstage passes to see soul-brother number one James Brown at the Odeon in Hammersmith, no small feat. James Brown was terrific, but he was getting old and his show was predictable. To demonstrate our savvy, I got us in to see Generation X at the Roxy. Gen X were terrible in comparison to James Brown, but they were young and exciting, and there was nothing predictable about their amateurish performance. The sweaty club was packed to the rafters, and there was electricity in the air, an unexplainable threat of violence. The slam-dancing audience thrashed about and jumped up and down, and banged headlong into each other with wild abandon, walking a thin line between fun and danger. It was impossible not to get involved, or to ignore the intensity of the music. The incredibly charismatic teen-ager Billy Idol proved that singing was not his strong suit. His attitude and belief in himself more than made up for it. His band weren't great musicians either, but they had enough arrogance to convince you otherwise. That, it seemed to me, was what the punk scene was all about. Just about anyone that wanted to could give it a go.

Mom and Dad on
their wedding day.
London, England,
1943.

2

Baby Ian and CIA bodyguards. Damascus, Syria, 1949.

1

Brother Miles at the Step Pyramids in 1952, the year Stewart was born.

The Copeland kids in Cairo, 1954: Ian, Stewart, my sister Lennie, and Miles.

Stewart on drums, age twelve. Beirut, Lebanon, 1964.

The Beirut Wild Bunch, 1965.

'Nam, '68.

7

8

The First Infantry "Pheons" left to right: Me, Jarvis Jasper, Jay Anklam, and Tom Goodwin.

9

Ronald "Magic Man" Jaragosky. Di An, Vietnam, 1969.

Marianne Faithfull and Sonja Kristina of Curved Air. London, England, in the summer of '75.

Alex Hodges, head of Paragon Agency, overlooking me and fellow agent Buck Williams. Macon, Georgia, 1977.

12

The Police would sometimes come to my apartment in Manhattan to escape the hordes of fans at their hotel. Here they are watching themselves on the news.

World-wide success. Joan Jett & the Blackhearts, with manager Kenny Laguna and his family, celebrate platinum album status in Australia. Sydney, 1982.

13

14

The FBI family in 1982. Behind me, front row: Marlene Passaro, Linda Langford, Pamela Burton, Paula Leone, Connie, Patti La Magna. Rear, from left: Maria Torrente, Buck Williams, Theresa Lowery, Jim Longstretch, Dawn Harris, Dan Koppel, Rick Shoor, John Huie.

15a

The Copeland brothers must be the only people that *Playboy* magazine ever put clothes *on*. When this photo (below) appeared in their November issue in 1982, they dressed us up by giving us our father's suit and hands. Nice ties, too!

15b

16

Sting and Stewart's famous fighting was playful but rough. Just before going on stage at Shea Stadium, Sting broke a rib.

Me and daughter Barbara on stage at Shea Stadium.

Me, Miles, and Stewart at a wedding.

19

When *Forbes* magazine asked me to pose for a picture in 1985, I brought along Courteney Cox (FBI's first acting client) to share in the publicity. Manhattan Pier, N.Y., 1985.

Courteney Cox and me in Long Island, New York, 1984. Approximately twenty-four seconds in a Bruce Springsteen video was enough to launch her career.

20

21

Courteney and me in Malibu, California, while she was Michael J. Fox's girl-friend on *Family Ties*.

22

FBI acting client Sean Nelson received rave reviews and prestigious awards for his debut performance, starring in the Miramax film *Fresh*, written and directed by Boaz Yakim and produced by Randy Ostrow and Lawrence Bender. His next role was starring alongside Dustin Hoffman and Dennis Franz in the movie *American Buffalo*, filmed in 1995.

23

Mike Mills was the bass player in my band The Frustrations. He then went on to join his own band, R.E.M.

Sting and me.

24

My lovely daughters, Barbara and Chandra.

25

The FBI detected a similarity in our logos, but as everyone knows, at the center of my logo is a nose.

Not that that's what did it, but Sting, in any event, did decide to stay in London, and The Police was born. Sting decided to move his family down to London from Newcastle, and they began to rehearse in our apartment. At some point Stewart asked me to provide him with some lyrics for the riffs they were working on. I wrote down some heavy lyrics, really meaningful stuff. He threw them back at me. Then I wrote love songs, dripping with metaphor, all of which rhymed beautifully. He threw up.

"I want nihilistic, antisocial lyrics about hatred and other dark human emotions," he said. So, I wrote down a load of rubbish about being a dropout and hopeless loser, which Stewart put to music and transformed into a really great song called "Nothing Achieving." I wrote some simple rhymes about how it wasn't cool to dance, how I was too weird to watusi, and too tough to tango. Stewart turned those lyrics into a song called "Too Kool to Kalypso." I mention these because both of them were eventually recorded and released on vinyl. "Nothing Achieving" was the B-side to the first Police single ("Fallout" was the A-side), and "Too Kool to Kalypso" was recorded by Stewart under the alias of Klark Kent, and released on his own Krypton label. Still later, Sting took some more of my scribbles and turned them into a song called "Dead-End Job." That song came out in America on the B-side to the first pressing of the second Police single, "Roxanne," and on the B-side to "Can't Stand Losing You," the third single released in the United Kingdom.

Miles too was inspired by the whole new scene. While Stewart was busy forming a band, he was transforming his office into a haven for punk bands, setting up an independent company called Faulty Products to manage them, and printing up their records to release on a number of his own different labels. He signed up a group of young kids that he and I both went to see at a rehearsal in their basement out in Deptford, on the outskirts of London. They called their band Squeeze, and Miles put out their record on Deptford Fun City Records. He then signed Chelsea, and released a number of their singles on a label called Step Forward. At some point, Mark Perry (and the whole staff of *Sniffin' Glue*) sort of moved into the office to take advantage of Miles's generosity, trading Mark's knowledge of the scene for the use of the phones and electricity. One of Miles's earliest record releases was, in fact, an EP by a band that Mark Perry had put together called Alternative Television, which was also released on Deptford Fun City Records. None of them sold many records, but it was a start.

As for my situation, things went from bad to worse. In no time at all my money began to run out, what little I had to start with. Inside our posh penthouse Mayfair flat, Stewart, Sonja, and I considered a shared can of baked-beans-on-toast a hearty meal, if not exactly a feast, and between us we could rarely scrounge up enough money to buy even a packet of fags. Eventually we took to selling off Marcy's furniture to raise some cash. The landlord, however, was now seriously threatening to throw our stuff out into the street and change the locks. This meant that someone always had to be there, and we took turns leaving the house. Week by week the situation just got worse, until Stewart and Sonja finally found another place to stay. That was great for them, but not too groovy for me.

For some strange reason I went back up to Primrose Hill and sat down on the bench I had sat on nearly ten years before, when I made the desperate decision to join the U.S. Army. It seemed to me the only thing that had changed was the weather. It was a gloriously sunny day. Otherwise, I was basically back where I'd started, without a pot to piss in!

Examining my options, I realized my choices were few. At the age of twenty-eight I could easily start up again in London, but the thought of it didn't exactly turn me on. I felt I had already done it all, at least to a large extent, and just to do it again would not be the same the second time around. If my heart wasn't into it, I couldn't see the point.

Somehow, I just knew it was time for me to start a new life in America. It would mean making it on my own, without any help from my family, but that was something else I still wanted to prove— that I could.

I reconsidered going to find work in New York, but I had not been inspired by the agencies I'd visited, and the feeling was no doubt mutual. The fact is, no one in New York had actually offered me a job. So, with seemingly only one option open to me, I went back to the Mayfair flat and made one last call on Marcy's phone bill. I called Alex Hodges at Paragon Agency, way down yonder in Macon, Georgia. My whole future was literally on the line.

"Hello, Mr. Hodges?" I said. "About that job . . . ?"

CHAPTER 17

SOUTHERN COMFORT

The Devil went down to Georgia . . .
—THE CHARLIE DANIELS BAND

I ARRIVED IN America with my cat, Yassir, a suitcase of old clothes, a small collection of rare punk singles, a bass guitar, and a few hundred dollars that I made by selling off everything else I owned in London. I had no idea what I was in for at my new job, and only an inkling of what was expected of me. Alex Hodges, the boss at Paragon, had told me he wanted me for my ability to sign bands, but to start out I'd be booking the ones he already had on the Paragon roster, all of which were Southern rock bands, like The Charlie Daniels Band, The Outlaws, Atlanta Rhythm Section, Lynyrd Skynyrd, Marshall Tucker Band, and The Allman Brothers Band. I'd never heard of most of them but I was to discover that these bands were huge in America.

I was greeted at the Atlanta Airport by a tall teenager in a chauffeur's cap holding up a sign with my name on it. He had the bushiest eyebrows I've ever seen, like one big eyebrow across his forehead, and a firm handshake that matched his athletic build. He introduced himself as Bill Berry, and as I climbed into the back seat of the huge company Cadillac he explained that he was not only Paragon's chauffeur, but also the gofer, mail clerk, tea boy, messenger, and odd-jobs man. His workload might have been easier had his employers known a little bit about his future. Five years later he would be playing drums at Shea Stadium with his band R.E.M.

Bill Berry, I soon realized, probably knew more about Paragon than anyone else on the payroll. Curious to know more about my new job, I grilled him about the agency all the ninety miles to Macon, and he gave me a full rundown on all the people who worked there. He was a compulsive talker, and before long I knew the whole company's chain of command and all of the players. That's when I found out exactly what I was getting into. Bill told me, to my horror, that I was filling the shoes of the number-two man at Paragon.

Terry Rhodes, who was the agent responsible for Lynyrd Skynyrd and Marshall Tucker Band, among others, had convinced Alex Hodges to allow him to open a Paragon branch office on the West Coast, for the purpose of signing new acts, but only a few months after it opened he skipped to join I.C.M., a rival agency. According to Bill, Paragon's plan was for me to spend a few months in Macon getting to know the acts, then transfer out to L.A. to pick up where Terry left off.

My shocked expression must have been easy to see, even in the rearview mirror. When it dawned on Bill that all this was news to me, he kept his mouth shut, not wanting to tell me anything that might get him into trouble with Alex Hodges, for whom he obviously had a lot of respect. But not for long.

"I'll tell you this much," he said. "It's not just that Terry Rhodes's leaving meant losing some of our big acts. Fact is, Alex thinks the Southern rock thing has seen its day, and that if we're to survive into the eighties, we've got to expand our roster. That's where *you* come in. To put it bluntly, Alex is counting on you to save the agency."

"And how does he suppose I'm going to do that?" I asked.

"Simple," he said. "By signing bands from England."

"From England?! How am I going to convince a band from Britain to sign with an agency down in Macon, Georgia, with a roster full of Southern rock bands no one ever heard of?"

"Sir?!" I could see Bill looking at me in the rearview mirror, with an expression like "You're asking me??" That's when I decided to clam up. I didn't want Bill to realize I was terrified by his revelations. Meanwhile, I was thinking Holy moley! This time I've really bitten off more than I can chew!

Macon, Georgia (population 90,000), was culture shock for me. It could hardly have been more different from what I was used to in "swinging" London. A rural town of majestic old Southern mansions preserved from before the Civil War, when it was spared by General Sherman on his devastating march to the sea, Macon had grown into a small city while most of its population remained country folks just as before, going to the Methodist church on Sunday, eating corn pone and turnip greens for noonday "dinner," and preferring country-and-western music to what I was listening to at the time.

Small as it was, however, Macon was considered by many to be a capital city of American music, as the home of Southern rock and soul. The number of America's musical favorites that either came from Macon or got started there was way out of proportion to the size or commercial importance of the place—Otis Redding, Sam and Dave, Wet Willie, Lena Horne, Little Richard, most of James Brown's band, The Allman Brothers, Charlie Daniels, The Outlaws, Lynyrd Skynyrd, and Sea Level, to name but a few.

There was a lot to get used to in my new home. The whole town had only two half-decent restaurants. Neither of them was Indian, which had been my food of preference in London, and which I couldn't imagine living without. There were no traffic jams in Macon, no crowded tube trains, no throngs of busy people filling the sidewalks. At night, there was virtually nothing to do. Naught! By eleven o'clock it was as if they rolled up the sidewalks and sent everyone home. Aside from the people who worked at Capricorn Records and at Paragon, it seemed like the rest of Macon's population were old folks.

I did find right away that there were a good many things in favor of life in America, however, not the least of which were the improved climate, good food, and friendly female natives.

I was beginning to comprehend how lucky I was to have landed my job in America. My flash new BMW, secondhand but "like new," was to me a dream come true, and a vast improvement over the faulty junk heaps I'd had in the past. My new pad was top class, at least by London's standards: two large bedrooms, a full kitchen, and a bathroom with a shower that had enough water pressure so you didn't have to run around in it to get wet. I was so happy with my new apartment that I considered the fact that it flooded every time it rained to be a minor inconvenience. I now had a new car, a bad pad, and a great job with all the perks that went with it. I was overjoyed that I had successfully immigrated to the land of promise and plenty.

The Paragon offices were impressive, clean, and spacious, not at all what I was used to in London. Unlike the cramped, gloomy, and run-down pisshole at Dryden Chambers, Paragon was housed in a magnificent old Southern mansion, with polished wood floors, crystal chandeliers, cut-glass doors, and rocking chairs on the porch out front. My own office was enormous. My glass-topped antique mahogany desk was nearly as big as the small room in London I shared with four other agents. I had an ultra-modern stereo system, top-quality stuff with a volume switch that I swear went up to eleven. My phone actually connected me to the right number every time I dialed, which nearly never happened back in England. Best of all, I had a secretary of my very own. I'd never had one before, and it took some getting used to, having someone to make my calls for me, to take dictation and type out my letters. I was fortunate to get a great one. Darnise Maness had been the assistant for my predecessor, Terry Rhodes, and she was therefore able to cover my ass while I found out what in the hell I was supposed to be doing. The fact is, she should have had my job. She knew more than I did.

From day one I was under pressure. I felt as if I had somehow landed this job on the higher rungs of the ladder, and yet, secretly, I didn't have a clue what to do. I'd never actually booked a tour in America. My five-or-so years of experience booking Europe helped only a little, since things were done so differently in the United States. I wasn't sure where to begin.

Alex had given me the office next to his that had previously belonged to Terry Rhodes, and it was the plushest office in the place except for Alex's. I was afraid this would cause resentment from the other bookers, all of whom had more going for them than I did, or so it seemed to me. All I had going was my London contacts and experience in Europe, which wouldn't be of much use to me, at least not until I had my feet on the ground in America. But if there was any resentment from the others it never showed. They were all very helpful to me, especially the agent who handled the Southern states, a real good ol' boy from North Carolina named James (Buck) Williams.

Buck was an army veteran too, having served with the legendary Green Berets during the Vietnam War, and he possessed a quiet confidence in everything he did. I would secretly consult with him whenever I had a problem that was beyond my experience. I went to great lengths to hide my ignorance from Alex and the other agents, but Buck was the kind of guy who inspired immediate trust. He taught me how to structure intricate percentage deals (fees in Europe were almost always a flat fee in those days), where the artist could make lots more money if the show did well, and he helped acquaint me with who was who in the music business in America. In short, he generally saved me from making any serious fuckups while I got my act together.

I wasn't convinced I was fooling Alex Hodges. It occurred to me that he might well have given me the best office in the place so that he could keep the door open between us and keep an eye on what I was doing. Knowing that the boss could listen to my every conversation was nerve-racking, but, apart from that, the open door was beneficial because it let me watch a true master in action. Alex was far and away the most thorough and aggressive booking agent I had ever seen. He was also the loudest shouter. At least once a week I heard him screaming at some poor bastard on the other end of the phone, hurling profanities and delivering threats, with his veins popping out of his neck and forehead. When Alex started screaming, the chandeliers shook and the rest of the office staff went deathly quiet. We could always see it coming. Alex would increase in volume slowly, until finally he had worked himself into a rage, then he would explode like a great volcano.

I once saw him throw a manager* bodily out of his office, after an argument about The Charlie Daniels Band. On that occasion, the manager had announced to Alex that he was arbitrarily raising the band's sound and light fees from $2,500 to $15,000 (or thereabouts, I forget the exact numbers), even though this meant a corresponding reduction in the band's performance fee. In other words, the band went from earning an average of $15,000 per night (plus $2,500 for sound and lights) to a mere $2,500 per night (plus $15,000 for S&L). Since the agency didn't claim a commission for sound-and-light fees, but only on performance fees, and since the band owned the sound and lights themselves, it seemed clear to Alex that the new manager was pulling a fast one at his expense by trying to cheat him out of his commission. The result was a very pissed off Alex, and a manager's hasty exit from his office.

Alex ran a tight ship at Paragon, and the fact that he was an ex-army officer was evident in the way he ran his company. He had agents' meetings each week that were like torture sessions. Anyone coming late was fined twenty-five dollars for each five minutes missed, as if incurring Alex's wrath wasn't bad enough. We gathered around a huge conference table, with Alex at its head, while each agent was given a detailed grilling over every booking and every contract—and heaven help the poor slob who overlooked a possible booking or who failed to get a sufficient deposit for each date. At my first such meeting, one of the other agents admitted to making a "simple mistake." Alex nearly reamed him out.

"Simple mistake!" he yelled. "There's no such thing as a simple mistake! Let me remind you that Lynyrd Skynyrd just went down in a plane crash *simply* because somebody underestimated the weight of equipment, or miscalculated the fuel consumption. The airplane *simply* ran out of gas just short of the airport." Alex was serious. "Gentlemen. You are not allowed to make simple mistakes."

The first chore Alex assigned to me was to study the rider contracts for all the Paragon bands. A rider contract is attached to each standard contract of engagement, and in it are all the special requirements needed for each band to perform its show; i.e., stage dimen-

---

* Robert Stewart, I later learned, was actually more accurately defined as a "management representative" who worked for Joe Sullivan's management firm.

sions, dressing room requirements, and so on. Alex gave me a huge pile of them, one for each band, and then he gave me an oral test to make sure I had memorized them all, down to the smallest detail. The Allman Brothers Band's rider included a clause that I didn't understand, words to the effect: "Promoter will ensure a snowstorm immediately upon the band's arrival." I asked Alex what it meant, and he looked at me like I had two heads. Some of the bands I worked with in Europe smoked hashish, but cocaine was new to me.

Next, Alex introduced me over the phone to all the major promoters around the country, one by one: Ron Delsener, whose turf was Manhattan; John Scher, across the river in New Jersey; Larry Vaugn, on Long Island; Don Law, who controlled Boston; Bill Douthat, in the Virginias; Cecil Corbett, in the Carolinas; Alex Cooley, in Atlanta; Jack Boyle and Jon Stoll, rivals in Florida; Don Fox, in New Orleans; Louis Messina, in Texas; Rick Kay and Rick Franks, in Detroit; Irv Zuckerman, in St. Louis; Jerry Mickelson and Arny Granat, who together owned Chicago; Randy Levy, in Minneapolis; Barry Fey, in Denver; John Bauer, in the Northwest; Brian Murphy and his rivals, Steve Wolf and Jim Rissmiller, who competed for the Los Angeles market; and, last but not least, the famous Bill Graham, in San Francisco. Nervous though I was at times, I was doing fine until we got to Larry Magid, the major promoter in Philadelphia, considered to be the number-five market in America. Alex introduced me to Larry, then he got off the line and left me to it. Larry first asked if I was any relation to Miles Copeland, and I admitted I was.

The tirade that Magid went into took me completely by surprise. He cursed, he shouted, he ranted and raved, and, in eighteen eloquent ways, told me to go fuck myself. Then he hung up.

I had no way of knowing beforehand that Miles and Larry were sworn enemies. It had transpired that Magid refused to make an offer for Miles's band Renaissance some time before I had arrived in America, and Miles made the mistake of listening to another promoter, a young fellow named Rick Green, who was eager to promote the band. Larry Magid, not one to look kindly upon competition, simply bought the building Rick Green was offering, and blew off the show. Rick Green accused Magid of trying to enforce a monopoly on the market, and took the unusual step of suing

WILD THING

him for restraint of trade. Miles, of course, was caught in the middle, but based largely upon his testimony in affidavits, Magid was forced to settle out of court.

Now I was expected to pay for it, or at least share Magid's animosity. I certainly didn't need any enemies this early in the game, and being a "new boy" I let it worry me more than it should. To make matters worse, almost immediately after that I had an unfortunate confrontation with the mighty Bill Graham himself. Graham was renowned for his promotions at the Fillmores, and for his involvement in the careers of many of the bands from the "Woodstock generation." Operating out of San Francisco, his influence in the music community spread much farther than the Bay Area he controlled. Bill Graham was probably the most powerful promoter in the world.

It was all much ado over nothing, really, but it grew to be a major row between us, and Alex Hodges was brought into the middle. Alex had put me to work trying to book a West Coast tour for The Outlaws, and I was diligently busting my ass on it, trying to find enough bookings to make it worthwhile. It was then that Buck informed me. "I hate to be the one to tell you," he said, "but I suspect they've sent you on a snipe hunt."

I said "What's a snipe hunt?"

"That," explained Buck, "is where you take some damn Yankee—actually a limey jus' might be even more groovy—anyway, you take him out into the woods, you give him a ol' burlap sack, put him under some thorny bush where you know he'll be cold and uncomfortable, and you tell him to give bird calls all night—you know, like 'snipe! 'snipe!—while the rest of you go downwind and chase the birds to him. 'Course, then you go on home and leave the poor bastard out in the wilderness all night."

That was Buck's way of explaining that I was wasting my time. Alex and The Outlaws' manager, Charlie Bruscoe, had considered a West Coast run many times, but they'd always concluded that it was not financially feasible. Alex had apparently assigned me to a dummy run so that I could "get my feet wet" booking a tour that wouldn't cost Paragon anything if I made mistakes. In fact, I found out, the other agents at Paragon were simultaneously booking dates in their territories, even though The Outlaws had already been overexposed in all of them. Even after I knew all this, however, I still busted my ass trying to put together a West Coast run, if only to impress my new boss with my ability to break new ground.

There were only a handful of promoters on the West Coast and they enjoyed a virtual monopoly on the major markets. This meant that they could offer whatever guaranteed fees they wanted, and the bands had to accept them to play in that market. But I was unhappy with the low offers these promoters were giving me for The Outlaws, since they didn't add up to enough to warrant a trip west. So, naturally, I started turning over rocks to find others, calling some promoters and colleges Paragon had never done business with before. It wasn't long before I was able to find a number of people willing to work with me, particularly at the colleges, where they rarely, if ever, got phone calls from agents. There was a young college kid at Stanford University who was more than eager to book The Outlaws. Better still, he had an entertainment budget from the college, money to burn.

Bill Graham was offering a $1,000 guarantee against a percentage for a show in San Francisco. The kid at Stanford College offered me $10,000 flat. Obviously, this made a big difference to the touring budget. I knew what to do; I booked it. But, out of courtesy, I first called Danny Scher back at Bill Graham's office, and told him about the offer from Stanford. I was hoping I could do both shows. As I expected, he told me I couldn't do it, that Stanford was too close to San Francisco. I told him I didn't agree, but that if I had to make a choice I might be forced financially to go with Stanford. He told me I was making a mistake. He said that the venue at Stanford was one where no respectable group would want to play, that the stage was too small, that it was out of doors and therefore risky because it might rain, and so on. So I got pictures of the building from the college to learn that a stage could be built to our specifications, and I checked with the weather service as well as the almanac to learn that the chance of rain there at that time of year was only minimal.

None of the other reasons seemed to hold much water either. Danny was only doing his job, which was to try and keep the act away from his competition. The bottom line was, with Stanford and no San Francisco, the tour was financially feasible. With San Francisco and no Stanford, it wasn't. The Outlaws' manager approved

WILD THING

my tour, without San Francisco. With a tour of the West Coast that made sense, and would actually happen, I thought to myself, "Fucking 'ell, I caught a bloody snipe!" Again out of courtesy, I called Danny Scher to inform him of our decision. "I appreciate your letting me know," he said. "But, before you do anything, maybe you better talk to Bill Graham."

Bill didn't call me. Instead, he was on the phone to Charlie Bruscoe within minutes, screaming and shouting bloody murder. Bruscoe, in extreme awe of Bill Graham, was immediately on the phone to Alex, demanding that he pull me off the case. Alex called me into his office and told me I was to back off.

As new to the game as I was, the last thing I wanted to do was mess with Bill Graham, argue with a manager, or make life difficult for Alex. But I also knew I had no choice. Apart from the principle of the thing, I told Alex, "If promoters can go over my head to you, or call on managers direct, and you don't back me up, I might as well just quit, 'cause I can't do my job." Alex knew I was right. After talking it over with Bruscoe, the decision was made for the tour to go on, and Bill Graham would have to get over it.

Bill was furious. He sent us a six-page telegram, a tirade of angry threats mixed with long diatribes about loyalty, and greed, and the importance of paying dues, the latter in reference to my inexperience. In the end, however, we did play the date at Stanford, and it was a great success. The Outlaws made a profit on their West Coast run, for the first time ever, and from then on both Bill Graham and Charlie Bruscoe showed me a bit more respect. The next time The Outlaws came to the Bay Area I gave them to Bill in San Francisco, and they were paid, funnily enough, ten grand as a guarantee.

I was to find, in subsequent dealings with Graham over the years, that Bill loved a good shout now and again, and that more often than not it got him whatever he wanted. I learned that you could have a no-holds-barred shouting match with Bill in the morning, then in the afternoon he'd call you up about something else, another artist perhaps, as if nothing happened.

There was one other little benefit I enjoyed about living in America I feel I have to mention. In London I was invariably recognized as an American, but upon arrival in Macon I was thought of as unmistakably British. I won't try to explain it, but in most parts of America even the slightest suggestion of a British accent opens the door to romance and an active love life. So for a while you might say I made out like the proverbial fat rat in a cheese factory. I mention it because I believe this may have had something to do with my keeping my job, at least in the early months. On my first out-of-town trip together with one of my bosses I somehow managed to hook him up with one of two voluptuous young ladies whom we met in a restaurant and who ended up staying the night in our hotel, and after that he never went anywhere without me.

Miles, meanwhile, was back in England, still selling badges, buttons, and posters at concerts to pay all the bills from the Startruckin' Tour. His company, BTM (British Talent Managers) had folded completely, along with his sound-and-light company and everything else. But when all his other bands deserted him, Miles went to Climax Blues Band and promised them that if they'd stick with him for just one more year, he'd deliver them a hit record. Well, they did. And he did. "Couldn't Get It Right" became a monstrous hit all over the world within the year.

Miles had given the band to Alex at Paragon, and now that they had a hit record, it was time to book them a tour. It seemed only natural that I should be assigned to coordinate the tour of the U.S. as their "responsible agent."

Alex had a first-class team of agents at Paragon, each with his own territory to book. Together they put a lot of work into making this the best tour possible, and basically all I did was watch, learn, and pretend to be on top of it. The tour that was booked was a masterpiece. Whatever his faith in me, Alex still covered everything himself, just to make sure. And everything seemed to fall into perfect place. The money we got for the band was top dollar. The routing was excellent from one city to the next. All the promotion was in place. Then I got a phone call from Miles with unbelievably bad news. Climax Blues Band had left him, despite the fact that he had fulfilled his promise of delivering them a hit record, and they now had a new manager and a new agent. The tour Paragon had booked so diligently was blown out.

WILD THING

Miles was devastated, and so was I. I had to go back to everyone and tell them all their efforts had been a waste of time. The promoters had gone to great lengths to shuffle dates around for us to make everything fit just right, and now they were left with a dead night and unrecoverable promotional expenses. Alex Hodges was supportive, but he had hired me to build up the roster with British acts, and I had just lost one. Right then the honeymoon at Paragon was over, and the pressure was on for me to sign a band.

I made several trips to London to revive my old contacts, and mostly came up empty-handed. None of the big acts in London wanted to sign with an agency in a hick town in Georgia they'd never heard of. It did no good to drop names like The Charlie Daniels Band, who were huge in America but unknown in Britain, and not the sort of thing a band on the British *Top of the Pops* would want to tour with anyway.

All the same, I was able to sign some tasty acts. Frankie Miller's Full House, for example. Although they hadn't made it to the charts in America, meaning that they were a long shot and wouldn't immediately justify my fancy office, this was one of the best groups I'd heard in a long time, and at least everyone at Paragon loved it. That gave a boost to my credibility, but nothing more. And I blew that by signing two acts that never even toured. I booked tours for Ian Gillan, the singer in Deep Purple, and for Roger Chapman's Streetwalkers, but their record companies pulled financial support for their tours when their records stiffed, and we had to cancel them. After a whole year, the closest I got to signing a "big" act was Root Boy Slim and the Sex Change Band, but their one single we thought would be a hit ("Boogie 'Til You Puke") didn't get off the ground. Again, the record company bailed out, this time right in the middle of the tour.

I was about to give up. I met with hundreds of bands, or their managers, and I visited all the record companies. I beat the bushes until they looked like they'd been hit with Agent Orange. No luck. I did stir up a bit of interest, though, and I even managed to convince a few bands they should sign with us, only to see them back down at the last minute to sign up with a New York and L.A. agency. Even my old friend Luke O'Reilly, who I was hoping would give me Al Stewart when his contracts expired with his current agency—an agency he was unhappy with—ended up taking him to another agency in Los Angeles.

I was by this time slightly nervous about keeping my job. To make matters worse, Alex made me the responsible agent for Fandango, Stillwater, Grinderswitch, and every other band on the Paragon roster that it was nearly impossible to book. They were great bands, but the barn door had evidently closed on Southern rock. The pressure was on for me to sign a major British act, something more conventional, something with a record on the charts. Unfortunately, I wasn't having much luck with that.

Paragon Agency was a sister company to Capricorn Records in Macon, the label to which many of our bands were signed. Capricorn was owned by Phil Walden, a local millionaire who'd made his fortune with Southern bands. Phil was in the same boat as Alex, of course, and he needed something to pull him out of the nose-diving Southern rock scene. I tried to call his attention to The Police and Squeeze, the two bands Miles was now managing, and to many other struggling punk bands from London that were looking for a record deal in the States. But Phil was never the least bit interested. This was no great surprise to me, of course, since no one in America at the time was interested in them either.

One time, however, I found something that would have been perfect for Phil Walden. As the owner of Capricorn Records (and according to Alex, secretly the principal owner of Paragon Agency) he was the only person in Macon that ranked higher than Alex Hodges, and if fate and I had been on the same side we could have saved the whole Macon music scene.

I had what appeared to be an enormous stroke of luck; an act called Gerry Rafferty went shooting up the charts, and I discovered that he was being managed by my old friend and mentor, Ed Bicknell, the same guy that taught me how to be an agent back in London. I was immediately on the next plane to Heathrow.

Ed Bicknell was glad to see me, and I him. We went for lunch and a laugh, exchanging stories of what we'd been up to since the last we'd seen each other. But as we settled down for a serious talk, Ed told me right away I was wasting my time. Gerry Rafferty hated going on the road, he informed me, and would never tour America, "not in a million years."

"It's downright embarrassing!" said Ed. "I've been invited to lunch or dinner by every hot-shot agent in America. Honestly, I've gained at least ten stone in the last fortnight. I have to tell you the same thing I told them. I enjoy having you all wine and dine me at greatly overpriced restaurants so you can show off your company expense accounts, and I'd love for you to tell me all the sordid details of your seedy sex life and so on. But there is absolutely no point in discussing Gerry Rafferty."

As I was paying the bill, he gave me a tape recorded by another band he managed. "This is the group you should be going after," he said. "They're going to be absolutely enormous! They're the kind of band you and I both can appreciate 'cause they love to work. They're an agent's wet dream. But I haven't been able to swing a record deal in America. If you get them a deal with Capricorn Records," he said, "they're yours for your agency."

I was deeply disappointed. I had been counting on signing Gerry Rafferty as a means of saving my ass. I had rented a Jaguar upon arrival at Heathrow so as to impress Bicknell, and it came equipped with a cassette player. The only tape I had with me, it so happened, was the one that Ed gave me. To get my mind off my troubles I played it. I was only a minute or two into it when I saw that Ed's "ears" were right on the money. The more I listened the more I liked what I heard. It was clear to me this band *was* going to be enormous! With their clever lyrics and amazing guitar playing they sounded like Bob Dylan meets The Allman Brothers, just perfect for Capricorn Records. The band was called Dire Straits.

I was so excited by the tape that I could hardly wait to get back to Macon. Bill Berry met me at the airport and I had him drive me straight to Capricorn to drop off the tape for Phil Walden. I was happy with myself for I was sure that he'd love it. Several days passed, however, and I grew impatient for a response. I tried to catch Phil after work in the Capricorn steam room, where we often met for informal conferences and listened to new recordings. He seemed to be avoiding me. I eventually had Buck drive me out to his house. Since Buck knew Phil better than I did, I asked him to hand deliver another copy of the tape. I gave Buck instructions to tell Phil to pay particular attention to the third track on the tape, titled "Sultans of Swing."

Two days later I got the tape back, with a note from Walden's office: "PASS. Please don't send me anymore of this punk crap."

Punk? Crap? I couldn't believe it! To this day, I'm convinced he never listened to the tape. "Sultans of Swing" was a monster hit. Dire Straits was soon to be the most commercially successful group in the world for the next decade, selling millions of records (over 65 million to date), and their tours would also gross many millions of dollars, more than any other group in history. Unfortunately for me, they were signed to a New York–based record company, who gave them to a New York agent.

That did it! For the first time I realized the truth of what I'd long suspected. Phil Walden might have been a shrewd businessman, but in judging the new musical trends he didn't know punk from Frank Sinatra. His arrogant note only increased my resolve, making me realize that my only hope at Paragon or anywhere else was to follow my own ears. It was pointless for me to rely on anyone else, especially the so-called experts, whose ears were obsolete. I knew what was happening, and I determined that I was going to have to go for it on my own.

◆◆◆

That week, as if to make the statement, I shaved off my shaggy beard, and cut off all my hair, which hadn't been cut in years. What happened was very strange. I experienced a complete reversal from a generation earlier. When I first grew it long I was treated like a social outcast. Now I had short hair, and in Macon I was considered to be a freak. Oddly, it felt good.

Punk music was generally ignored in America, but it had taken a firm hold in England, and I could see that the punk scene there was really happening. What had started as a tiny underground movement, a motley bunch of garage bands who could barely play their instruments, who scorned fancy lighting and massive banks of equipment, and who spat in the faces of the music establishment, had ended up taking it over.

In May 1977, I flew over to England to see The Police, with the original guitar player, Henri Padovani, at their first headline show at the Railway Hotel, in Putney, London. I was very impressed. Their

WILD THING

sets were only ten or fifteen minutes each, but it was an incredibly intense fifteen minutes, and the band was exhausted by the time they came off the stage. Sting seemed to have shed any shyness he may have had when I met him, and as a front man he was excellent. Henri wasn't bad either, though his guitar playing was weak in comparison to Sting's bass playing and Stewart's drumming. I was, of course, extremely proud of Stewart. He had always been impressive in Curved Air, but in The Police he played with the power of the possessed.

Paul Mulligan, my old friend from Beirut, was also at the show. Paul was proudly calling himself The Police's manager, basing part of his claim on the fact that he had donated one of his flight suits to Sting, the very suit that Sting was wearing on stage that night—and every night for nearly the following year, for that matter—and loaned Stewart a few hundred pounds to make the first Police record. Flight suit or no flight suit, the band was good, and certainly showed great potential. But beyond that, none of us knew it would one day be the biggest band of the decade. That's not to say we didn't realize they'd be successful, even at this early stage, but we didn't really know what that meant. We never quantified success, we just believed.

Well, since I couldn't get the established bands to sign with me, and the punk bands weren't being signed by the establishment, I soon figured punk and I were perfect for each other. Back in Macon, I began to collect all the punk records I could get my hands on and I played them continuously. Stewart sent me care packages every so often with the latest stuff. Then I found a guy up in Atlanta, Danny Beard, who ran an import record store called Wax 'n' Facts, and who was only too glad to keep me up to date. He sent me 45s like "New Rose" by The Damned, "Right to Work" by Chelsea, and "God Save the Queen" and "Pretty Vacant" by The Sex Pistols. When The Police recorded a single called "Fallout," Stewart sent me a box full, and I was pleased to see that a song I had written the lyrics for, a song called "Nothing Achieving," was put on the B-side.

I sent copies of it to all the radio stations within a hundred-mile radius of Macon, and listened every day to hear it played. To the best of my knowledge, nobody played it once. I finally went down to the local radio station personally, and the DJ there met with me because I was with Paragon. But when I explained that I was trying to promote punk in America, he tore into me. To my surprise, he went into a rage, shouting he didn't want that punk shit on his station, or any other station for that matter. He was really over the top about it. I asked him for my records back, and he told me he had thrown them out. Luckily, I was ushered out before I could tear off his head.

On January 5, 1978, The Sex Pistols came to Atlanta. Hoping they would finally convince everyone at Paragon that punk was the wave of the future, I dragged the whole office to Atlanta to see their show. But, as it happened, The Sex Pistols blew it. Atlanta was their warm-up gig, the first of their dates in America as arranged by their record company, so they went on stage with jet lag and equipment problems, several hours late. When they finally got started, it was clear that they had already thrown in the towel. Not to put too fine a point on it, they sucked. Johnny Rotten spent much of the performance throwing up on the side of the stage, and the rest of it spitting on the audience. At the start, the place was packed with the curious, but by the time the concert was over the hall was practically empty. And *none* of the agents I dragged up to Atlanta could see any future in either The Sex Pistols or the kind of music they were supposed to represent. All my Paragon associates could talk about on the ride back to Macon was how they'd seen a usually uncritical audience walking out of the concert. It did no good for me to point out that this was because any kids who showed up even resembling punk were refused entry to the club. I'd seen a group of them who did manage to sneak in for part of the show, but they were quickly ushered out the back door and beaten up. One of them, I found out much later, was a young fan of punk music called Peter Buck, the future guitar player with R.E.M.

By this time almost everyone in Macon that knew me was steering a clear path away from my house. At every opportunity, I would play this punk music, subjecting all those who might drop by to large doses at high volume. If they didn't seem to like it the first time—and nobody in Macon did—I'd play it to them again even louder. I was sure that it would grow on them. I was so determined to turn people

WILD THING

on that I was driving them away in droves. Phil Walden threw a party one night and I slid some punk music on the record player when no one was watching, figuring that since the guests were all record biz at least one or two of them would be astute enough to recognize Big Opportunity when they saw it. But no, they all hated it, and after that I wasn't invited to many Capricorn barbecues and get-togethers.

Before long, Bill Berry and his roommate, Mike Mills, were just about the only two people in Macon who would mix with me socially. They shared an apartment together over by the Paragon offices on Cherry Street, but more often than not they were over my place listening to punk records. At age eighteen, Bill was already what you might call a real "character," although to me at age twenty-eight he was just a kid. After leaving high school, he had played drums in several local bands, but he became discouraged with the local scene and put away his drums for a "real" job. His love for music led him to get a job in the music business, working for Paragon. He was ambitious, but he was willing to work his way up from the bottom. He got a job at Paragon running the mail room and doubling as office boy, chauffeur, and messenger. In fact, working from a shack at the back of the Paragon parking lot, he did whatever anyone in the front office dreamed up for him to do.

Mike Mills's story was pretty much the same as Bill's. He played bass guitar in various local bands long enough to become bored with them, then he quit the scene to work for Sears & Roebuck. Coincidentally, he sold me his guitar amp when I first arrived in Macon, but now that he was renewing his interest in music he was anxious to play, so he'd hang out at my house and play on my see-through Dan Armstrong Ampeg bass that I had brought with me from London. Years later, he bought himself one just like it, but at the time there was nothing about his playing, or Bill Berry's for that matter, to indicate that they would one day be superstars.

Bill and Mike were intrigued by this new music, so they came over to my place almost every night for jam sessions, and the three of us played along to 45s of Klark Kent, The Police, The Damned, The Stranglers, The Ramones, The Sex Pistols, and, of course, Richard Hell and the Voidoids. This, of course, did nothing to better my popularity ratings in the neighborhood.

One of the big events in Macon was the Capricorn picnic that Phil Walden organized every year. He would set up free bars and barbecues at one of the town's parks, invite a lot of music-business heavies from around the country, add a sprinkling of local political bigwigs, and then have his Capricorn bands play a set or two each, giving the guests the thrill of mixing with the stars.

That year, the Capricorn picnic was going to be an extra-special event. Since Phil Walden and Alex Hodges had helped Jimmy Carter in his presidential campaign, it was rumored that the President of the United States was going to be attending. It was also going to be the first time The Allman Brothers Band played together in years, since Greg Allman had fled the scene. The event was to be of national importance, the sort of thing that wouldn't be missed by *Time* and *Newsweek*. But that didn't impress me: all I saw in it was possibly a way to capitalize on it to promote my new obsession. I wanted all those promoters who were going to be in town to have at least a taste of punk.

I knew, though, that Bunky Odom, who was to be in charge of entertainment, wouldn't allow me anywhere near his music system with anything like punk music. So I figured that maybe I could somehow get a punk band onto the stage. And since there weren't any local punk bands, I figured I'd have to form one. When I told my idea to Bill Berry and Mike Mills they immediately volunteered, and I went to work on getting some of the others at the office to join in. When we started jamming out in Bill's mail shack behind Paragon right after work, it turned out that practically everyone in the office was a frustrated musician. We ended up with Jeff ("The Whale") Siroty on guitar; Buck Williams on the harmonica; and Darnise Maness (my secretary), Pat Rawlings (Rogers Redding's secretary), and Kathy Kitchen (Buck Williams's secretary) on backup vocals. We called the band—Macon's first and only punk band—"The Frustrations."

At first we just went out back to Bill's shack and jammed. I managed to decipher the lyrics to a few Ramones songs ("I Don't Care" and "I Wanna Be Your Boyfriend") and forced everybody to play them over and over until, on the third day, we could actually play the songs to the end, beginning at the same time and ending at the same time. Roughly.

The day of the picnic, our guitarist Jeff Siroty came up to me with his chin hanging down to the ground to tell me he couldn't go through with it. I asked him what, at this eleventh hour, he could possibly be worried about. "It's not me," he said, "it's my wife."

It figured. Jeff's wife was regarded by the rest of us as a notorious bitch. Jeff shared a large booking room with some of the agents, and on many occasions Jeff's wife would call him up and yell at him with everyone in the office watching him squirm.

"She says she'll divorce me if I get up there," he said.

"Then Jeff, I owe it to you to get you up there."

I was halfway joking, of course, but I wasn't going to let my great plan be sabotaged by some wimp's wife. But with Jeff out of it, some of the others started flaking out. In the end, however, Buck, Bill Berry, and Mike Mills agreed to go on with it, so I did too.

Meeting the President of the United States should have been the most exciting event in my life, but it was nothing compared to the excitement I felt about going on stage in front of that huge audience, and a highly critical audience at that. I had watched many a band perform, but I'd never been up there myself. The Outlaws played first, then The Allman Brothers Band. Both groups were magic. By this time my stomach was churning, and I was in a cold sweat. These were tough acts to follow, and we were due on stage next—playing punk!

It's probably all for the best, but just as we were ready to go on it started to rain. Despite that fact, we were determined to play, but The Allman Brothers' roadies stopped us. They didn't want their equipment to get wet, but more than anything they didn't want to see us electrocute ourselves. So, the first, and only, Frustrations gig was rained out, and I lost my chance to play punk . . . for the President.

After this I became more resolved to turn on Macon and the rest of America to the new generation of music. On subsequent trips to London and New York I began to seek out the managers of punk bands to try to convince them to tour the States. I was having no luck with anything else, as a matter of fact, but I was firmly convinced that punk could happen in America. From where I sat, I seemed to be the only person in America that thought so.

In early 1978, Miles called me from England to tell me that he'd managed to get a record deal for Squeeze, a band of kids he and I had gone to see play a year or so earlier in their basement in Blackheath, on the outskirts of London, but in order to get A&M to release their record in America, Miles had to get them a tour. Miles wanted to know if it could be done.

At that time all the record companies were reluctant to finance tours for any bands, much less bands that were considered punk. Tours cost too much money, and record companies preferred to spend it on radio, which certainly wasn't playing punk or anything remotely like it. Disco was all they played, even though the disco scene, the record companies' hope for saving a plummeting market, was already dead or dying.

The budgets for touring that the big bands were demanding were full of frills: massive tour buses and private planes to get them from city to city, limos to get them to and from the show, expensive hotels and lavish backstage parties. The fact was, however, that the record companies were not spending *their* money on these tours; the money was the bands in the end, although only a few of the bands actually realized it. Thinking that they were spending record company money, most of the British bands tried to outdo each other to see who could get the biggest tour budget. Then, later, not fully understanding that the record companies took costs of the tours from royalties, they wondered why they made peanuts off their albums. Miles, of course, knew the score.

He told me that Squeeze was willing to forsake the luxuries, and he asked me to budget out a tour in which the band would go from gig to gig in a station wagon and stay in cheap motels. His plan was to go to the record company with a low budget they couldn't turn down.

John Lay, Squeeze's hardworking tour manager, had never toured America before, so he hadn't been spoiled by previous experience and he was ready for anything. This was fortunate, because there were all sorts of problems ahead, and it was a bitch putting the tour together.

A club circuit did not exist at the time, although many of the major markets had "showcase" clubs that put on national acts. Bands were expected to break by getting on a major tour supporting another headline act, and the showcase clubs were used mainly for promotion by the record companies. When I offered them Squeeze, and they asked me what the record company was going to do to promote it, I said "You're the promoter, not the record company." To the showcase clubs in America, this appeared to be a new concept. Normally, they were inundated with promotional material from the record companies, and they had to do very little promotional work themselves. The record company would buy promotional spots on whatever radio station was playing their record, but in Squeeze's case there weren't any.

Squeeze was unlikely to get on a tour with any of the major acts of the day, and it would have been too expensive anyway, so a club tour was the only choice we had. Somehow, I had to make it work. To make it even more difficult, all the club promoters wanted the same nights of the week, favoring weekends, which left me with gaps in the datesheet. With a band willing to work every night, it didn't make sense to leave it sitting in a hotel with no income on the off nights, so I filled these with whatever I could, often in clubs that had never had a band from Britain.

Miles went along for much of the tour, lining up old radio friends wherever he could and inviting them down to see the show. While John Lay took care of soundcheck and stage production, Miles got out the old glue bucket and put up posters all over town, hitting the local record stores especially. In the process, he weeded out the ones that would also be useful to us in the future, having in mind not only Squeeze but also other projects that would be coming up.

The tour included one major achievement for me. I was able to route the group through Macon with a show at a local bar called Flaming Sally's. This was important, because I felt if any group could turn everyone at Paragon around, Squeeze could. By its strictest definition, Squeeze wasn't really a punk band anyway, but at the time any band from England whose members were under the age of thirty was immediately labeled punk. But Squeeze was the acceptable side of punk. Their album was brilliant, and, most important to me, they were first-rate on stage. They were well rehearsed and professional, just what was needed to shatter the myths and preconceptions about punk harbored by my colleagues.

Having booked them a date at Flaming Sally's, I then had to figure out how to get a crowd to come watch them. It would serve no purpose if the band were to play to an empty room, since this would make it all the more difficult for them to impress my coworkers. Once again, I turned to Bill Berry and Mike Mills, converts to punk and my partners in crime. We went all over Macon to wherever the kids hung out and spray-painted "U.K. Squeeze" (the U.K. was added to avoid a lawsuit from another band in Philadelphia with that name, who later broke up, and the U.K. was dropped) over every blank space we could find. We sprayed it on the walls at high schools, and on the sidewalks outside every club and bar in town, including The Cottage, where all the Capricorn and Paragon people hung out. Holding me by my feet, Bill and Mike hung me upside down over a bridge where I spray painted U.K. Squeeze, (with the ee's the wrong way round), on the overpass to the interstate. Then we climbed up on an enormous billboard out by the airport as you come into town, and sprayed it in big letters on top of where they had just freshly painted it white. It stayed there for several months after that.

Squeeze played their gig in Macon on June 16, 1978, and it was the regional pop event of the year. They performed amazingly well, and the crowd in the packed bar loved them. More important, so did everyone at Paragon. After the show I dragged the agents back to meet the band, and again they were surprised. Expecting to meet a bunch of obnoxious punks, they found instead some of the nicest people you'd ever want to meet. Gilson Lavis, the drummer, got into a drinking contest with our star beer drinker, John Huie, an ex-college football player who was twice Gilson's size, and came out the winner. They were even a hit with the local cops, one of whom let Gilson pose for a photograph with one of his pistols. Being English, Gilson had never handled a real gun before, and he was waving it around like a toy, causing everyone in the room to hit the floor.

It was hard to hide anything in a small town like Macon, and it soon became obvious who the culprits were who'd vandalized the neighborhood with Squeeze logos, so Mike Mills, Bill Berry, and I were thereafter barred from The Cottage and other local clubs in Macon. But I considered it a small price to pay. Although the

WILD THING

Squeeze tour was a relatively modest success in the eyes of the music industry, I saw it as a major breakthrough. Squeeze pleased enough of the people at Paragon, and elsewhere around the country, to set the stage for me to bring in The Police, and after them, a whole wave of new bands from England.

CHAPTER 18

The End of the Beginning

Roxxxxaaaaanne . . .
—The Police

BACK in Britain, The Police were making some headway, but it was rough going. Record companies remained reluctant to sign punk bands, so many of the early punk bands were forced to put out their own records. The first Police single, "Fall Out"/"Nothing Achieving," was recorded for $300, which Stewart borrowed from my old friend and guru from Beirut, Paul Mulligan (who had helped to smuggle me out of Beirut as a runaway juvenile). Stewart released it in May, 1977 on his own Illegal Records label, which Miles distributed through his independent record company Faulty Products, and though it met with mainly negative reviews, the initial pressing of two thousand copies sold out immediately, simply on the strength of the punk artwork on the record sleeve. It was a start.

Miles was trying to find work for the band, but it certainly wasn't easy. The British press hated them. As far as they were concerned, the band was too professional, and way too old to be punk. Sting was considered a jazz man, and Stewart and Andy were hippies. But Miles was able to find them the occasional support slot on tours he was booking in Europe (Wayne County and the Electric Chairs, and Spirit). He also got them on the Cherry Vanilla tour, where The Police doubled as the opening act and her backing band.

With the money they made from that, and another couple of thousand dollars they borrowed from Miles, they went back into the studio, this time with Andy Summers taking the place of Henri Padovani on guitar, and began recording their first album, *Outlandos d'Amour*.

When he visited them in the studio, and they played him the material they'd been working on, Miles was fairly unimpressed. Then, reluctantly, the band played him a song Sting had written as a throwaway, a slow, melodic song that could hardly be termed punk, and therefore not something they were considering putting on the album. The song was called "Roxanne," and Miles flipped over it.

The next day Miles took the tape of "Roxanne" to Mike Noble at A&M Records, with whom he had signed Squeeze. Realizing that he would not need massive amounts of money for recording and touring, he offered A&M a deal they couldn't refuse. They could have the single for free. Almost. The deal that Miles made did not involve a large advance, so it was a no-risk venture for the record company. In return, however, he asked for, and got, a fairly high royalty rate, much higher than other bands of The Police's stature were getting, and, much more importantly, the promise that the record would be released in America. Miles knew that for The Police record to have any chance of success, it had to come out in the States.

"Roxanne" was first released in the U.K. on April 7, 1978, and this time the reviews were amazing. Unfortunately, the only radio station that really mattered in Britain, the BBC, refused to play it. They objected to the lyrics, saying they didn't want a song about a French whore on their playlist. As a result, the single only sold around ten thousand copies.

In July, Stewart recorded his own single under the alias Klark Kent, and put it out on his Krypton label. His song "Don't Care" had been rehearsed by The Police but Sting couldn't identify with it, so Stewart did it himself, singing as well as playing all the instruments. This time the BBC added the record to their playlist, and it began to sell so well it was reissued by A&M Records, hit the charts, and ended up selling thirty-five thousand copies. Klark Kent was invited to perform on the television show *Top of the Pops,* which was a problem since Stewart wanted to keep Klark Kent's identity a secret. But it was too important an opportunity to miss, so Stewart called some friends, made a band, and went down to the television station. When he, Miles, Sting, Kim Turner, and our old friend Florian Pilkington-Miksa showed up at the *Top of the Pops* studio wearing horrendous masks, the stuffy producer of the show freaked. He refused to let them perform on the grounds that it would frighten the kids in the audience, but in fact, he was more interested in exposing Klark Kent. Miles, himself under the alias of Melvin Milktoast, was unable to change the producer's mind. In the end, Stewart performed with his face painted, but his cover was blown.*

In August of 1978, The Police finished recording *Outlandos d'Amour,* and released their third single, "Can't Stand Losing You." Again the BBC refused to play The Police's record. This time, they objected to the suicidal theme of the record sleeve, which was a picture of Stewart with a noose around his neck, standing on a block of ice that was melting fast in front of an electric heater. Being black-listed by the BBC made it hard for the band to get the proper exposure, and it became difficult for them to find live gigs. On the trendy London music circuit, it's possible for bands to rise in popularity very quickly, but if a band loses their momentum, it can be all over just as fast. In desperation to make something happen for the band, Miles called me up in Macon, Georgia.

"Ian," he asked, "A&M in America are contracted to release 'Roxanne,' but they aren't committed to the album. I think if we can get the band to the States, and the people at the record company get a chance to see the band, we might be able to get them to go for it. Do you think you could book a tour for The Police in the States?"

"With just a single? Are you nuts? Miles, I don't have to tell you, it's hard enough to find tours for bands with albums out."

"I know," he said. "But can you do it?"

"Will we get any support from the record company?" I knew the answer.

"No. Not for a single. The Police's live show is so exciting, though,

---

* Stewart later recorded an album under the alias Klark Kent, playing all the instruments and vocals himself, and another single called "Too Kool to Kalypso" that I wrote the lyrics to.

WILD THING

if we can just get them over there, I'm hoping we can create a buzz on the band. Maybe then A&M will decide to release the album. Don't forget," he said, "this band is willing to work their asses off. As a three-piece, with one roadie, we could tour them on the cheap."

"All right," I said. "Let me see what I can do."

The Police tour was much more difficult to book than the Squeeze tour. Whenever Squeeze came to a town, A&M routinely did whatever it was they were supposed to do, but for The Police, with a single that wasn't even getting any radio airplay, they weren't in a position to do anything. The showcase club circuit, therefore, which relied on the record companies to promote their shows for them, wasn't at all interested. Even the clubs that I coerced to go along with me on Squeeze balked at booking The Police as soon as they found out they weren't going to get any help from A&M. Obviously, I *had* to find some alternative.

I began to work on some of the contacts Miles and I had put together during the Squeeze tour, people who were interested in the new generation of music, like Danny Beard in Atlanta, Gary Cormier in Canada, Vince Bannon in Detroit, David Carroll in Philadelphia, Jim Harold in Boston, and Hilly Kristal in New York. One by one, I was able to find someone in each of the major cities in the Northeast that was willing to promote the band, or direct me to a club that would. In many cases I was calling up discos that were going out of business, as a lot of them were at the time, and promising them something new, something they'd never been offered before. A real live band from England.

When I first started booking the tour, a woman from the record company in New York, Gail Davis, called me complaining, saying I was crazy to even think of bringing the band over. "What the hell do you think you're doing?" she asked me. As I tried to explain our objectives, she interrupted me: "Ian, you're not listening to me. This tour is not happening. We're not paying for it."

"With all due respect," I said, "you aren't listening to *me*. You won't have to pay for a thing. All I ask is that you try to get some of your people to come to the shows." Since no act had ever come over from Europe before and toured the United States without financial tour support from the record companies, she still thought I was crazy. But at least the A&M reps did start turning up when the band came over. And to be fair, there were supporters at A&M. Phil Quartararo and Bob Garcia come to mind, and Jerry Moss, the boss.*

The Police were a three-piece, lean and mean, and ready to conquer the world. Miles and I figured that if anyone could turn America on to new music, The Police could, and if we cracked the American market, more bands would have a chance to do the same. To all of us, it was more than just a matter of breaking The Police. In the bigger picture, it was a way of saving the music business from the stagnation that had set in, a way to revive the excitement that once defined rock and roll.

I wasn't able to get a lot of money for the band, but I did manage to round up a tour of twenty-three shows in twenty-five days, starting with two shows at CBGB's, the only club in New York that was willing to present punk bands. I concentrated on the major cities in the Northeast and nearby (New York, Boston, Philadelphia, Washington, D.C., Toronto, Detroit, Cleveland), but in order to fill up the Mondays and Tuesdays, the most difficult nights to fill, and to pay for the hotels every night along the way, I was forced to find dates in some peculiar places.

As if to make things even more difficult, The Police insisted I find local support in each market, and it had to be a punk band. What they didn't realize is that there weren't any in most places the band was playing.

The Police's first tour of North America:

1978

OCTOBER

20—CBGB's, New York City
21—CBGB's, New York City
22—Grendel's Lair, Philadelphia, Pennsylvania
23—The Last Chance Saloon, Poughkeepsie, New York
24—The Firebarn, Syracuse, New York
25—The Shaboo, Willimantic, Connecticut

---

* Phil Quartararo is now President/CEO of Virgin Records, Bob Garcia is Director of Artist Relations at A&M, and Jerry Moss has since sold A&M to PolyGram.

WILD THING

26—The Rat, Boston, Massachusetts
27—The Rat, Boston, Massachusetts
28—The Rat, Boston, Massachusetts
29—The Rat, Boston, Massachusetts
31—Phase III, Swissvale, Pennsylvania

NOVEMBER

1—Stage I, Buffalo, New York
2—The Horseshoe, Toronto, Canada
3—The Horseshoe, Toronto, Canada
5—Bookies 870, Detroit, Michigan
6—Pirate's Cove, Cleveland, Ohio
7—Baliwicks, Centerville, Ohio
9—University of Pittsburgh, Johnstown, Pennsylvania
10—Atlantis, Washington, D.C.
11—Atlantis, Washington, D.C.
13—Grendel's Lair, Philadelphia, Pennsylvania
14—CBGB's, New York City
15—CBGB's, New York City

To be sure of at least breaking even on The Police tour, we had to cut costs every way we could think of. Fortunately, The Police was only three people, and they decided to bring only one other person with them on the road. It was unheard of at the time for a self-respecting band to come over with less than a fair-sized entourage of roadies, tour managers, lighting technicians, wardrobe girls, and so on, but the band hired our old friend Kim Turner, of Cat Iron fame, to do everything. By having only four people on the road, and by using a few tricks learned from old Joe Newman, the hotel bills were kept way down, and the band sometimes slept in the van on the long hauls. Alex Hodges loaned Miles some money up front, and so, rather than pay exorbitant rental costs, I bought an eight-passenger Econoline van in Macon and drove it to Manny's Music Shop in New York, where I picked up the backline equipment. Then I met Miles, Kim, and the band at the airport and took them straight to CBGB'S. Because they carried all their own instruments on the plane (to save shipping costs), they were so late getting through customs they had to change into their stage clothes in the van on the way and go directly on stage.

They were late, but they were great. The tour was an incredible success, even though there were a few shows where almost no one came to see them. But most of the major cities were sold out, and even in Syracuse, the show where there were seven in the audience, including the bartender, the band put on a great performance. It so happened that one of the four paying customers was a curious DJ who was blown away. The next day he started playing The Police's record on heavy rotation at his radio station. It was happening everywhere the band played, and the record company was starting to notice it big-time. What's more, it wasn't costing them anything, because the tour was breaking even.

The A&M representatives that came to the shows had to be impressed by the audience reaction the band was getting. Most of them were expecting to see a band like The Sex Pistols, and they didn't know much about The Police. In fact, most of the record company reps had never heard of the band. There was one guy in Philadelphia that came backstage raving about the band. "You guys were fucking amazing!" he said. "Awesome!" Only problem was, The Police hadn't gone on yet.

In booking the tour, there had been the odd occasion where I was offered the favor of a support slot with a big band, but the band decided against it every time. As champions of the new punk scene in Britain, they felt it was important to disassociate themselves from "dinosaur" bands of the old generation. Their decision to headline was a good one. As Stewart himself said during the tour:

> Something we've discovered on this tour is that we get much better exposure and make much more of an impression on a city doing it this way. If we'd played Boston, say, as a support act at a bigger theater to several thousand people, with the record company hustling people in, giving free tickets away, people would probably have got there just in time to catch one number of our set and maybe given us a line in their reviews. But this way, going out and doing it ourselves, we get journalists and radio people who really do care, who really are turned on to "Roxanne," and we dominate the gig. It's our gig and I'm sure we get much better exposure because of that.*

---

* *The Police—A Visual Documentary* by Miles (no relation), published by Omnibus Press in the U.K., 1984.

243

By the time The Police completed the tour, ending with another two nights at CBGB's, Jerry Moss at A&M had already decided to pick up his option on the band. *Outlandos d'Amour* was scheduled for release early in the new year. With that news I knew I'd be booking a return tour to promote the album, and I knew from the callbacks I was getting from promoters that this time it would be a lot easier. Even promoters that lost money on their shows were eager for a return date on the band. Those that were not interested in booking the band before suddenly were.

Having blown everyone away in America, The Police finished their tour and went back to Britain, where they were suddenly being taken a lot more seriously. Until then, the British press had been slagging them mercilessly, and in Britain the press can make or break you. The Police's success in America, where even The Sex Pistols had failed, gave them a new-found credibility and respect. The album was released in Britain the day the band got back from the States, and it immediately started to take off.

Meanwhile, back in Macon I felt like Jack coming home with the beans. I knew I had found the Golden Goose, the way to make Macon happen again. Actually, I was still the only one who thought so. My "punk project" was doing well, but only on a very small scale. The new promoters I had dug up to do my bands were different from those the other agents dealt with, so the others weren't receiving the feedback I was.

But Squeeze and The Police *had* caused excitement everywhere they played, and, although their dates were not all sellouts, the interest started to spread to clubs and discos across the country that had never been offered a band from England before. People were calling me up asking if I was bringing over any more British groups. In the process, I discovered that there were a few more people in the music business who shared my interest in promoting new music. We felt it was time for a changing of the guard.

With the success of the Squeeze and Police tours under my belt, I went back to London to try and convince more bands to come over. This time I went looking for punk bands with a proper record deal in America, and found them to be few and far between. Whenever I did track down a band that showed interest, after talking to their record companies the trail went cold. In the end I had to settle for a band that was relatively big in Europe and was getting radio play in America on their imported albums. By the strictest definition, Ultravox was not a punk band, but its members were young, British, and very exciting performers on stage. American record companies had passed them up, but when I checked with the promoters on my club circuit I found strong interest. I found that even some of the clubs that had been unmoved by punk were attracted to Ultravox.

All the same, the manager of Ultravox remained skeptical. I tried to show him that their tour could be profitable even without record company support, but he wouldn't believe it. They were perfectly willing to cram in the van and rough it, the way The Police did, but there were five in the band and two roadies, so they'd still need a truck for the equipment. Their hotel and other expenses were obviously going to be greater than those for a three-piece band. Furthermore, the manager, Richard Griffiths,* had been told over and over again by every other agent in America that it was impossible to tour without a shortfall, paid for by a record company. The problem was, they didn't have a record company in America.

I got back to Macon and started calling the clubs to see exactly what I could get for Ultravox, trying to make it work. To my surprise I found strong interest on the West Coast. The problem would be how to get the bands out there. Huge areas of the country were still turned off the minute they heard the word "punk." Since I was already talking to promoters about my hopes for bringing a whole new wave of British bands over, I began to refer to Ultravox and all the bands after that as "new wave."

Through a great deal of effort I was able to put together a run of clubs that started in New York and ended in Los Angeles, covering almost all of the major markets in between. Since they were much better known, the total in guarantees was much higher for Ultravox

---

* Richard Griffiths went to work for Island Records after Ultravox split up. He is now president of Epic Records.

Wild Thing

than I'd gotten for The Police, yet it was still not quite enough. No matter how much we trimmed the budget and cut the frills, we were still below the bottom line.

The problem was CBGB's in New York. Hilly Kristal, like many other club promoters, booked all his bands on a percentage of the door, with no fee. So although a band like Ultravox *should* do well, there was no guarantee. If for any reason the show stiffed, the band was shit out of luck.

There was a disco in New York called Hurrah's that had lost all its business to Studio 54. Robert Boykin, the owner, had talked to me about making his club into a showcase for live bands, so I offered him Ultravox. Robert had never heard of them, but his DJ, Jim Fourrat, was a huge fan, so he called me back to offer a guarantee of two thousand dollars, more than enough to put us into the black. With that, I was able to convince the band to come.

The Ultravox tour was a huge success for me, because everyone made money, including the promoters. Hurrah's was packed for the first time in ages. At the Whisky a Go Go in Los Angeles there were lines around the block, and hysteria at the box office. The band broke percentages everywhere, and went home with a huge profit in their pockets, something few bands had ever done before. More importantly, record companies in America were now lining up to sign the band.

Word of this spread around management companies in New York and London, and soon my phone started ringing. People who wouldn't talk to me before were suddenly interested in what I could do for them. Best of all, I now had clubs stretching across America that were hungry for more, and I also had a van and a set of equipment in my garage from The Police tour.

Since no one else was after them, I began to sign the best of the new bands on the punk scene—Buzzcocks, Siouxsie & The Banshees, XTC, Magazine, Eddie and the Hotrods, 999, The Only Ones, Penetration—and, one by one, we sent them off on tours. As a band was dropped off at the airport by the van, another band would fly in on Freddie Laker's cut-rate airlines to start its tour. I found that I could also take my pick of the bands on the New York club scene. Nobody else was booking them. From right under the noses of the New York agents, I signed Johnny Thunders, Iggy Pop, and then

John Cale, and through Cale's manager, Jane Friedman, I signed
The Ramones.

None of these bands meant anything at the time, but Alex Hodges
let me run with them. Gradually I expanded the club circuit and
added more cities. In the middle of Gang of Four's tour I added another couple of weeks, leaving me with overlapping tour schedules.
So when The Police came back for their second tour I had to buy
them yet another van. Now I had two vans, allowing me to bring in
two bands at a time. The new wave invasion was well under way,
and yet, even then there was incredible resistance from the music-
business establishment. Despite the fact that America was in a deep
recession, and for the first time ever concert sales were down, most
of the major promoters were still not interested enough to try and
develop this new scene. And record companies, who I thought
would be only too pleased to be relieved of the financial burden of
supporting tours for these young bands, seemed to be resentful of
the loss of control that would result from my economics. They didn't
employ the people who understood the genre of music I was selling,
so they felt threatened by it.

I even had resistance inside my own company. In my own neck of
the woods, up in Athens, Georgia, I discovered the B-52's, one of the
most important bands of the decade, but it almost got away from us.
The band had pressed several hundred copies of their own record, a
zany song called "Rock Lobster," a copy of which Danny Beard sent
me from Atlanta. I loved it. Danny gave me their number in Athens.
I talked to Kate Pierson in the band, who told me she'd been booking
a run of dates herself, and that she'd be only too glad for me to
relieve her of that chore. But since I had to be in New York on the
day the B-52's were doing a show in Athens, I sent another young
agent from Paragon to check them out.

I figured John Huie would be perfect. He was fresh out of college
himself, having been a buyer for Duke University, and he had only
been at Paragon several weeks. But I couldn't really blame John for
not getting it; few people did at first. At an agents' meeting the following Monday, he reported that the B-52's were the worst piece of
shit he had ever seen. He jokingly threatened to quit if we signed
them, and given his description, we had no choice but to pass.

But then Miles, all the way from London, called me to rave about

WILD THING

the band. He said the buzz on the band in Britain was intense. I asked him to have a word with Alex. So he did, hitting poor Alex below the belt. "Alex," he said, "are you going to let some New York agent discover this band in your own backyard?" That did it. We took on the B-52's.

For all the success I was having in the signing of new wave bands, Alex still felt we needed an office in New York or Los Angeles in order to sign the more "commercial" acts. In order to cut overheads, he decided to take a partner in New York. So he joined forces with Jonny Podell, the famous agent for Alice Cooper and Blondie. At the time I fully approved. More than anyone else in Paragon, I felt that a New York office would enable us to sign more acts, even punk bands. There were a few that actually had record deals, such as The Clash, and I was still losing out when it came to signing those acts. Alex had discussed with me the possibility that I might open a Paragon office in New York, but my reaction had been entirely negative. I'd grown to love living in Macon.

Instead, Jonny Podell seemed the perfect choice. Young and handsome, looking like a rock star himself, he was the first rock-and-roll booking agent that wasn't bald and fat and smoking a cigar. He was a star in a business where there are few stars. He was admired for his career-oriented planning, and for his brilliance at cutting deals. But though he was famous for his success, his excesses were also well known. Although now he was supposed to be clean and reformed, he was generally known to have been a junkie.

I was particularly pleased that Alex had chosen to partner up with Podell, because that meant we would be adding his act Blondie to our roster, an act I considered to be a valuable addition to our growing list of punk bands. Blondie was shooting up the charts at the time, and I felt that could only help our cause. Unfortunately, I made the mistake of telling Jonny how I felt, and that's when I realized there was trouble ahead. Jonny informed me, in no uncertain terms, that Blondie was *not* a punk band. Furthermore, I was not to mention them in the same breath as my other punk bands. In fact, he didn't want me talking to promoters about Blondie at all.

In his New York office, Paragon East, Jonny had an assistant, a booker named Jim Cramer. Jim was into the new music, but Jonny wasn't, and Jonny was the boss. Jim did the best he could for me, but when I was forced to put the pressure on him to deliver dates on my bands, he owned up that he had been instructed by Jonny to give my bands a low priority. I said "Jim, I can understand that, but I've been waiting for weeks to get something, anything."

"Well, if you want to know the truth," he said, lowering his voice, "I'm not supposed to bother with them at all."

Since we booked the country by territories, the New York office naturally took on the Northeast as theirs. The Northeast, however, was the nucleus of my club circuit. When I couldn't get the New York office to book the dates, I went ahead and booked them myself. This was no problem, since I had done so quite nicely up to then, and I knew places and promoters no one else did. But Jonny Podell didn't like this a bit. He called me up and chewed me out, demanding that I stop calling promoters in his territory. When I argued that I had to book my band if he wouldn't, he answered that I didn't have anything to say in the matter, since he was now my boss.

But "my boss" was slurring his words, having trouble with whole sentences, and obviously not all there. Anyway, since I figured that at this particular point in time I should have some say in Paragon's organizational concerns, especially the little matter of who was and who wasn't my boss, I hung up on him, something I never, ever do.

Jonny was immediately on the phone to Alex demanding that I be fired. I could hear Alex's side of the conversation from my office, and to my dismay Alex wasn't jumping in Jonny's shit. Instead, he was trying to reason with him, promising to talk to me about it. I had the frightening thought that maybe I had underestimated Jonny's weight.

It just so happened that I was just about to leave for London on a mission to sign The Clash, and would be going to New York to catch a Laker flight, so I agreed with Alex to meet with Jonny in Manhattan between flights. When I got to the Paragon office on Fifty-seventh Street and Broadway, Jonny's snooty secretary had me wait in the reception area for nearly an hour. Finally, over her objections, I took over one of the phones and started making long-distance calls to London. This made her finally go into Jonny's office and get him.

When Jonny came out of his office he looked a mess. He could hardly stand up, and Jim Cramer had to assist him into a cab to The

WILD THING

Palm restaurant, a favorite music-business steak-and-lobster restaurant over on the East Side. Whenever the cabdriver touched his brakes, even lightly, Jonny would fall off his seat and slam into the partition of the cab. Jim and I had to virtually sit on him to keep him from breaking his face.

At the restaurant Jonny ordered enough food for a week, and he particularly wanted several helpings of The Palm's world-famous creamed spinach, insisting we try it even though neither Jim nor I cared for it. Then, in garbled sentences, he proceeded to lecture me. It was hard to understand what he was going on about due to the fact that he kept nodding off mid-sentence. He had an amazing ability, though, to pick up his thoughts after long moments of nodding out, and carry on where he'd left off. I'd seen it too often before. Heroin.

With a great deal of patience, I was able to figure out what he was trying to tell me. He said that, first of all, I was just going to have to accept the unalterable fact that he was my boss.

"Ian, you were . . . in the army, you . . . know how it is. There are generals . . . and . . . privates, and you happen to be . . . a private."

The bottom line was that he was ordering me to drop my punk bands. He said the other Paragon bands, the ones that earned the money that paid my salary, didn't like being associated with punk bands, so I'd just have to take them off the roster. He told me he thought my brother's band was a waste of time, and that I shouldn't let nepotism get in the way of what was good for the company.

But he was careful not to hurt my feelings. He said, "Don't get me wrong, I . . . think your brother's a great singer . . . , but the drummer is terrible."

Just when I could take no more of it, Jonny nodded out completely. Jim Cramer, who had been nudging Jonny every now and then to keep him awake, got too involved in conversation with me, and neither of us were able to catch Jonny before he fell face-first in the creamed spinach.

After my horrendous meeting with Jonny, I flew to London and met with The Clash's manager, Bernie Rhodes, who immediately informed me that he had decided against Paragon Agency. He said he wanted to be with an agency based in New York, and wouldn't even consider going with an agency in Macon. My heart sank. I asked him, "Then why did you meet with me?"

"Because I want to know how the CIA is involved in the music business." He was nuts! He seriously thought that Miles, Stewart, and I were part of some conspiracy hatched by my father and backed by the CIA. I explained to him that my father had left the CIA many years before and was now an ordinary retired businessman, but Bernie refused to believe me.

All the same, I really wanted The Clash, with or without its eccentric manager. As the first punk band to sign a record deal with a major label in America, they had a major commitment for promotion, and a considerable tour support budget. It seemed only fair that I should get this plum when I had worked so hard on nurturing their audience in America. I couldn't stand to see them handed over on a platter to some undeserving agent.

"Wait a minute. We do have an office in New York," I told Bernie truthfully, adding that I worked out of there on occasion myself, this being at least partly true; I had managed to make a few phone calls while Jonny's snotty secretary was keeping me waiting. Bernie may have been a nut but he was no fool (nuts, I have found, can sometimes be awfully canny when it comes to signing business deals), so he insisted on meeting the people in the New York office before considering to come with us. I knew I was kissing good-bye my chance of getting the hottest new band in the world at that time, but I put in a phone call to New York and set up the meeting. Jonny, however, never showed up.*

As I was to learn years later, Bernie was less nuts than I thought. I had been told that my father *was* retired, but evidently he was still working with his old cronies from the CIA, and was involved at the time with attempts to win the release of our American Embassy hostages in Iran. President Carter's inept handling of the situation had led to disaster, and Dad was determined to find a way of solving

---

* Podell's biggest client, Alice Cooper, was also a heroin user. Both have since undergone treatment and cleaned up their act. Podell is currently Senior Vice President of the concert department at ICM.

WILD THING

the problem. In December of 1979, he assembled some of his old CIA pals and their associates to discuss it. The group included William Casey, a former intelligence officer and close associate of Republican presidential candidate Ronald Reagan, Robert McFarlane, a former Marine colonel who had served in Vietnam, and a number of others with CIA connections.

The group concluded that the Carter government was unable to deal with the Iranian issue, and that something had to be done to resolve the problem. They also saw eye to eye with Israel on the strategic situation in Iran. The Israeli government considered it essential that the Iranians were not defeated if and when Iraq attacked, and to make sure that President Carter's blunders were not repeated. A subsequent meeting was arranged between my father and Israeli intelligence in Washington, D.C., at a house in Georgetown.

In his controversial book *Profits of War*, Ari Ben-Menashe, an ex-agent of Israel's secret service, Mossad, described the meeting as follows:

> A good friend of the late Egyptian president Gamal Abdel Nasser, Copeland was known for his anti-Israel stand. Israeli intelligence believed him to be the man responsible for the U.S. pressure put on Israel, Britain, and France in 1956 to pull out of the Suez Canal area. He was also thought to have been the man behind the push for the Israelis to withdraw from the Sinai. While the United States was pressuring the Israelis over the Sinai, the Soviet Union invaded Hungary without U.S. reaction. Copeland was criticized for this. Nevertheless, he was still highly regarded for his analytical abilities, . . . [and] the Israelis were happy to deal with any initiative but Carter's.*

Apparently the old man was up to his neck in intrigue, and, as always, kept his family in the dark as to his activities for our own protection. I never knew what he was up to, and as I'd learned from an early age, it was never wise to ask.

Meanwhile, back in Macon, my optimism was at an all-time high. Despite my setbacks, I felt that things were on the move. I even took

---

* My father was neither anti- nor pro-Israel. He was merely pro-American.

some pleasure from The Clash signing with a major agency in New York, since I read that as proof that I wasn't wrong in my conviction that punk bands could happen in America. And Macon had been good to me, overall. I had arrived there with nothing going for me, but by this time I had really laid down roots.

Soon after arriving in Macon, I walked into a diner and immediately fell in love with a beautiful Southern belle behind the counter. I was so taken by her that when she came over to me I was completely at a loss for words. Gone was the hip language of rock and roll, and all my savvy went AWOL. To my own amazement, the only line I could come up with was "What's a nice girl like you doing in a place like this?" Three months later we were married.

We had a lovely daughter named Chandra, who, unlike me, was one of the best-behaved kids imaginable. Not long after I was married, I fulfilled every American's dream by putting money down for my first home, a newly built house on the banks of beautiful Lake Wildwood, where I could play my music as loud as I wanted, and catch fish right from my backyard.

When disaster struck, it couldn't have come at a worse time. When I got back to Macon from a trip to London and New York, having racked up a few thousand dollars of expenses on my American Express card, entertaining and signing acts, I got twelve hours of sleep before going to the Paragon Agency to count my blessings. I found the parking lot full of moving vans and furniture removers. I went into my office, and my desk was gone. Even the Persian carpets were rolled up and ready to go. Thinking maybe I'd been fired and no one had bothered to tell me, I went into Alex Hodges's office to see what was going on. But his office was missing some furniture too, so now I was totally confused. Alex didn't look good at all.

The way he told it, Capricorn Records had been helping themselves to Paragon's money in their joint bank accounts, including the deposits held in escrow belonging to the bands. Now Paragon couldn't pay the bands their money. Alex sat me down, and explained Capricorn Records and Paragon Agency were both out of business. Once again, I was out of a job.

CHAPTER 19

FBI—The Booking Agency

You say you want a revolution?
— John Lennon

It took a few weeks for them to cut the phones off at Paragon, and we used them to take care of business as best we could, servicing the bands we had out on the road. Any money that came in went straight to paying off the debts to the bands, so all of us worked for free. To cover The Police, and some of my American Express bill, we were given the vans as compensation. The formal closing of the Paragon Agency finally came on a Friday in late July 1979.

On Monday, I flew to New York to find a job with one of the major agencies, this time a little more confident than the time before, when I had nothing to offer. At least this time I had some experience booking in America, and I had acts I could bring with me. To my dismay, I was to find that no one wanted them. Or me.

I was able to set up interviews with most of the big agencies, but once again I was getting the run-around. And worse, they all seemed to be pumping me for information, asking me questions about my acts and the circuit I had built up under their noses, inside information I wasn't keen to give before they'd at least made me an offer of employment. And none of them did. I was eventually offered a job at one of the secondary agencies, called Magna Agency, but it was on a trial basis, and though they wanted me to make my bands sign long-term contracts with them, they weren't willing to give me one. If they wanted to, after six months they could keep my acts and say "see you later" to me.

I was at a major fork in the road and didn't even see it. I was pretty good at handling other people's careers, while giving little thought for my own. All my life I'd plowed ahead, going with the flow and jumping into things with both feet. With my bands I considered every option before I made a move, but for myself I just followed the clearest path in front of me. And now, since I had only one job offer, it seemed obvious that I should accept it. I didn't stop to consider the alternatives, or ponder any opportunities I might have to change a little of the world—or, anyway, my particular piece of it.

Jane Friedman saved my life. Jane was John Cale's manager, and about my only real friend in New York. I never spent much time in the city, only when I was passing through with various bands a couple of times, and when I was selling posters on the street outside of Bloomingdale's. When I would call her from Macon, we'd end up talking for hours about the state of the whole music scene, about how fucked up things were, and how we could improve them. Jane was a general in the new wave army. As the manager of Television, one of the first American new wave bands, she was very much in tune with the new music scene, and perhaps a bit fanatic about it. She was also the publicist for Frank Zappa, Stevie Wonder, and several other big acts, so she knew her way around the music business. I went to see her in New York, after my meeting with Magna. I told her about the job I was offered. I wanted to make sure she'd keep John Cale with me.

"Big mistake," she said. "Let me tell you what I think. You want to know what I think?"

You can't stop Jane from telling you what she thinks, and she always gives it to you straight. Just to piss you off, she's invariably right. But at the moment I couldn't see what she might be talking about. The inescapable fact was that since Paragon folded I didn't have but one offer.

Jane had more confidence in me than I had in myself. She said I should start my own agency. I couldn't believe what I was hearing. I made her repeat what she had said.

"Start your own agency," she said, serious as a heart attack. "Why work for someone else? You'll only get fucked."

I found that offensive, but she followed it with flattery. "Look, Ian. You created the club circuit, and in so doing, you created a whole new way for bands to break in this country. You are on to something important, a new frontier. Look at what's going on in this business; there's a changing of the guard. This is a new scene, and a new music, and only a few people understand it. Ian, the other agencies are not interested in helping the scene. They just want to steal your bands."

"Well, it's not exactly stealing. They're offering me a lot of money, nearly twice what I was making in Macon!" I was already on the defensive.

"They're offering good money for Ultravox, and maybe The Police, and Squeeze, but what about the rest? How about XTC and Gang of Four, or John Cale? When they don't start making money right away, they'll make you drop them. Without new bands, the new clubs can't exist. The club circuit you're building will dry up, and we'll be right back to where we started. The accountants at the record companies will be dictating who tours, or, much more often, who doesn't."

A depressing thought, but one that certainly got my attention. All the same, agencies are started by heavies with huge acts and lots of capital, and nobody had opened a new agency in over ten years. I didn't see how it made sense for me to jump into competition with the fat cats.

"Just *do* it!" Jane said. "Look, you're not in competition with the other agencies anyway. Those old farts aren't even in the same game. You are the only agent in America booking the new wave."

I was still far from convinced. Start my own agency, with no money, no office, and a handful of acts that weren't exactly headliners? It didn't make any sense.

"But *all* your acts are headliners," Jane insisted, "and you're not putting them on tour with those dinosaur bands at the other agencies anyway. That means they can't steal your acts when they start happening. You said so yourself. Because your bands are so alien to theirs, the big guys can't threaten you. That's what makes this such a unique opportunity."

Jane knew how to get me fired up. She was making me an offer I couldn't refuse. She said I could use her phones and, for offices, she would clear out one of her rooms that she wasn't using. "I've got two rooms full of junk and old posters," she said. "You put it all in one and take the other. Look, I'll show you."

I looked. I was grateful for the kind offer, but it was a far cry from the nice plush offices I'd have at Magna Agency, and certainly not what I was used to in Macon.

I flew back to Macon with a lot on my mind. The move to New York would be yet another culture shock, and I wasn't ready for it. The thought of living and working in the big city was intimidating enough to me, and I knew it would be worse for my wife, who'd only traveled a few hundred miles from Macon in her life, and never north of the Mason-Dixon line. Nevertheless, I'd have to find a place to live, then sell my newly acquired house, and move my family up to New York.

At first I didn't consider Jane's suggestion as a serious option, but her words kept coming back to me. She was certainly correct about the other agencies—they were fast asleep. There was a revolution going on, and they didn't even know it. One thing was clear to me. The window of opportunity to form my own agency would come and go, then the window would close forever. There was no doubt in my mind that the new wave was going to happen, and that a new British invasion was upon us. The other agents were going to have to wake up to it eventually. The element of surprise had been my advantage so far, and I was getting the cream of the new bands without much competition. But once the other agencies realized what I was on to, they would come down like a pack of wolves. If I moved to Magna, taking my acts with me, it would be a long time before I could make another change. The contracts my bands would have to sign with Magna held me for three years, and in three years it would be too late for me to go it on my own.

Another factor that frightened me was the problem of clout. I didn't have any. I'd been an agent in America for a very short time, so who'd take my calls if I wasn't with an established agency? The buddy system with the major promoters gave the big agents the power to force their bands into dates, sometimes even those already booked by a smaller agent, like myself. If I went out on my own, I'd have to use persuasion instead of clout, and I'd have to cultivate my own promoters.

On the airplane back to Macon I fretted about the biggest question: where would I find the money to get started? While I was paying for a drink to help me think this through, the stewardess noticed my "Police" badge, a souvenir from the Japanese record company that I had pinned to the inside of my wallet. She asked me if I was a policeman. I said, "No, but my little brother is in The Police."

"Your brother's a policeman? How nice. Is he your only brother?"

"No," I said. With all that I had on my mind, I wasn't really interested in small talk with her. "I have an older brother, too."

She wasn't really that interested either. But it was a long flight. "How interesting," she said. "And what does he do?"

"I guess you could say he works for the IRS."

"How fascinating!" she said, barely concealing a yawn. "Both in the same kind of business. That's unusual, if you know what I mean. And what do you do?"

"I'm an agent."

"Oh, really? An FBI agent?" She was serious—and now genuinely impressed. But she thought I was trying to put her on, and before I could answer, she said "I suppose next you're going to tell me your father's in the CIA."

"Well, as a matter of fact . . ." I couldn't resist. "He is."

She left me alone for a while after that, thinking I was a wise guy. I had a laugh to myself about it, then got back to worrying about what to do with my life. That's when the idea struck me. FBI! It was as simple as that. With Dad and the CIA, Stewart and The Police, and Miles having just formed a new record label with A&M called IRS, it was up to me to form an "FBI." A few Bacardi-and-cokes later I had made up my mind. When I told the stewardess that, yes, I was an FBI agent, a whole new world opened up. The stewardess started treating me special, and I felt *special*. From what little I knew of the FBI, I figured that they are all good guys and wouldn't begrudge a harmless booker of pop groups the use of their initials, especially if they stood for "Frontier Booking International."

My wife thought I was nuts. It took some time to convince her that I knew what I was doing. She eventually got into it though. Connie was a Walden, Phil's cousin, and therefore part of a big family in Macon, so it wasn't going to be easy for her to leave the family behind. She decided to stay in Macon for a while where our baby, to be named Barbara Lorraine, was to be delivered by the same doctor that had delivered her.

Back in Macon I spent one last week tying up the loose ends, both at home and at the agency. I got rid of a few things to raise some cash. Mike Mills, who (along with Bill Berry) was by now enrolled at The University of Georgia in Athens, had decided to get back into music, and he wanted his bass amp back. But he was nearly broke, so I sold it to him for lots less than I paid for it. Luckily, I found that the value of my house had gone up in the few months I'd owned it, and I sold it for a profit of nearly five thousand dollars. After paying off the bank, this was all the money I had in the world. Considering what was ahead, it was a pitiful amount. Most of it went to pay off my credit card debts and various expense account bills that Paragon would never repay me for. Yet it was the most money I'd ever had to my own, and once again I reflected that, on balance, America had been good to me.

On Monday, August 1, 1979, I was back in New York, and Frontier Booking International was open for business. I was, indeed, an FBI agent. At Jane Friedman's, in the Fisk Building on Fifty-seventh and Broadway, the office had to be cleared out and the junk piled in another room. I found an old table with one leg missing, propped it up on a cardboard box, sat on another one, picked up the phone, and started booking.

I took up temporary residence on Forty-fourth street at the Iroquois Hotel, right next door to the Algonquin Hotel, the internationally famous meeting place of *New Yorker* magazine intelligentsia—James Thurber, Dorothy Parker, Alexander Woollcott, and the others. But unlike the Algonquin, the Iroquois was a dump. On the door to my room there was a flimsy lock at nose level and marks all up and down where previous locks had been torn off. It had obviously been kicked in a few times. The place was overrun with monstrous roaches. It was the B-52's who had put me on to the Iroquois Hotel, which was only a slight improvement on the first hotel I'd stayed in when I was in New York on leave from basic training, where I paid by the hour.

The Iroquois became a regular stop on all my tours, and, along with Laker Air, it was an essential ingredient in the formula that made it possible for the new wave bands to tour the U.S. without support from the record companies. The greatest thing about the Iroquois was that they didn't mind how many people you put into a room. For fifty dollars you could get a two-room suite and sleep ten people. It only had one dilapidated elevator, which usually broke down just as the bands arrived to check into the seventh floor, but what the hell, it was cheap, decent enough, well located, and most important, it had a bar that stayed open late.

Not all the bands I'd had at Paragon were willing to risk going with me, and, in the transition, I lost some of my favorites. The Fall were out on the road during the confusion in Macon, and their tour suffered for it. I did the best I could for them, and I was sorry that they were unhappy, but I didn't blame them for leaving. The B-52's wanted to stay with me but their recently acquired New York manager, Gary Kurfirst, took the opportunity of my misfortune to pull them away and take them to Premier Agency, where he had a long-standing relationship with Frank Barcelona. So did Linda Stein, the new manager of The Ramones. But most of the others did stay, a few because no one else wanted them—not, anyhow, at the time.

I had Magazine, Gang of Four, The Cramps, Pere Ubu, and Fashion out on the road doing club tours. Iggy Pop, Squeeze, The Police, and Ultravox were all set to go out in the next few months. My first task was to let them know the situation, and convince them to have faith in my new agency.

Then I had to figure how to pay for it! The costs of setting up a legitimate business in New York City came near to putting me out of business before I'd got started. I had to be licensed, bonded, and approved by the Musicians Union and the Department of Labor. The lawyer's fees alone were enough to use up all my capital. Fortunately, due to their relationship with Miles, and a farsighted desire

WILD THING

to start one with me, attorneys Alan Grubman and Paul Schindler came to the party. They agreed to defray their cost, or legal obstacles might have prevented me from getting started at all. Over the years, their firm has continued to serve the FBI well. And what comes around, goes around; over the years I've steered many a client their way.

The projection I made of upcoming tours and incoming revenue showed that I was headed for trouble. As the first month's bills came in I saw that, like all entrepreneurs optimistic about their new businesses, I had figured on the bills being about half of what they turned out to be. Some of them were clearly rip-offs, like the one from the artist who helped me design my company logo, a simple takeoff on the Federal Bureau of Investigation's logo. He hit me with a bill for two thousand dollars, claiming that he was letting me off cheap.*

As I got a clearer picture of what my expenses were going to be, I realized that I couldn't make it through the first year without borrowing money. Any way I figured it, I was going to be short twenty to thirty grand. I firmly believed that the bands I was building would one day be bringing in enough to pay the overheads, but it was going to be a tough battle on any budget. Iggy Pop was my biggest act, and he was only worth five thousand dollars a night in his best markets. The Police and Squeeze were earning a couple of grand on a good night. But at least I knew they would tour for most of the year. To keep up the circuit of clubs, to keep my own doors open, and to meet my overheads, it became obvious that I'd have to book a massive volume of acts.

Borrowing what I was to need seemed impossible. The banks were out of reach. I had no credit, no property, no collateral, and I didn't know anybody who had money to lend. Miles suggested that I call Jerry Moss, the "M" of A&M Records, but I couldn't bring myself to do it. But, on second thought, I remembered what seemed a genuine interest by him in what I was doing, as well as a strong belief in the future of Squeeze and The Police. There were two other acts on

---

*He was. John Vogel did the artwork for the FBI logo as a favor to Jane Friedman, and I have since found out that the going rate for a corporate logo was about five times what he charged me.

A&M that I was planning to bring over, a reggae band from England called UB40 and a zany pop band from New Zealand called Split Enz. So I went ahead and called him.

At first I couldn't get through to him; he's a very busy man, and I couldn't get past the secretaries. He was always "out to lunch" or "in a meeting" but they would take a message.

I said, "Just ask him to call me, please."

"And you said your name was Len Copeland?"

"No, I'm sorry, that's Ian, I-A-N."

"E-n-i-a-n. Okay, Enian, and what company are you with?"

"No, that's . . . Oh well, never mind. I'm with FBI."

"You're with the FBI? Wait, hold on a minute!" And sure enough, Jerry Moss himself came on the line.

Fortunately, he thought it was funny. I gave Jerry my story, and how I thought I had to do what I was doing to keep the movement going, and that it could only benefit the whole music business. I pointed out that Squeeze and The Police, both A&M acts, were showing the promise of selling a lot of records, and that my tours had helped to make that possible at great savings to the record company. When I finished my spiel, I laid out my problem, the costs, and so on. Jerry quietly listened through the whole thing.

Then he said, "Ian, believe me, I know the problems of starting up a company, and I certainly appreciate what you've done. What's the bottom line?"

"Twenty thousand." I gulped, my tongue sticking to the top of my mouth. It seemed such a lot of money.

Jerry was quiet for a moment, then he laughed. "You must be kidding." I wished I was. But then he said: "Do me a favor, give me a call back in the morning."

Now, if there is such a thing as a "true gentleman," Jerry is that person. I called him the next morning, and without further discussion he gave me a personal loan of *fifty* thousand dollars, twenty thousand up front, with an additional thirty grand should I need it. As luck would have it, I didn't.

A report on my situation would have been like that of the Arab scout sent into the desert in search of food, who, upon returning, reports first the bad news then the good. The bad news is that the

263   WILD THING

only thing to eat is sand. The good news is . . . there's plenty of it. My first advertisement was in *Performance* magazine, announcing that the agency had thirty-three acts on the roster:

BUZZCOCKS	999
JOHN CALE	THE ONLY ONES
CHELSEA	JOHN OTWAY
THE CRAMPS	PENETRATION
THE CURE	PERE UBU
EDDIE & THE HOTRODS	THE POLICE
THE FALL	THE RUTS
FASHION	SKAFISH
FINGERPRINTZ	SIOUXSIE & THE BANSHEES
JOHN FOXX	THE SPECIALS
GANG OF FOUR	SQUEEZE
IGGY POP	STEEL PULSE
BRIAN JAMES	SVT
KLARK KENT	U.K. SUBS
MAGAZINE	ULTRAVOX
MONOCHROME SET	XTC
WAZMO NARIZ	

All day long and half the night I had two telephones to my ear. Within the next few months I signed a number of new acts, keeping the vans rotating with tours up and around the club circuit, which by now stretched into a full circle all the way out to the West Coast and back again. For a while I handled everything myself, but then I got some volunteers to help. Louis Tropia, a big, lovable bald-headed guy who worked for Jane Friedman as John Cale's tour manager, pitched in to help out. If I was on another phone, he'd tackle an incoming call and deal with it, and gradually he began booking dates.

For a while it was wonderful. But you get what you pay for, and Louis was free. Soon the bands started calling me to complain that they were turning up for dates that Louis booked only to find that they were to be paid much less than Louis had specified, or worse, that the clubs were closed tight on specific nights. On checking with

Louis, I discovered that some of the dates he said were confirmed weren't and that the fees the groups were expecting were only the fees he had asked for, and not necessarily what the club owner had agreed to. He'd watch me screaming at promoters and making demands without realizing that demands are meaningless until the other party agrees to them. It was like déjà vu, but unlike the little creep who'd ripped Miles off back in London, Louis honestly meant well and his heart was in the right place. All the same I was glad when John Cale went back on tour, taking Louis with him. I made sure that it would be a long one.

Then there was Katie. Looking like a cat caught in the rain, she wandered in one day to ask for information on my bands, and when she saw us trying to juggle all the phone calls, she immediately offered her services at the switchboard. She was willing to work for next to nothing, just so she could get into the shows for free. Katie was a real live punk, safety pins in her nose and all, and quite a shock to anyone coming into the office. But she was gung ho, and she knew all the bands (some of them intimately) and could help me decide which to sign. An extra set of ears comes in handy, especially if they belong to someone who is representative of the ears in the audiences.

Eventually, though, I knew I needed experienced help with both the administration and the booking. Word about the agency was spreading, and just being in New York gave me access to a lot more talent. I clearly needed professional help. The realization had just dawned on me when I got a phone call from a Ms. Pamela Burton, who I remembered was Jonny Podell's snooty ex-secretary from the New York Paragon office. She called on some other pretext, but I knew right away she was after a job. Still, I figured that anyone who could handle a maniac like Jonny could surely handle me. I knew she was a ball-buster, and that was just what I needed. I told her to come down to my office for a meeting.

Pam arrived all set to come on strong, like she was doing me a favor. In her best "finishing school" accent, she began by giving me a list of demands stating all the things she would and wouldn't do. She would work only four days a week, and a half a day on Friday. On top of her lunch hour, she wanted a half hour for meditation, and every Wednesday she had to leave early for yoga class. She

WILD THING

wouldn't start right away because she wanted to go to "The Cape" for a couple of weeks, and she wouldn't take less than six hundred dollars a week.

I said, "Pam, I need a good assistant. But I want someone who can help me deal with my problems, not add to them. To start with, I can only offer you about half that, and if you work for me, you'll work seven days a week, sometimes eight, starting tomorrow. You'll do whatever is required, with one limitation: I will never ask you to do anything that I wouldn't do myself."

"Where do I sit?" she replied. When I told her, she went straight to her new desk and began arranging all her secretarial materials. From then on, we made a great team. Having covered for Jonny Podell for so long, she could deal with any dilemma. She knew everyone in the city, and knew how to get things done. She was a great organizer, and, in time, she so transformed the office that it was almost professional.

Oh, she needed a bit of retraining—rather, reorientation. For example, she saw herself as sort of a human moat, protecting her boss from pointless interruptions, and she took almost sadistic pleasure in screening telephone calls. Sometimes it went to the extreme. To my wife's extreme annoyance whenever she called me from down in Macon, Pam would tell her "I'll see if he's in," then put her on hold. I had told my wife that we were working from one room, so when I picked up the phone, she would ask me what the hell was going on between me and my secretary.

Connie was several months pregnant with Barbara, and perhaps a touch sensitive, but Pam didn't help. One night I worked late, and so did Pam. As we were leaving I offered to buy her dinner, since I was grateful for her working late. She accepted, and we went to a little French restaurant that just happened to be the only one I hadn't tried yet on our street, and that I'd been planning to go to anyway. As we sat down at the table, a smart-ass waiter came over to light the candles, and for no reason at all asked if we were newlyweds. I looked at him like he had two fucking heads. But the next day Pam told Connie all about it. Within minutes she was on to me, wanting to know what we were doing to prompt the waiter's question.

To find help with the bookings, I interviewed several agents in New York, but the money they were asking was so far beyond the pay scales I'd been used to in Georgia that I thought they saw me as an ignorant rube and were trying to rip me off—a reasonable conjecture since they were all sleazeballs.

I called down to Macon and asked Buck Williams, my old friend at Paragon, if he could come up and join me, but he said he couldn't afford to move, especially not to New York. He had a wife, two kids, two dogs, and a house with a mortgage to think of. Buck was polite enough not to say it, but at the time the idea of running my own agency in New York was considered a risky venture at best, and most people thought I was out of my mind.

I then called John Huie. He was single, young, and energetic. He had a minimum of experience but he was a good kid, and he was hungry to make something happen. He had only been an agent at Paragon for a short time but he was eager to learn, and he showed a lot of potential for becoming a great agent. More than anything, John had nothing to lose. I thought he'd jump at the chance to join me.

But Huie wasn't interested. He said he wanted to promote what he called "Christian music," and he had booked the first of what he hoped to be many Christian rock concerts in Macon. I told Huie it didn't make much sense, but, having heard the "calling of the Lord," he wasn't listening to me.

He did listen, however, when I pointed out that his concert was a few months away and he'd need something to do in the meantime. I asked him, "Why don't you come on up here and check it out? What have you got to lose? The worst that could happen is that you might like it and decide to stay." He wasn't convinced, but he did agree to come to New York to help out for just one month. A few days later, he moved into the Iroqouis Hotel with me and the cockroaches.

A month later, John went back to Macon, and two months later his Christian rock show was an unmitigated disaster. Ticket sales were dismal and he couldn't pay the bands out of the door receipts. None of the bands were willing to renegotiate their fees, and John was wiped out and disillusioned. But not lacking in faith. He called me up, and he said "Leroy, I guess the Lord has other plans for me. It seems he wants me to work for you a while." Holy shit, I thought, now even He's on my side!

WILD THING

John turned into a great booker, one of the best in the business, and Pam turned into a terrific assistant. I made John the vice president of FBI, and I gave both of them a percentage of profits. But, with all due respect, they both lacked the ears for the agency's kind of music. They didn't have a clue, at first, of what the new bands were all about. John's favorite band at the time, in fact, was Earth, Wind and Fire, and he had learned to play air guitar and lip-synch to all their songs. Pam's idea of a great punk group was Blotto, and she played their awful single "I Wanna Be a Lifeguard" over and over until I finally had to ban it.

The shortcomings of these two made Katie of particular value to me, and gave her a certain amount of secret power. Sometimes when I needed a second opinion on whether or not to sign a band, I'd ask her and she'd respond without a word, just by turning a thumb up or down. By this time we were getting inundated with tapes from garage bands all over the world, so her help was invaluable. But Katie kept disappearing. She'd go running off with bands on tour, then call us from the road to let us know she would be gone for a while. So we eventually had to replace her at the switchboard with a beautiful young girl named Theresa Lowery, our token New Yorker. She was only eighteen, but she took shit from nobody. Except Pam— from whom, of course, we all had to take it, including myself. Pam was the office bitch in a way that made me the office Mr. Nice Guy. I liked that.

In the first year the roster of FBI acts nearly doubled in size, and the office staff grew in numbers accordingly. Every couple of months or so someone new would join the staff. For example there were two more agents, Rick Shoor and Dan Koppel, and their assistant, Patty LaMagna.

Rick Shoor was a doorman at the Bottom Line, a showcase club in downtown Manhattan, and whenever John and I went to shows there Rick would take special care of us. One day he went up to John Huie and said he desperately wanted to be an agent.

"What makes you think you'd be a good agent?" asked John.

"I'm hungry," said Rick. "I'll do anything to get out of here."

John said, "I don't blame you, I can't eat the food here either. Ahyah, ahyah!" It was that simple: Rick got the job. It was purely a matter of timing, since only that afternoon I had agreed to let John find an assistant booker. And Rick became a great booker in almost no time at all. Before long, however, we were in need of even more help.

To further illustrate how tough it was to get hired at FBI in those days, the next person to ask got the job. Dan Koppel had some experience, at least. Danny had been on the buying end of the business, booking bands for a club called The Malibu in Long Island. He had to be retrained slightly so that he got used to the idea of getting the band's fees up instead of down. Once he got the hang of that he too turned out to be a damn good agent.

Next aboard was Paula Leone, hired to organize and run our newly formed "contract department." Paula had been the assistant to a well-known agent named Jeff Franklin, owner of ATI (American Talent International), so we finally got someone who knew what they were doing.

By the end of our second year we actually started to make some money. It dawned on me that I wasn't just fooling around, and that I might be headed for what my brother Miles called "the Big Time." FBI needed an office manager who was a true professional to keep a keen eye on our cash flow, someone who would round out the team and administrate the office while John and I flew around the world by the seat of our pants. Most of all, I needed someone I could trust. I called up my old friend and mentor Buck Williams down in Macon.

"Buck, old buddy," I said, "how would you like to come to New York?"

"I'd rather watch hogs fuck," he said.

Buck had been keeping himself busy since the collapse of the Paragon Agency by running a successful investment business, while his wife, Patti, was dealing in real estate, so apparently they were doing quite well for themselves. But fortunately for me Buck was bored! The music business was in his blood. And by now it was clear that FBI was not such a risky venture as it was when I first asked him to join me. A week or so later Buck called me back and agreed to come up, and soon he was in New York as just the office and business manager that the agency needed.

By the end of our third year in business, FBI had a staff of ten and a roster of over sixty acts. Jane Friedman's office wasn't nearly big enough to handle our growth, so Buck's first job was to find new

WILD THING

office space. After managing to finagle an amazing rent deal, he moved us into a whole floor of a building on Fifty-seventh Street and Broadway, across the street from the old offices. As part of the deal, we were able to redesign the space, and we turned it into one of the best places to throw a party I've ever seen.

The team at FBI was gung ho, and it always felt like family. To encourage this atmosphere, and to provide more reason for our bands to visit us, I installed a hot tub, a steam room, and a fully equipped gym, complete with Ping-Pong table, Soloflex, stationary bicycle, and a dumb gravity boot contraption, something that was all the rage at the time. In the reception area I put two pinball machines for the amusement of any visitors that might be kept waiting.

We were in our new offices less than a week when I got a rather rude phone call. I was first in the office one morning, and, as was my habit at the time, I answered the phone with "This is the FBI."

The voice on the other end of the line said, "No, *this* is the FBI!"

CHAPTER 20

THE POLICE—THE BAND

Too Kool to Kalypso.
— KLARK KENT AND IAN COPELAND

I DIDN'T HAVE enough to deal with—now the FBI was on my case. Three incredibly straight-looking G-men came to visit me in my fancy new offices, and they obviously weren't there to play the KISS pinball machine, or to try out the office steam room. They flashed their badges at my receptionist and demanded to see me. I can't say I wasn't expecting them. The fact is, I was wondering what took them so long.

What brought me to the FBI's attention was an innocuous advertisement I had placed in *Billboard* magazine, a music trade paper, in which I listed my current roster of acts. The G-men pointed to my company logo, which bore an uncanny resemblance to theirs, and they objected to my bold use of the letters FBI. I explained that I was merely poking fun at all the agencies who used the letters of their corporate names, such as ABC (Associated Booking Corporation), ICM (International Creative Management), ATI (American Talent International), APA (Agency for the Performing Arts), and so on, and that I didn't know of any laws I was breaking. Since I had legally registered the name and logo, I suggested it was just possible that they were the ones that were breaking the law. Believe me, they failed to see the humor in that.

The FBI agents came back a few times after that, each time with more lawyers. But in the end they gave up, since the closest thing they could find to charge me with was impersonating a federal agent, and I sure as hell wasn't guilty of that. Eventually we worked out a compromise. So as not to confuse anyone that might be calling by accident with information that was vital to the nation, I agreed that I would answer my phone with "Frontier Booking" rather than "FBI."

Meanwhile, as I was getting my office in order, the bands were out on the road doing the really hard work. Since everything ran on a very low budget, and since the economics allowed for very few nights off along the way, the tours were true endurance tests. By now it was obvious that punk, or new wave as we now called it, had indeed taken hold in America. Even so, it was still difficult to find decent venues for the bands to play in many of the major markets.

At first most promoters were leery of getting involved with the punk or new wave scene. They were afraid of punk crowds, or what they had heard of them. It didn't make sense to them to book bands that spat on the audience, assuming, incorrectly, that all punk bands did. Among the promoters there was a widely held opinion that the punk movement was a passing phase that would never go anywhere in the U.S. The attitude was, let's ignore it and it'll go away. The record companies were even less receptive to what I saw as an impending musical revolution. Top executives were highly paid for their "ears," and their ears were both offended and threatened by this new stuff. The bands all sounded the same to them, all of them being just noise.

Slowly but surely, however, as more and more young people turned on to the new alternative music, the network began to grow. We made it a policy to try and stay loyal to the promoters who helped us in the early stages of a band's career, and wherever possible we stuck to it. It wasn't always possible, since many of the early promoters had a hard time staying in business. As the bands got bigger in stature and the venues got larger in size, there came times that some of the small club promoters couldn't handle it. But that wasn't a problem yet.

When The Police came back for their second tour of North America, in March 1979, they were easier to book, since this time A&M decided to release their album. This meant I could promise promoters at least *some* help with promotional materials, and perhaps even hope for some radio play here and there. In any case, the buzz that the band had created from the first tour was enough to entice enough people into giving them a shot in their venues. But the album, *Outlandos d'Amour,* was starting to happen in Europe, and the band was needed in London for the *Top of the Pops* TV show. I therefore had to cover as many major markets as we could in a short space of time.

Still crammed in their van, with Kim Turner at the wheel, The Police traveled a total of 7,200 miles on this tour, playing thirty-seven shows in forty days, covering twenty-one cities, beginning at the Whisky a Go Go in Los Angeles (which I arranged with the help of the now famous disc jockey Rodney Bingenheimer) and ending up back in New York, where they played four shows at the Bottom Line (the established showcase club) to appease the press-hungry record company, and another two shows at CBGB's (the punk club) to please the fans. As if that wasn't enough, they filled their one day off with a free show at the Walnut Street Theater in Philadelphia before flying home to England.

The Police's second tour of North America:

1979

MARCH

1—THE WHISKY, LOS ANGELES
2—THE WHISKY, LOS ANGELES
3—THE WHISKY, LOS ANGELES
4—UNIVERSITY OF CALIFORNIA, BERKELEY
5—UNIVERSITY OF CALIFORNIA, DAVIS
7—THE ARMADILLO, AUSTIN
8—OPRY HOUSE, HOUSTON
9—PALLADIUM, DALLAS
10—UNIVERSITY OF ILLINOIS, CHAMPAIGN

273 WILD THING

12—The Palms, Madison
13—Beginnings, Chicago
15—One Block West, Kansas City
16—Mississippi Nights, St. Louis
18—Bogart's, Cincinnati
20—The Decade, Pittsburgh
21—The Agora, Cleveland
22—Center Stage, Detroit
23—The Edge, Toronto
24—The Edge, Toronto
25—Stage One, Buffalo
27—Uncle Sam's, Syracuse
28—Hullabaloo, Albany
29—My Father's Place, Long Island

APRIL

3—Bottom Line, New York City
4—Bottom Line, New York City
6—Paradise, Boston
7—Paradise, Boston
8—CBGB's, New York City
9—Walnut Street Theater, Philadelphia

The Police tour ended on the ninth of April, and on the tenth the band flew out on low-budget Laker Air. That same afternoon, Squeeze flew in to pick up the van and start their second tour of the United States. Only this time, I succumbed to pressure from the record company to put them on a tour supporting one of their major headliners, the theory being that they would therefore play to more people, and hence sell more records. This was the established way of breaking an act in America, and it was still considered to be the only way. Since the record company seemed to be so gung ho this time round, after much resistance I let them have their way. With A&M's help we were able to get Squeeze on a tour with The Tubes, the closest thing we could find to be at all compatible. The Tubes, featuring Fee Waybill and a massive production of dancers and rock musicians, were nowhere near new wave, but at least their single was called "White Punks on Dope."

It didn't work. From day one it was a disaster. Due to The Tubes' elaborate stage set, and a tyrannical stage manager with an obnoxious attitude, Squeeze was left to play in front of a curtain on a stage not much bigger than a large table. Since the sound system and stage lights were set and focused for the headliner, Squeeze had to settle for a weak sound and hardly any illumination. Very few of The Tubes' fans had ever heard of Squeeze, so most of them were still finding their seats while the band was struggling for an encore. The whole fiasco earned Squeeze a grand total of $10,700 for twenty-three shows, which couldn't cover the costs, and left them in debt to the record company, since "tour support" is recoupable from record sales.

More determined than ever to headline my bands whenever possible, and to avoid playing with dinosaur bands, I brought Squeeze back two months later for another headline tour of the clubs. This time they played to fewer people, but they were people who appreciated their kind of music, and who were more likely to buy their album. In a headline environment the band could really shine, and their ability to charm an audience could show itself. With full control over the PA and the lights, the band could play their music with more force, and the show was more exciting. This tour earned a total of $22,150—more than twice as much—for only nineteen shows, easily covering the costs. For many years after that I refused to put my bands on supporting others, unless they were my own and I had some control over how they'd be treated.

Meanwhile, The Police just kept working. In the wake of their previous tours they had left behind a lot of excited fans, among them a number of disc jockeys who began playing "Roxanne," enough for it to enter the record sales charts and start to climb. The album *Outlandos d'Amour* also entered the album charts, not enough to go all the way, but enough to warrant bringing the band back to promote it some more. After just two weeks in England, the band returned for their third tour of America, which took them through the month of May.

In June they began their first headline tour of Europe, with The Cramps as support, and in August they recorded their second album, *Regatta de Blanc*. By now, the record company was fully behind them, and the record was given the push that can only come from people who believe in the project. The band was suddenly in great demand

275   WILD THING

for radio shows, press interviews, and photo opportunities, all of which they handled with amazing aplomb. In September they were back out on the road, and they would stay out for a full eight months. This time we were going for the world.

If finding places for The Police to play was difficult in North America, it was even harder to find them in all other parts of the world, especially since the band wasn't really big enough yet to warrant it. Just to make it even more interesting, they decided to play in countries where no bands had ever played before. But that's what made it fun, for them as well as for Miles and me.

The world tour began in England on September 10, 1979, coinciding with the release of "Message in a Bottle," the first single from the second album. Wherever possible, we would try to create an event out of Police shows by playing in halls that no bands had played before. Their first date back in America, on September 27, they headlined in New York City at a previously unused ballroom in the Diplomat Hotel that Miles and I promoted ourselves, and the first thousand tickets sold so fast we added another two days of shows. The show was significant to me because it was proof that new wave bands could rise out of playing the clubs.

The Police played forty-seven dates in unusual venues across the States until December 1, when they ended the tour with a sold-out show at the 3,300-capacity Palladium back in New York City. Then two months touring Europe, and back to America for another sixteen dates, the last of which was at the University of Hawaii. From there they flew to Tokyo, for a tour of Japan that lasted two weeks.

In Japan the band was treated as if they were already superstars, simply because they came. Since only the biggest stars ever made it to Japan, it followed that The Police must be big. There were mob scenes at the airport, and scores of screaming female fans in a crowd outside the hotel. It was impractical to leave the hotel, even for me, and the band was mostly confined to their rooms. Even the hotel restaurant was impossible to eat in without being surrounded by autograph-seeking fans. It wasn't long before they began knocking on the doors to our rooms.

Japan was an established stop on most world tours, and I knew the promoters from years before, when I was booking tours for bands in England. As proof of the value of maintaining relationships, Mr.

Udo, the top promoter in Japan, offered to help me with The Police even though he'd never heard of them before. It was the same in Australia, with the top promoter there, Michael Gudinsky. These were countries that had established concert circuits, paths well-trodden by other bands of the past. But the real challenge The Police presented was to find shows in the countries in between, where no bands had been before.

I was determined for The Police to be the first Western rock band to play in China. Unfortunately, however, I couldn't find a way to establish contact in the United States through diplomatic channels, since we didn't recognize the Communist regime on the mainland, but rather the People's Republic of China now located on the tiny island of Taiwan. I desperately tried to find a link between contacts in Japan, or Australia, or England, anywhere that might have relations with China. I painstakingly exhausted every lead, and still came up with nothing. My father put me in touch with an old crony of his who claimed to be able to pull it off, but this soon proved to be bogus. So, I finally settled for second best. Through a worthy Oriental gentleman named Rigo Jesu who claimed to be an illegitimate relative of China's ruler, General Chiang Kai-shek, and who was therefore able to finagle the work permits, I booked The Police for three shows at the China Sports and Cultural Center in Taipei, Taiwan. For good measure, I also booked them for two days in Hong Kong, at a disco called Today's World, and through the promoters in Australia we added five shows in New Zealand.

The next four stops on the tour were all to be places that no one ever played. When we discussed the tour, The Police said they wanted to play in the Third World, and even the Fourth World if possible, so it had been my mission to come up with concerts in places off the beaten path. In Bangkok, Thailand, I located an old friend that had served with me in Vietnam, who led me to a local promoter willing to put on a show at a downtown Bangkok bar called the Kit Kat Klub. It didn't take a great deal of research to discover that the Kit Kat Club was actually a glorified whorehouse, but when I talked it over with the band they thought it would be a good enough place to play "Roxanne." I found another club in Singapore that wasn't much better. Miles came up with some little old ladies that ran a social club in Bombay, India, and through them

WILD THING

organized a concert there at a place called the Homi Bha Bha Auditorium. In Egypt we contacted the American University in Cairo, and offered them the show for free, since our expenses were covered by the promoters in the next stop, which was in Athens, Greece. The Police wouldn't be the first band to play in Greece, but they'd be the first band to play there since The Rolling Stones back in 1969, after which the generals took over and rock concerts were banned.

Booking the world tour was one thing, pulling it off was quite another, and we had our fair share of problems. To begin with, Sting picked up a throat infection in Hong Kong that left him voiceless for nearly a week. We were forced to cancel the shows in Taipei as a result, as well as all but one of the shows in New Zealand. Also, the first few shows in Australia had to be rescheduled, which meant blowing out Bangkok and Singapore. We were able to keep in the Bombay show, but when we got there we found there was only enough power for the lights, or the amplifiers, or the PA system, but not enough for all at the same time. The little old ladies that organized the show had all the best intentions, providing their services for charity, but they clearly hadn't a clue when it came to putting on a concert. Since this was the first time any band had played in Bombay, it quickly turned into a mob scene as thousands of Indians came to see The Police. To keep from causing a riot, the venue was moved to the much larger Rang Bhawan Stadium, solving some problems but creating others. But just to watch this crowd as they enjoyed their first, probably only, rock concert made the whole thing worthwhile. In spite of the enormous cultural gap between the musicians and their audience, in many ways they lit up like a crowd from New Jersey. Music is truly an international language.

In Cairo the band arrived on a Saturday to do a show that evening, only to find that the customs office was closed for a religious holiday. The Egyptian airport officials refused to clear our equipment, and we were told that nothing could be released until the following Monday. We tried to impress them with our Arabic, but still we failed to get through. We tried to persuade them, we tried to bribe them, we tried every trick in the book. All to no avail.

Miles had employed a local fix-it man to advance the show who met us at the airport. He explained that he was helpless. Half-jokingly, he asked if there was someone we might know through my father's old connections that could pull some strings for us. Miles thought about that for a minute. Then he said:

"I do know someone that might be able to help us. It's a long shot, but maybe it's worth a try. There was a man that lived next door to us in Cairo that had something to do with the government. I remember that as a child I used to go over and play with his guns. His name was Hassan Touhaimi."

The effect of his name was remarkable. Every Egyptian within earshot looked startled, and the fix-it man's eyes nearly left his head.

"You know this man?!" he said, aghast. "This man is a god!"

It turned out that Hassan Touhaimi, who had been Gamal Abdel Nasser's bodyguard when we were children, was now the vice prime minister of Egypt. Miles placed a call to his office, and to his surprise he was put straight through. Touhaimi had mistaken the call to be coming from my father, but was glad to hear from young Miles once he explained. He promised he would help.

"Don't worry, *ya khayou,*" he said. "I'll take care of it."

It didn't take long to witness his power. In no time at all the border officials went from complete indifference, even disdain, to groveling helpfulness. Despite the holdup, we managed to get the equipment cleared in time for the show.

From Egypt the band went to perform in Greece, then in Italy, Germany, France, Spain, Belgium, Holland, and back to Britain, ending in Sting's hometown of Newcastle on April 28, 1980. After spending a few months writing and recording their third album, *Zenyatta Mondatta,* they were back out on the road in August for a tour of Europe, and for another grueling tour of North America in October, November, and part of December. We followed that with a tour of South America, another territory untapped by other bands, playing in Venezuela, Argentina, and Brazil.

The BBC sent a camera crew along on the world tour, accompanied by Annie Nightingale, their top music correspondent, and they documented the whole trip, which, when shown on TV, displayed better than any video possibly could what the band was about, and the end result of the whole exercise was that the band was now perceived to be a world-class act. The fact is they were. By the end of

1980 they had won nearly every top award that the music business and the press had to give, including Best Band, Best Album, Best Single, Best Live Show, etc., etc., etc.

On January 10, 1981, a year and a half after I started the FBI, The Police came back to America yet again, only this time it would be a short tour. Short, but big. Just to demonstrate to everyone how big the band was, and to thumb our collective noses at all the people who doubted that punk would prevail in America, we headlined the band at two of the most renowned venues in the world, Madison Square Garden in New York and the Sports Arena in Los Angeles.

As at almost every step of the way, we first had to convince the venues and promoters, and also the record company, that The Police were a big enough attraction to do it. The Police's press and critical acclaim were outstanding, but as yet their record sales didn't exactly justify it. Nobody, in fact, was confident about the dates. Madison Square Garden held twenty thousand people, or six times as many as the Palladium, where they had last played.

But before any of that, as usual we had to deal with the band, who weren't worried with any such trivia. They just didn't want to do it. Sting in particular, being the front man of the band, was concerned that they would lose rapport with the audience in a big building like that. Ron Delsener, the New York promoter, suggested we take the whole band down to see Bruce Springsteen's show at the Garden. As we watched the show I could see from Sting's face that our show was on. Sting saw Bruce take that huge venue and turn it into a club atmosphere, and he rose to the challenge to do the same.

The management, Miles and Kim, were also worried that the band would lose their "street credibility" by playing such a cavernous place, so we added an unannounced show at the Ritz in New York for the day after the Garden event, and in Los Angeles, we added a show at the Variety Arts Theater, an 1,100-seater that no one ever played. Just to make that show extra-special, Miles made it a requirement that in order to get in one had to be blond, like the band. Even Jerry Moss, the head of the record company, the "M" in A&M,

had to dye his hair blond to get in. The Police, of course, came out on stage all wearing black wigs.

To everyone's surprise The Police concerts in the big buildings sold out in a matter of hours, and to no one's surprise, the smaller ones sold out in minutes. It was official. The Police had made it! How can I describe the feeling of finally putting an act in Madison Square Garden, and the elation at selling it out? Any pride I had in past achievements paled in comparison to how I felt that night. I paraded around the building like I owned it. I was mingling with the crowd like they were my personal friends who'd come to see me as well as the band, and the same backstage, hobnobbing on a first-name basis with the rock stars, film stars, and otherwise famous people who'd come to witness the excitement of The Police show. Hell, I was flying!

But while this was a major victory for The Police, and for the whole new music movement in general, the battle for me had only just begun. Despite The Police's apparent success, FBI still had a long way to go.

CHAPTER 21

IRS—The Record Company

It's the end of the world as we know it (and I feel fine).
—R.E.M.

By now I was on a mission. Breaking new wave in America had become a burning crusade, and there was a growing number of people getting involved in the movement. The Police's achievements only served to fuel the fires. Even so, the naysayers of new wave were claiming that The Police was a fluke, that they were never a punk band in the first place. True enough, perhaps, but they opened the floodgates in America for the next generation of music to come through.

For my purposes, the bands I signed did not have to fit any particular criteria, other than they had to be unique. That ruled out all the old-fart bands, who all seemed to sound alike. I signed young bands that ranged in style from hard-core to avant-garde folk, from The Dead Boys and The Stranglers to John Cooper Clarke and Pere Ubu, and everything in between, as long as they fit one simple standard: they had to be different. The more difficulty I had in comparing them to any other band the more I liked it.

The other major agencies were still slow to show interest in the new bands, primarily since most of the bands were still finding it hard to get a record released. Without a record in the charts, and no record company to finance a tour, the other agencies didn't know what to do. The club tour established by FBI as a tool for breaking acts remained exclusive to us for quite some time. By convincing the bands to keep their expenses down, and to live within their means, we were able to tour bands from as far away as New Zealand (Split Enz), Australia (Midnight Oil), Japan (The Plastics), and Africa (King Sunny Ade), as well as from the U.K. (Echo & The Bunnymen, Psychedelic Furs, The Cure, Joy Division, Bow Wow Wow, Simple Minds, Thompson Twins, Robert Palmer, Adam Ant, etc.), Canada (Martha and The Muffins) and the U.S.A. (The Go-Go's, Oingo Boingo, Wall of Voodoo, Klaus Nomi, Joan Jett, etc.)* Not all of them were destined for greatness, but all of them were important. The main objective was to keep the movement supplied with a steady flow of exciting new talent. If we were going to challenge the old guard, we had to have troops.

At the same time as the early punk movement first reared its head in London another musical force, reggae, began to emerge. Reggae was not exactly new. Public interest in reggae was piqued years before by Bob Marley and the Wailers, but it had mostly gone underground since then, and could only be heard, oddly enough, in the same clubs that dared to play punk music. Punk DJs, such as Londoner Don Letts, refused to play music by dinosaur bands, yet there was a lack of product to choose from the new stuff, so they would spin reggae. In the same manner, reggae clubs were the only place where punks could go and not get beaten up. Violence was common in London at the time, and punks were the target for just about everybody from right-wing skinheads in the National Front to the working-class Teddy Boys, who were once the punks of their generation. On weekends in the summer, raging battles took place on Kings Road, with punks on one end and Teds at the other, much the same as had taken place between mods and rockers in the sixties. And it was common for the cops to join in on the side of the Teds. Punk bands were often stopped and searched and subjected to harassment from the cops, and their apartments were constantly being

---

* A full list of bands represented by FBI is provided at the end of this book.

IAп COPELAпD   284

raided for drugs. Perhaps that accounts for some of their eagerness to come to America, and in some ways it was the same for reggae bands.

The Police helped to make reggae reemerge in America. When they released "Roxanne," "So Lonely," and "Can't Stand Losing You," with their obvious reggae influences, reggae music was given a much-needed boost. On top of that, The Police had always insisted on having a local punk band support them on their shows, but when that proved to be an exercise in futility (sadly, most local punk bands in America at the time were simply awful), Sting asked that I put on reggae bands. From then on I began to put reggae bands on as support wherever possible, and FBI began to champion their cause.

Admittedly, because no one else was interested I had no competition in this field, so I was able to choose the cream of the crop, among them Steel Pulse, Peter Tosh, Black Uhuru, Dennis Brown, Third World, Sly and Robbie, and UB40. Not all of them toured with The Police, but one way or another I brought them in. This wasn't always easy, since most of them had a large number of people in the band and an equal number of road crew.

UB40, for instance, had seven people in the band, plus two horn players, five roadies, a manager, and an accountant. In order to put them on some of The Police shows (in November 1983), I had to pay them five thousand dollars per show. Fortunately for me, The Police were fanatical about making sure their shows were extra-special, and top value for their fans, so I was able to get away with such indulgences now and again. Ironically enough, UB40 was a big attraction in Europe, and they felt they should be getting twice as much money per show. At the time they were probably worth only a thousand dollars in the U.S.

Most of the reggae bands I dealt with smoked massive amounts of marijuana, especially since many of them were Rastafarian, and ganja was religion to them. Perhaps because of this, the reggae bands were generally an agent's nightmare to work with. Some were extremely professional, but as a general rule they would drive me crazy because everything was done in such a haphazard way and at a pace that tried my patience. To be fair, the tours would always come together, but at the eleventh hour. The reggae fans were the same, always showing up at the last minute, which drove the promoters crazy. On the day of the show advance ticket sales would spell disaster, but by night it would be all right.

Somewhere in between punk and reggae, an inspired offshoot developed musically, and several of the new bands in England adopted a style that was a hybrid of the reggae beat and pop, with the added angst of punk. The result was a sound called "ska." The Specials were the leaders of the pack, and their first album was produced by another up-and-coming superstar, Elvis Costello. I first heard a single from it called "Gangsters" in a Manhattan punk room called the Mudd Club, and the next day I booked a flight to London to check out this new scene. Since The Specials were still in rehearsals, I took a train ride up to Birmingham and caught a show by a band who were considered to be next in line for the ska throne, called The Beat.* Their show was so amazing, and the crowd reaction so awe-inspiring, I went back to their dressing room and signed them on the spot. They were surprised to see me at this early stage of their career; they didn't yet have an agent in England.

With The Specials on my roster, the first ska band to tour America, and The (English) Beat, who toured behind them, I went after the third of the most popular ska bands, a nutty bunch of English guys called Madness. As if to show me I couldn't get everything I wanted, their manager turned me down on the grounds that he didn't want to be on the same roster as the other two ska bands. Managers can decide to go with one agent or the next for any number of reasons, but I'd never heard that one before. Acts tend to gravitate toward agencies with a roster of acts similar to their own. Competition and jealousy between the new wave acts in Britain was fierce, however, so I would hear this reasoning a few times again in the future.

Johnny Rotten may have been a case in point. When he called me about his new band Public Image Limited (The Sex Pistols had broken up immediately after their disastrous first and only U.S. tour

---

*Due to a band of the same name in San Francisco, they were called The English Beat in the U.S.

early in 1978), he told me straight away that he was not impressed by my roster of mainly punk bands. It was my reggae acts that attracted him. "If you can handle that bunch of lunatics," he said, "there's a chance, just a chance, that you can handle us lot. Why don't you invite me to dinner and we'll discuss it?"

I was delighted to do so. As the leader of the whole punk revolution, and therefore the one person most responsible for my current success, Johnny Rotten was nothing short of being the messiah in my eyes. As far as I was concerned, it was like getting a call from Elvis Presley.

It was one of the only times I've ever been nervous to meet anyone. I took great care in choosing the restaurant. I had read somewhere that Rotten was vegetarian, so I chose a place that served no meat. Because of his reputation for shunning the wasteful extravagances of dinosaur bands, I decided to forego a limo ride to a fancier place downtown, and instead I chose a place a short walk from his hotel. Imagining him to be all decked out in outrageous punk gear, I went to pick him up from his hotel straight from the office, dressed in casual attire.

Johnny Rotten was all decked out in an expensive suit. He took one look at me and said "I suppose that means I can expect a cheap meal." I told him I had picked a nice place nearby.

"Walk!?" he asked. "Walk? Surely you jest."

"Well, it's not far," I said, "but we could take a taxi . . ."

"Uuungh, oh noooo!" he exclaimed with disgust. "Not a fucking taxi. Where's the fucking limo?"

When we sat down at the restaurant, the first thing Johnny did was order a steak. I didn't know whether he was fucking with me, but I offered to take him to another place. While he went to the toilet, I went outside to catch a cab. Along came a limo to save my life. When he had dropped off his customer, I convinced the driver to take us downtown to the best steakhouse in the city. When Johnny came out, the limo was waiting.

It turned out that Johnny Rotten was now John Lydon, his real name. After the demise of The Sex Pistols he had totally changed his image. He had learned a lot from that experience and he was serious about his new band. He played me a tape of his new album in the limo on the ride downtown, and it was great if not what I expected,

WILD THING

which made me like it even more. Fortunately for me, the rest of the evening went well, despite Lydon's attempts to unnerve me and challenge my intelligence, something he apparently did with everyone. He decided to work with me in America.

Although FBI concentrated on new wave bands, we didn't completely rule out the possibility of working with bands that weren't. My receptionist buzzed me in my office one day, and told me that Donny Osmond was on the line.

"Donny Osmond? You've got to be kidding!"

"Well, I asked him twice, and that's who he says he is," she replied.

I was sure it was Sting or someone, just trying to fuck with my head. "Put him on," I said.

"Donny, you old wanker," I said when she put the call through. "How's Marie?" I asked.

"Fine, thanks . . . fine," said the voice on the phone, sounding somewhat surprised. "You know Marie?" he asked.

"Sheeyit! Do I know Marie? Boy, do I know Marie! You better belieeeeeve I know Marie! Hell, only four or five guys on my rugby team know her better."

". . . This isn't really Ian Copeland, is it?" asked the voice, after some hesitation.

It started to dawn on me that I might've made a mistake.

"This isn't really Donny Osmond, is it?" I asked.

"Yes, it is," said the voice. It was.

After accepting my profuse apologies, Donny explained that he had recorded a new album of material that was harder-edged than his previous work, and he wanted me to represent him for touring. "Why me?" I asked, slightly flattered and extremely curious.

"I've got a rock 'n' roll album, and a rockin' band, and I want to go out on the road. The problem is, I want to be taken seriously." Donny was aware of his apple-pie image, which by now had become a burden. In order to increase his credibility, he wanted to align himself with a more street-level operation than he'd previously surrounded himself with. I agreed to meet with him to discuss it.

I can say without qualification that Donny Osmond is simply the nicest person I've ever met. We spent a few days hanging around together in New York, where I took him for a tour of the happening clubs and educated him on the new scene. To my surprise he was recognized everywhere we went, and he was universally admired or adored by even the funkiest of punks. His genuine warmth of character and his humble yet magnetic demeanor gave him a natural charisma that couldn't be denied. Unfortunately, I was unable to work with him. I added him to my roster, then I received a call from the William Morris Agency's lawyers. Donny had a firm contract with them that he'd forgotten existed, and I was forced to bow out.

Grand Funk was another example of a band that we handled that could hardly be called new wave. I was recommended to them by my friend Jane Friedman, who was their publicist. I wanted to do them because I considered it a challenge to prove that we could do as good a job on a band that was out of our musical domain, and also on the grounds that they had been a favorite of mine in the bunkers of Vietnam. Grand Funk was no slouch signing; it wasn't easy convincing them to come with my agency. After all, Grand Funk was one of only two bands to have headlined a show at Shea Stadium. The other band was The Beatles.

Miles, meanwhile, was building his record label, IRS, into a major musical force. Headquartered in Los Angeles, and headed up by Jay Boberg, a young entrepreneurial music fanatic fresh out of college, IRS cornered a niche of the record market by signing up many of the new wave bands that other record companies were too nervous to run with, and by discovering talent undetected by the others. The beauty of it was that IRS bands didn't have to sell platinum records in order to make money and be successful. The concept we were using at FBI was the one they used at IRS—keep the costs down and live within your means. So IRS had their fair share of hit records, even with such obscure records as "Mexican Radio" by Wall of Voodoo, and ska records by The English Beat. But bands like The Cramps, Buzzcocks, and Magazine could put out their records and still make a profit even though they didn't reach the high end of the charts, mainly because they could tour for a profit while promoting them. This enabled both Miles and me to be involved with bands we liked, that we considered important, even though they might never be monstrous commercially. For me, that luxury, more than any potential for making money, is what made it all worthwhile.

The Go-Go's were just such a band, and it so happened that Miles and I discovered them simultaneously. While he was chasing them to sign with IRS for recording, I was after them to sign with FBI for agency, and luckily we got them for both. I'm not sure either of us realized just how successful they would be, nor how quickly it would happen, but we knew there was something special about them. The idea of an all-girl band wasn't exactly unique, but The Go-Go's weren't just a great all-girl band, they were a great band, period.

The Go-Go's rise to the big time was the fastest I would ever witness. My first booking on the band was early in 1981, after they returned from a tour in England they had booked by themselves, and I worked them in clubs across America throughout the year. By the end of that year they had built up enough of a following to where they were already doing theaters in some cities. They headlined three nights at the Greek Theater in their hometown of Los Angeles in October, then headlined the Palladium in New York in November, with clubs, small halls, and a tour of Europe in between.

Meanwhile, The Go-Go's record was released on IRS, and to everyone's amazement, it quickly climbed the charts to number one. By January of 1982, their album had gone gold (500,000 copies). In January and February of 1982 we put them on as a support act to The Police, who were by this time playing in large arenas, including a show at Madison Square Garden on January 22. In the summer we sent The Go-Go's on tour to Japan and Australia. By the end of that year, with their album now a platinum record–seller (1 million copies), The Go-Go's were headlining in arenas themselves. On October 19, 1982, the same year they had been support for The Police, they sold out their own show at Madison Square Garden.

Working with an all-girl band was a pleasure in most regards, but it did have its pitfalls. Especially out on the road. Girls on tour get just as lonely as guys on tour, and when you've been on the road for a long time it gets to where *anything* starts to look good. Even for The

Go-Go's. It was very late in the tour when I showed up, and one of them made advances.

It was harmless flirting at first, and nothing to be ashamed of. The fact of my marriage kept me safe. But at some point the other girls began teasing her, and what otherwise would have been nothing more than a passing fancy became a challenge, or possibly a dare. With each day she became more aggressive. One night, after a show, we were all getting plastered in the bar of the local Holiday Inn, and she had more than the rest of us. Late in the night, she hinted loudly to the others to leave us alone. No sooner had they done so when she indicated to me that I had a choice to make. I could take her to bed, or The Go-Go's were going to find another agent.

Not knowing quite how to deal with the situation, and not wanting to lose The Go-Go's, I took the most obvious course of action. I ordered more drinks. And lots more after that. By the time we got to her room, she was legless. By the time we got to her bed she was out. I took all her clothes off, put her under the sheets, and left a note saying how much I'd enjoyed our night together. I don't know what she told the others, but she walked around the next day with a glow I wish I got from girls I *did* sleep with, and all her aggression was gone.

For a time, FBI was the only major agency in America that was willing to take on bands that were unsigned to a record label. This made the job more difficult at first, needless to say, but the result was a greater sense of pride in their ultimate success. Joan Jett and the Blackhearts, for instance, was turned down by twenty-four different record companies. We took her on and put her in clubs. Within two years of touring, beginning in small clubs and working her way up to larger halls, she managed to get a record deal with a small but adventurous label called Boardwalk Records. Soon after its release, her single "I Love Rock and Roll" went to number one on the charts. By the end of 1982, Joan Jett had earned a platinum album in most countries of the world. Meanwhile, I was booking her for guarantees of fifty thousand dollars per show.

About this time, I was visited in my office by an old friend from London, an agent-turned-manager named Geoff Jukes. Geoff managed an unsigned English pop band called The Fixx. He brought me a demo tape of their music, what he hoped would be their forthcoming first album. One listen and I agreed to be their agent. I heard at least two hits on the tape, so I was confident they would eventually be signed. Sure enough they were. Their two classic hits "Red Skies at Night" and "Stand or Fall" from their first album continue to be played regularly on radio to this day. That first album went gold (over a half million copies sold), and their second album *Reach the Beach* went platinum (selling over a million copies). That album was top ten in the charts for over four months. The Fixx went on to become a major success on the touring circuit, selling out large venues such as the Reunion Arena in Dallas, which holds twenty thousand people.

Even though IRS and some of the others were starting to have success with new wave acts, many of the other record companies in America were still not interested. As a result, many of the bands that were signed in England to worldwide deals couldn't get their records released in the States. A Flock of Seagulls, for instance, were signed to Jive Records in Britain, which meant they were automatically on Arista in America. Arista was unimpressed with their record and decided not to put it out. It so happened I loved the record, and I decided to bring the band in anyway.

I first brought them over in April of 1982 as the support band on the first leg of a Squeeze tour. It lasted for less than a month, but we were able to persuade enough Arista reps to come to the shows that we caused a buzz at the company. They changed their minds and decided to release the record, and to keep the band in America to make a video. That gave me time to book them a headline tour of their own in the clubs. That ran for six weeks, by which time Squeeze returned for the second leg of their tour, so I put A Flock of Seagulls back on that, including a show at Madison Square Garden. That took us to to the end of July, and by then the record was out and starting to get some action on radio. So, I filled the rest of July and all of August with a mixture of headline shows, some festival shows with The Police, Joan Jett, The Specials, and The (English) Beat, and a one-off show in front of ninety thousand people at JFK Stadium in Philadelphia with Genesis, Blondie, and Elvis Costello. By now their record was taking off, so I added them to The Go-Go's tour for all of September and October, including yet another show at the Garden. I finished the tour with a week of headline shows at the Peppermint Lounge in Manhattan.

Having originally planned to come to America for only three weeks, A Flock Of Seagulls stayed for a full six months. They played more than a hundred and thirty shows to an audience of approximately 650,000 fans. And just to wind up the year I arranged for the band to headline at The First Annual New Year's Eve Party in New York that was being organized and televised by a newly formed national music channel called MTV. The band was flown in, put up, and paid $25,000 for that show, and they returned to Liverpool with a platinum album under their belts.

I never tried to steal acts from the other agencies. I liked to discover them and build them up. Being a bit idealistic, I eventually came to realize that some of the bands we championed, the so-called punk bands, *really were* punks, irresponsible kids who took pleasure in wrecking our vans and in otherwise making costly nuisances of themselves. Here we were, supplying vans to help out the bands, and they were wrecking them. Being appreciative and taking care of them was just foreign to their nature, which was what made them punks in the first place. They had no more respect for my vans than they had for anything else. To them, bookers and promoters were mere businessmen to be ripped off.

It dawned on me that we were supporting a revolution for a lot of maniacs when The Lurkers called me after their last show in New York to report that our van and equipment had been stolen. They claimed to have parked the loaded van on the street outside the Iroquois Hotel overnight, an incredibly dumb thing to do. I later found out what really happened. The Lurkers had gone berserk on stage on their last night, completely trashing the equipment as a grand finale to the tour. They then left the van on the street, with the equipment in full view and the doors unlocked. They weren't dumb. They knew it would be gone by morning.

The other van was abandoned at the airport in L.A. by Gang of Four, who were late for a flight and couldn't be bothered to leave it in a parking lot. Instead, they left it parked on the curb in front of their terminal, and ran off to catch their flight home to England. By the time we managed to track it down, the parking tickets and storage charges exceeded the value of the van. After that, we decided we'd better get out of the transportation business, and let the bands get their own vans.

WILD THING

♦♦♦

Meanwhile, the enormous success of The Police put huge demands on Miles's time, which eventually caused strains between him and his other management act, Squeeze. Miles divided up his time as best he could, but while on tour with The Police, another manager began to hang out with Squeeze at the studio in England, bending their ears and feeding their insecurities. He told them how they were being neglected, and that they deserved more attention. His name was Jake Rivera. He owned the ultra-hip Stiff Records and he also managed Elvis Costello, so he was considered to be the dog's bollocks in London at the time. Squeeze decided to give him a try, and Miles was fired.

As I've mentioned, when a manager is fired the agent is often the next to go. Aware of the open hostility between Rivera and Miles, I was almost certain to lose the band. I could only hope that the band would feel a loyalty for all the sweat we'd put into their past, and that they would insist on staying with FBI, but I knew that a band would never go against a manager's decision to change agents. That's considered to be the manager's job, and Jake was a big-shot manager.

My fears were fueled further when he refused to take my phone calls. In fact, he would not acknowledge my existence. This led to a standoff. Squeeze had a new album recorded, so I was already in the process of booking their tour. Without communication with management, that was extremely difficult if not impossible to do. Luckily for me, just as the Squeeze album was released, at a time when the band most needed management, Jake Rivera simply lost interest in the whole thing. Before I was officially fired, he unceremoniously dropped the band.

The next manager they chose was much more friendly. An English chap named David Endhoven, he had once been a "heavy manager," with King Crimson as one of his clients, but he had dropped out of the business for several years before returning to manage Squeeze. He had no loyalties to any other agent, and he understood that I was much more cognizant of the band's problems, knowing their strengths and weaknesses in the marketplace better than anyone else. He bravely admitted that he was out of touch with the new music scene, and he was perfectly willing to listen to all the advice he could get.

While The Police were taking off in America and their music was all over the radio, for some reason Squeeze wasn't quite getting much airplay. They toured extensively and drew appreciative crowds and rave reviews wherever they went, yet in many markets they still couldn't pull enough of an audience to get out of the clubs and into the halls. Outside of New York, they just weren't getting the respect they deserved. They needed publicity. They needed a stunt.

Endhoven asked what we should do about it. I told him, "Start the tour in New York. At Madison Square Garden."

"What?" said David. To be honest, he nearly choked. "I say, old chap! I'm not sure I heard you correctly. Did you say Madison Square Garden?"

By this time I had become a little bit ballsy, but I was genuinely confident we could do it. Squeeze had built up a devoted following in many cities across America, but nowhere as strong as in New York. There we had a radio station (WPLJ) that was playing their records on heavy rotation, and, although the station soon went off the air, Squeeze was already considered "cool for cats" in New York. They had already sold out multiple nights at all the clubs in Manhattan, Long Island, and New Jersey. When I added up the tickets sold in the New York area on their previous tour, it far exceeded the capacity of Madison Square Garden. When I checked with the promoters, they said the band was the most requested band at all the ticket outlets. Nevertheless, when I asked where they thought Squeeze should play, they were still offering me theater shows like the Beacon, which held less than three thousand, or the Roseland Ballroom, which held about the same. They felt that Squeeze fans were following the band from club to club, and therefore their ticket sales were deceptively high. I pointed out that most of the places they played served liquor and had age limits, and therefore their ticket sales were deceptively low. At Madison Square Garden their younger fans would be able to come, and since it sits on top of Penn Station they could come from anywhere in the tri-state area.

I discussed my idea with the others in the office, and almost everyone else was skeptical. John Huie, and even Pamela Burton, who

295   WILD THING

never doubted me, were openly nervous. They seemed to think that my success at the Garden with The Police had gone to my head, and now I was trying to duplicate it with Squeeze when Squeeze was not quite ready.

David took my idea over to the record company, and their reaction was even more predictable. He called me after the meeting and said, "I'm not sure who to believe. They don't seem to think it's such a great idea. And that's putting it politely."

"What exactly did they say?" I asked.

"Well, they think you've been dropping acid."

"Look," I said, "I don't tell them what songs to put on the album, and I'm not going to tell them how to promote your record. But when it comes to live shows I know what I'm talking about. Playing Madison Square Garden is like getting the Oscar of live concerts. It's just the stunt we need. If we can sell out the Garden, all the other markets will wake up and take notice."

David was still not totally convinced. But I had talked myself into it, and now I was determined. I said, "Forget your record sales, and forget the charts. I'm not going by them. I'm going by the vibes on the street, and by how many Squeeze badges they're selling down at Irving Plaza." I finally hit David with the old standby. "David," I said, "trust me."

The show was set for June 18, 1982. The first announcement for the show was only a tiny ad in *The Village Voice*, about a square inch. Even that didn't exactly announce the show. It just said, "SQUEEZE FANS CALL," and it listed a phone number. That was all, nothing else. I had three reasons for advertising the show in such an unusual manner. First and foremost I wanted to make sure the most deserving fans got the best seats, and I figured that anyone responding to such an innocuous ad would surely be devoted. Second, I wanted to create a buzz. I hoped we could sell a majority of the tickets by word of mouth, thereby cutting advertising costs, which in turn lowered the promoter's risk. Third, I wanted to be able to really shove it in everyone's face if I was right.

Squeeze sold over nine thousand tickets the first week they went on sale, without a single radio station ad, which spelled an obvious and surefire triumphant home run. I couldn't believe it! When the posters came out, the show sold out instantly, and with the money that was saved on radio promotion, the band made a small fortune on their percentage deal. I was ecstatic that the band had finally made it, and the band was over the moon. The show they put on that night was one of the best performances I've ever seen from any band anywhere. The reviews of the show were excellent, and ticket sales for all the rest of the shows on the tour took a giant leap.

Two weeks after the tour, to my utter dismay, the band broke up.* This was not the first time or the last time that I would see such a thing happen. Strangely enough, it happens more often than not. The fibers that weave a band together are often fragile, and the strain of success can pull them apart. I can't count the number of bands I handled that were on the verge of making it big, or had just done so, then threw it all away. Bow Wow Wow, The Smiths, Split Enz, The Specials, Ultravox, The Go-Go's, The Bangles, The English Beat; the list seems endless.

Late in 1980, a year or so after I'd moved to New York to start up FBI, I got a phone call from Bill Berry and Mike Mills, who'd both moved from Macon to go to college at the University of Georgia. They called me from Athens just to say hello and shoot the shit, and "Oh, by the way, can you put us on the guest list for The Police show that's coming up at the Fox Theater in Atlanta?"

"No problem," I said, and I asked them how things were going. They said college was going great, and so on, and Bill mentioned that he had started playing the drums again, and that he and Mike Mills had joined up with two other guys from college to form a band. I asked him if his group was doing any live shows.

"Yeah," he said. "We started out playing at hangouts and fraternity parties, but then we progressed to playing the local bars. Here in Athens we pack the places we play. We've got a friend in North Carolina that's helping us get bookings in clubs up there, and I've been booking shows in between here and there myself, but that

---

* Squeeze's singer/songwriters Chris Difford and Glenn Tilbrook formed a band called, oddly enough, Difford and Tilbrook, and FBI booked their tour in 1984. Squeeze reformed in 1985 and returned to Miles for management. They sold out Madison Square Garden again on November 13, 1987.

WILD THING

part's not much fun. I even started my own agency here in town, called The Athens Agency, but I can't see it going anywhere. Nobody wants to play biker bars and pizzerias, and that's all there is down here."

"Bill, I always did say as an agent you'd make a great drummer." Just to show I was kidding, I asked him if he'd like play the support slot with The Police in Atlanta. "That way I can check out your band, and I won't have to bother with getting you backstage passes."

"Holy gopher fuck! Are you serious?" he asked.

"Yeah, I'm serious," said I. "And by the way, what's the name of the band?"

"R.E.M.," he said.

Their performance in Atlanta impressed me, but not so much for their talent. If they had any I barely noticed. It was enough for me just to see my old friends Mike and Bill up there on stage, and looking like they belonged there. When we had jammed at my apartment in Macon, and rehearsed as The Frustrations, even coming close to getting on stage at the Capricorn picnic, I never imagined that they would end up as professional musicians, and certainly not as teen idols, which they would one day become. Yet, here they were in front of four thousand people at the Fox Theater, and though they were only the opening act the crowd was so receptive that the singer, Michael Stipe, invited everyone up onto the stage, which got me into trouble with the promoter.

Early the next year in 1981, R.E.M. recorded a single called "Radio Free Europe," which they put out in July by themselves. In June, just prior to its release, I booked them a showcase gig in New York, putting them on for two days at the Ritz as the support band for Gang of Four. If R.E.M. had been slightly rough at the edges in Atlanta the first time I saw them, well, this time they were still rough at the edges, but that's what I liked about them. This time I was paying attention and noticed how good Mike and Bill really were. The singer, Michael Stipe, had an unusual voice but endearing charisma. The guitar player, Peter Buck, played intricate riffs while flailing around stage like a drunken Pete Townsend. Together, the four of them were terrific. What's more, the show received rave reviews in all the music press, confirming to me that they really were a great band, not just a band I liked for personal reasons. I decided to take them on.

When I told them I wanted to sign them to FBI, even though they didn't have a record deal yet, they were thrilled. Jefferson Holt, who had helped Berry get gigs in North Carolina, and who had since moved to Athens to become their manager and virtual fifth member of the group, asked me if I could also interest my brother Miles in signing them to IRS Records. I said I'd be glad to do that, but I also explained that since I had equally good relations with all of the record companies, it was my policy not to favor IRS over other labels. The majority of my acts had nothing to do with Miles or IRS Records, and it would be suicide for me to allow anyone to get the impression otherwise. I offered to shop them around to *all* of the record labels.

But Jefferson told me, "Leroy, we appreciate your concerns. We've all thought about it a lot, though, and we've checked it out pretty good. We want a label that's big enough to handle the job, but small enough to give us personal attention. We need people who can understand where we're coming from, and who can put up with our weird ways. There's no need to shop it around, 'cause we know what we want. We don't want to sign with anyone else. We want to be on IRS."

But I did shop it around, just to be on the safe side. I made up a list of the A&R men I knew at the various record labels, and sent out tapes to all of them. In my optimism, I envisioned a positive response from several, but having been in this position before, I only counted on one or two. Instead, I got none. Not even from my brother at IRS.

With Miles I made a near fatal mistake. In telling him about the band, I prefaced how great they were with an explanation of who Mike and Bill were, how I knew them from down in Macon. From that point on, Miles just thought these were friends of mine, and that I was just doing them a favor. Every time I asked Miles if he'd listened to the tape, he said that he'd meant to, but he hadn't had the chance. To be fair, Miles already had a lot on his plate; aside from running his record companies in the U.K. and the U.S., and managing The Police, Oingo Boingo, and Wall of Voodoo, he had just signed another L.A.-based all-girl group for management called The Bangs,

WILD THING

and that was proving to be a full-time job by itself. But whatever the reason, Miles never did listen to the tape.

Meanwhile, Jay Boberg, the president at IRS, had heard the tape and loved it. He had been sent the tape from his college radio rep in Atlanta, and he was aware that the band had been building a credible following, and that they weren't just friends of mine. Jay said he was interested in signing them, but not before seeing them play. So, mainly for Jay's sake, I arranged for R.E.M. to play at the Mudd Club in New York during a college radio conference in October when I knew he'd be in town. Unfortunately, he never showed up.

For the rest of that year and on into 1982, FBI booked R.E.M. up and down the East Coast and all across America. Since they didn't have an album out and were unknown in most parts, this was not an easy task. We put them on as a support act with one of our other bands whenever we could, but when there was no other choice we headlined them in whatever bar or club would have them, and, admittedly, many of these were dives and shitholes. It was in such a place that Jay Boberg finally saw them.

On March 12, at a seedy club in New Orleans called The Beat Exchange, R.E.M. delivered a set that was plagued with technical problems and power failures, playing to a mere handful of disinterested customers wasted on booze or drugs. They couldn't help noticing, however, that there was one smartly dressed young man in the crowd that seemed both sober and attentive. After the set, the band retreated to the dressing room to lick their wounds, and in walked the young man behind them.

"Hi," he said, extending his hand to the singer. "I'm Jay Boberg from IRS Records."

Michael Stipe groaned. "I was afraid of that."

Jay had been suitably impressed by the band despite the problems with the show, and he was eager to sign them to IRS, but he first needed Miles's approval. Miles had done all the signing for IRS up to that point, and he wanted to see them himself. The Catch-22 was that I couldn't get R.E.M. a showcase date in Los Angeles, and Miles was still too busy at the time to go to Georgia.

So, with Jay as an ally, I flew to L.A. to meet with the pair of them. Before we got into the subject of R.E.M., however, Miles said he needed me to help him with his new band The Bangs. The problem was that they didn't impress me all that much when I saw their show. I also thought it would not sit well with The Go-Go's for me to represent their direct competition, another all-girl band from L.A. And let's face it, I was kind of busy myself. I already had over seventy bands on my roster. But Miles wouldn't take no for an answer. He needed them to work on the road to improve their performance, and to keep them from costing him retainers while they sat around in L.A. In the end, we struck an informal deal. I would sign The Bangs to FBI if Miles would sign R.E.M. to IRS.

As it turned out, it was not a bad bargain! R.E.M. gave me a point on their albums for helping them to get their record deal. The Bangs, who were forced to change their name to The Bangles when another band called Bangs threatened a lawsuit, went on to become the most successful all-girl group in history, ultimately eclipsing even The Go-Go's in record sales. And, in time, both The Bangles and R.E.M. would be selling out shows in arenas such as Madison Square Garden. Miles didn't do so bad out of it either. IRS first released a rerecorded version of the tape as an EP called *Chronic Town,* and soon after that, an album called *Murmur.* These records were not exactly flying off the shelves, at first, but soon enough all of R.E.M's albums would sell multi-platinum.

In the beginning, however, and even for quite a while after they put out their first few albums, R.E.M. was not an easy band to book. For a start, they weren't English. This was a major disadvantage at a time when it was fairly easy to book any flavor-of-the-month band from London. They got very little airplay on any of the major radio stations, and the more courageous college stations that were playing them had very few listeners. So, the only way to promote their records was to go out on the road, and that was the dilemma. With no airplay, it's damned near impossible to find work.

But we managed to find dates for them somehow. After the first show supporting The Police in Atlanta, we put them on every date I could reasonably squeeze out of the bands I had on the road, putting them on as "special guests" to The English Beat, The Producers, Joe "King" Carrasco, Oingo Boingo, Steve Forbert, Suburban Lawns, The Motels, Lords of the New Church, Romeo Void, Thompson Twins, and the Gang of Four. On top of that, we booked them as headliners in clubs wherever we could. Eventually they began to

draw enough of a crowd of their own that they didn't have to support other bands, and at some point they decided to shun support
slots and would only headline their own shows. This made it all the
more difficult for us at the agency, but ultimately it was the wisest
choice. On their own, in front of their own audience, the band was
truly awesome.

As they started to become more and more popular I began to be
inundated with offers for them to play special guest slots on major
tours that would have put them in front of a lot more people than
they were playing to in the clubs as headliners. But always they
turned them down. Once, I called Bill Berry and insisted that they
consider opening for The Police.

"Leroy," Bill said, "I'll never forget what you told me back at
Paragon. It's better to play to ten of your own fans than a hundred of
someone else's."

I said "But Bill, that was then, this is now! The numbers have
changed. We're not talking hundreds, or even thousands. I'm offering you the whole Police tour in stadiums across the United States
and Canada. You'll be playing to more than a million people in less
than two months."

R.E.M. were initially against it, but eventually they let me have
my way. Or some of it, anyway. They agreed to accept five shows
with The Police for ten thousand dollars each. One of those shows
was at the rarest and most prestigious live-concert venue in the
world. Shea Stadium.

CHAPTER 22

SHEA STADIUM

I can see forever . . . walking on the moon.

—THE POLICE

AUGUST 18, 1983—NEW YORK, NEW YORK:

SHEA STADIUM HOLDS eighty thousand people, and when they're all screaming at once, let me tell you—it's *LOUD!* So loud, there were times I had to leave the stage. Even in the backstage area it was hard to hear yourself think, and the sheer electricity of this event permeated the air. Not since The Beatles' famous show there had there been such excitement. But The Beatles played from home plate and packed the bleachers. This show, we put the stage in center field and filled the whole stadium. Now that it was filled to its maximum capacity, there was only one small problem. As the fans clamored for The Police to come on stage, I knew the band wasn't even in the building.

Shea Stadium, the big kahuna of concerts. The Beatles and Grand Funk were the only bands ever to have played there, so it was to be a crowning achievement for The Police, as well as for everyone that worked for them. It had been less than five years since they began by playing in front of small audiences in tiny clubs, as the vanguard of bands promoting a new generation of music known as new wave, and now they were the biggest band in the world. At the Firebarn in Syracuse, one of the dates on their first tour of America, they played to only seven people, including the bartender and two waitresses. Since then they had continued to build a live following, from city to city, country to country, continent to continent. On this tour they were breaking attendance records in stadiums, and in Syracuse they sold out the Carrier Dome, one of the largest stadiums in America. And now this, the most prestigious venue of them all.

So where in the hell was the band? The stage was set, the crew was ready, and the natives were getting restless. I got a message from Miles to say that, ironically, the band couldn't get through to the stadium. Traffic jams around Shea Stadium had caused a backup of traffic the full length of the Long Island Expressway. The Police had returned to their headquarters in Long Island, a country estate provided for their use by Lenny Riggio, the famous book magnate. Billy Francis, the tour manager, was trying to commandeer a helicopter to bring the band in. That was the last we'd heard from them, and that was ages ago.

The show had been fraught with problems from the start. To begin with, the band didn't want to play stadiums. As usual, they wanted to play smaller venues, preferring a more intimate rapport with their audience. But I was able to change their minds just by showing them the numbers. In the smaller venues they'd have had to play for at least a week in each city, several weeks in some, just to appease the demand for tickets. Andy Summers, the guitarist, objected to that on the grounds that multiple nights in one city meant the first night would be great, and the rest of the shows would go downhill from there. The most rabid fans would scoop up the tickets for the first shows, the lazier or less interested would get to the later ones. More importantly, the tour would have gone on for years. Everyone objected to that. The Police had been on the road already for most of the last six years.

In the end, they agreed to play stadiums, but only if we stacked the show with bands that would ensure the fans got more than their money's worth, and that was fine with me. I had more than enough bands at FBI that fit the bill.

Having convinced the band, the next problem was picking the markets, and convincing the promoters in each city to go for it. Most of them were eager, but some were skeptical. As it happened, they became more interested when I told them we'd be stacking the bill with fantastic bands. Only problem was, some of the bands I had in mind they hadn't heard of yet. Bands like Joan Jett, The Fixx, A Flock of Seagulls, and R.E.M.

In New York there was never any question of where to play. Shea Stadium was it. I had my heart set on it from the outset. That's where my naiveté came into play. Having never done a stadium tour before, I didn't know you couldn't get into Shea Stadium. I wouldn't accept that it was impossible. Little did I know that the Mets would never let a rock show on their precious patch of grass.

But first, I had to figure out who would promote the show. This would be The Police's only concert in the tri-state area (New York/New Jersey/Connecticut), so there was more than one promoter that had a claim to the act, having played them before. In fact, there were four. I didn't want to offer the show to one promoter and have the others screaming down the phone at me. But at first that wasn't the problem. When I actually spoke to the promoters, none of them wanted the show.

They had reason to be skeptical. Not only was it considered impossible to get a rock show into Shea Stadium, but no one thought The Police were a big enough draw to fill it. John Scher knew how big they were in New Jersey, his home turf. Ron Delsener knew Manhattan, Jim Koplick knew Connecticut, and Larry Vaughn knew Long Island. All of them were willing to put us in their arenas. But we were hoping to do one big show, and draw from all of those places. We knew The Police's drawing power from the contact we had with kids on the street, and from the fan mail that came through my office. My Manhattan phone number was listed, so I knew from the phone calls I was getting at home from fans of Stewart's, begging for his number. And Sting and Andy's too. And I had another advantage. Miles called me from the studio where the band was recording on the island of Montserrat in the Caribbean. He heard the demo tape of the new album, *Synchronicity*, and he swore they'd

WILD THING

have a number-one single with a track called "Every Breath You Take." One thing about brothers, you know if they're bullshitting. I knew Miles wasn't.

With promoters there's one thing you can count on. None of them want to lose out on something to the other guy. You only have to hint to one that the other guy is interested, and the offers start flying in. Then, it's war!

And that's what happened. Ron Delsener, the adventurous Manhattan promoter, was the first to bite. In all his dealings, Ron Delsener has never been known to lose his sense of humor. "Ian," he said, "whatever you say. You want to do Shea Stadium? No problem. Who else is on the bill? Black Uhuru? Johnny Rotten? Great! Who's closing the show?"

Anyway, Ron may have been kidding, but it was enough to get the ball rolling. Jim Koplick remained disinterested and passed on doing the show, but Larry Vaugn and John Scher jumped on board, once I implied to them that Delsener would do it. To confuse the issue, John Scher counter-offered with a show at Giants Stadium. He pointed out how the band could make lots more money for a lot less hassle. At Giants Stadium the rent was about half, and so were most of the other expenses. Giants Stadium had better facilities and parking, and a lot of other advantages. More than anything, Giants Stadium was eager for concerts, while Shea Stadium was dead against it.

But I was determined to have The Police play at Shea. When "Every Breath You Take" came out, and did indeed climb to number one on the *Billboard* charts, the bidding reached ridiculous proportions between the three rival promoters. So we decided to cut them all in, and have them share the date no matter where we played. It had never been done before, but it seemed the obvious solution. It was not to be, however. Delsener and Vaugn agreed to a three-way split, wherever we decided to play. Scher did not. He was sure we couldn't get into Shea Stadium, so he refused to share his Giants Stadium show with the others. It was a gamble, and when we opted to ignore the money and go for Shea Stadium, John Scher was cut out.

Next, we had to secure the venue, which, in the end, meant talkng to the Mets. Once we got past city officials and stadium owners, the bottom line was the Mets contract with the stadium gave them control over everything that went on there.

Talking to them was tough, to say the least. Like talking to a brick wall. But they were used to dealing with businessmen on the basis that money was the *only* bottom line. In a situation where the concept, the statement, was more important than money, they were thrown for a loop.

We went to extraordinary lengths to overcome all the obstacles they put in our way. The rent was astronomical, the expenses were through the roof. We agreed to them all. They were worried about crowd control, so we agreed to hire thousands of security personnel, including hundreds of uniformed police. They made us employ plumbers, for what I don't know. Then there was the matter of insurance, and then it was something else. There were some legitimate concerns, indeed, but I had never experienced such logistics in such high figures.

After all was said and done, and all their problems solved, there remained one final obstacle that seemingly could not be overcome. The main thing the Mets were worried about was their precious field. They had a game coming up, and there wouldn't be time to re-sod the pitch.

Kim Turner, the Police's co-manager by this time, came up with the idea to cover the whole field with a massive tarpaulin. It would be expensive, but it could be done. Even then, the Mets said no. They were worried that the tarp would heat up under the sun and bake their grass.

Kim was determined. He took an astronomer out to the stadium to do a "shadow study" to tell us precisely when the sun would go behind the bleachers, allowing us to figure out when to start laying the tarp so that it was never too long in the sun. Ron Delsener worked out a system whereby we could let the crowd in and move them forward as we laid the tarp in stages, based on the setting sun. The Mets finally agreed.

One thing is for sure, The Police didn't play Shea Stadium for the money. It didn't look like there would be much left at the end of the day. Just the tarpaulin to cover the field cost $21,000, and we didn't even get to keep it. The "shadow study" cost $3,000, the plumbers were $14,500, electricians $38,000, stagehands $37,000, stage and barricades, $26,900, and backstage catering $14,000, just to give you an idea.

The union was making a killing. The forklift drivers were getting something like $10,000. They had to remain "on call" from the minute we started bringing in the stage until the show was over and the last truck was loaded. They actually only did about two hours of work. We paid $500 for a piano tuner that we didn't need since we had no piano. He got paid and didn't even have to show up. On top of everything else, if the concert ran into overtime, even by one minute, it would have cost us a fortune in union charges and rent. With three acts on the bill and an eleven o'clock curfew, that can be pretty hairy.

Once we got approval and the date was set, I came under pressure from all of the bands that wanted to be on the show. I had my own roster of acts to consider, but I was getting tapes sent to me from all over the place. It was well known I liked to discover my own bands, and I was proud of the fact that there was not one act on my roster that I had stolen from someone else, yet managers of big acts that were with other agencies offered to come to FBI if I could get them on the bill.

I chose Joan Jett and the Blackhearts because their single "I Love Rock and Roll" was hot, and they were insurance to sell tickets, but mainly because The Police preferred putting on local bands wherever they played, and Joan Jett was a Long Island native. I chose R.E.M. because they were simply the best of the up-and-coming new bands. And, because I remembered how appreciative R.E.M. drummer Bill Berry was when I offered him the first support slot they ever did, for The Police in Atlanta a few years before.

On the morning that the tickets went on sale, I got an early call from Larry Vaugn, one of the promoters.

"Ian, are you sitting down?" he said, sounding serious.

"Uh oh!" I said. "OK, I'm sitting down. What's the picture?"

"You're not going to believe this."

"How many tickets have we sold, Larry?"

"Have you poured yourself a drink?"

"Larry, it's too goddamn early in the morning. Now, don't fuck with my head," I said. "Tell it to me straight. How does it look?"

"I've never seen anything like it!" said Vaugn. "We've only been on sale an hour, and the machines can't handle it. Lines are around the block at all the outlets. The show is a stone-cold winner!"

The show sold out in less than three hours, and that was only because the computers were slow in coordinating between all the ticket outlets. But as I was getting over the shock from that, I soon found that my problems had only just begun. First of all, I got about a thousand phone calls from old and dear acquaintances, calling to renew our friendship. "Oh, by the way, can I get a couple of tickets to the show?"

I never knew I had so many friends. It was as if my life was flashing before my eyes. I even had some of my old Vietnam buddies call me up, guys I hadn't talked to since the war. Three weeks before the show I had to hire an extra person just to handle requests for tickets, and I still had to spend most of my time before the concert telling rock stars, movie stars, music business heavies, local politicians, and even friends that there were no more seats. People would get really uptight if they couldn't get tickets, even when they called up on the day before the show. There was nothing I could do, but if you want to know the truth, I loved saying it: "Sorry, it's sold out."

The day before the show, during soundcheck, we discovered another problem. The band could hardly hear themselves play above the noise of jets landing at La Guardia; they were flying overhead every few minutes. The band were concerned that it would ruin the show for the fans during the concert. So, the ever-resourceful Kim Turner, with golden tongue and tickets in hand, went out to the airport and persuaded some of the traffic controllers in the airport control tower to divert the planes to a different runway during the show.

Meanwhile, back at the stadium, Stewart and Sting were fooling around after soundcheck. They got into a playful wrestling match on stage that ended up with the pair of them tumbling off the stage and Sting falling on a flight case, breaking one of his ribs.

On the big day, the vibe of the event made up for any problems. When I arrived it was absolute pandemonium outside the stadium. Limos were lined up all around the building blocking the traffic, and

I wondered who the bigwigs were that were coming to witness The Police. As they emptied, I saw that it was all my own people, staff from the agency and friends who'd helped The Police along the way. It felt so good to see Katie, Jane Friedman, and Louis Tropia, all stepping from a limo. And to see the pride in the faces of all the people from FBI. John Huie, Pamela Burton, and Theresa Lowery, who helped start it all, to Courteney Cox, who was our newest employee, and also an FBI acting client.

I hung around for a while at the backstage entrance, just to make sure all my friends got in all right. That was a big mistake. For every person on the guest list there were ten people at the gate claiming to be on it. Once they found out who I was, everybody expected me to get them in for free, even people I'd never seen before in my life. There were some fans in the crowd too, not really trying to get in, just hoping to catch a glimpse of The Police. A couple of them asked me for my autograph, which I was thrilled to give. I got *them* in.

The rain started the minute R.E.M. walked on stage, and as they began their set the heavens opened up. It didn't just rain, it poured. In all the years of going to outdoor shows, I never saw it rain so hard. R.E.M. played on regardless, and the crowd loved it. This was the band's first time on such a big stage, in front of so many people, and though the elements were against them, I could sense from the crowd reaction that R.E.M. would one day be a huge act. In my euphoria, I made it a promise to myself that they too would headline Shea Stadium.

I had had a hard time convincing R.E.M. to be on the show in the first place. I pleaded with Jefferson Holt, their manager, as well as with the band. It had been their policy only to headline their own shows for quite some time, but they agreed to make an exception this once. So when they went on stage and it started raining, I wanted to crawl into a little hole and die. It rained solid, until almost precisely the end of R.E.M.'s performance, before it suddenly stopped. After the show I went back and told them how great I thought they were, and I told them "One day you guys will be playing here again," but before I could add "as the headliner," the band threw me out of the dressing room. I'm sure they wanted to kill me.

Joan Jett and the Blackhearts were the next band to take the stage, and they too went down extremely well. Long Island natives loved her, and her hit "I Love Rock and Roll" was virtually a national anthem at the time. By the time they came off, the crowd was worked into a fever pitch. Still stalling for time, I was just about to plead with Joan Jett to go back for another encore when I received word that The Police had finally arrived by helicopter.

With only half an hour before stage time, the band went straight to their dressing room, and I left them to do my rounds. Miles and I checked in at the box office to do the settlement and count the money.

Originally, before tickets went on sale, the promoters considered the show to be a high-risk venture. We were confident the show would do well. So when we negotiated the financial deal for the concert, we made a deal where we took a lower guaranteed fee from the promoters, but we got a much higher percentage of the profits if it happened there were any. If they were right, and the show stiffed, they wouldn't get hurt. If we were right, we'd make beaucoup bucks. As it turned out, the show sold out immediately, saving us the expense of advertising it. And, due to the cost-cutting methods employed by the band and crew, and the lack of unnecessary frills required by most big bands, the expenses were lower than projected, so the profits were even greater than we had hoped for. The Police came out with $444,731. And sixty-four cents, to be precise . . .

Next I stopped by the merchandise stalls, where their only problem was they were afraid they might run out. At the production office, my next stop, everyone was running around like crazy. You wouldn't think so to see it if you weren't used to it, but all was under control. I went back to the stage door to see if everyone got in that was supposed to. I was feeling so high, I was ready to let everyone in.

But there was this one asshole who pulled up in a Rolls-Royce and *demanded* to be let in. He said his name was Lord Somebody, and insisted that he was supposed to be on Miles's guest list. Furthermore, he informed me he was in the middle of some very serious business negotiations with Miles, and that Miles would be very pissed off if he didn't get in. He didn't look like a lord to me, and I wasn't aware of any such deal in the works. I got a hold of Miles on the walkie-talkie, and he said he'd come deal with it.

I was in the band's dressing room when Miles returned to tell us what happened. "Here's this dude in top hat and tails with a carload of girls, and he's demanding to see me. I walked over to the guy and said 'Excuse me, can I help you?' He looked me right in the face, and he says 'I'm Miles Copeland's closest personal friend, as well as a business colleague.' I never saw the guy in my life. He's standing there telling me 'Miles Copeland asked me to be here tonight to finalize a heavy deal we're doing.' Can you believe it?!"

"What a wanker," said Sting. "He can afford a Rolls, but can't afford a ticket?"

"You should have seen the look on his face when I told him 'I'm Miles Copeland, and I've never seen you before in my life.' "

Stewart looked up from taping his fingers with gaffer tape in preparation for the show. "So, what happened?" he asked.

"He went white and started sputtering. I went for him. 'Who the fuck do you think you are, showing up in a Rolls Royce, saying you're Lord Somebody, and expecting to get in for free when eighty thousand other kids had to stand in line and pay for their tickets?' He said, 'But the show's sold out.' "

"Well," said Miles. "I had some tickets in my pocket, so I pulled them out. I told him 'I just happen to have some twenty dollar tickets right here, and oh, there'll be a hundred dollar surcharge on each one for my time you've wasted.' I wasn't even expecting him to go for it, but the guy was so embarrassed he forked it over."

"Hey," said Sting. "He didn't do so bad. Danny Quatrochi told me that some guy on the street in Jersey tried to sell him tickets for a grand apiece. At least he got in to see the show."

"Yeah," said Miles. "But these were obstructed-view tickets that were pulled from the box office after the PA system was set up. They were seats that were blocked by the speakers. Can you imagine his face when he parades to his seats, only to find they can't see the stage?"

Nobody said anything for a minute. Then Andy, with a mischievous look, said, "So he paid you in cash, did he?"

"Yeah," replied Miles. "Cash in my hand."

"Then," asked Andy, "where is our share?"

"Yeah, Miles, where is it?" asked Sting and Stewart in unison. "Let's have it."

When Miles laid the cash out on the table and it was divided up, the guys were beaming. They didn't usually see the money they were making until months later, after the accountants had their fun with it, not like the old days when they used to divvy up the cash each night after the show in hopes there was enough to pay the rent. It was the first time in a long time they actually got paid cash in hand direct from the ticket, so they really seemed to get off on it. They never even asked what they were making for the show that night.

A few minutes before the band went on, it started getting out of hand backstage. That's when you see everyone jockey for position. The stick-on passes most guests are wearing suddenly don't mean a thing, because only a special laminated pass for the crew will get you on stage, and you can't see from anywhere else. You can't even see from up there unless you're in the way. I don't know why people bother with backstage passes. Regardless, I've sure seen people go to amazing lengths to get them.

It was a major hassle getting onto the stage, just getting past all the people I knew that wanted me to get them up. Like I had some special power to create some space for them once I got them up there. You'd think people would look at the tons of equipment being hauled around and realize there's not going to be any room on stage. But they don't. Instead, they wonder why they aren't being singled out for special treatment.

And, of course, anyone even remotely involved with any of the bands on the show has some inalienable right to get on stage for the headline act. There were so many friends of the bands, or "liggers," at this show that the backstage was a zoo. Miles, being much better at saying "no" than I, began to personally monitor who got on the stage.

At one point, Kenny Laguna, Joan Jett's manager, asked Miles for a place on the stage where his wife and daughter could watch the show. Miles expressed concern that the crowded stage might not be the safest place for such a small child. Kenny's bodyguard, meanwhile, thinking Miles was the regular security guy, came over and slid something into Miles's hand, saying "I'm sure you'll look after us." When Miles looked down, to his amusement he saw that he'd just been tipped fifty dollars. It must have been his lucky night. Seeing the humor in the situation, he turned around to one of the roadies, and shouted:

"Table for two in the corner."

Once the crew were done moving their equipment around and the stage was set, we were able to clear a safe space for people to see from, and just before the band came on I took my own two daughters, Chandra and Barbara, up to the front of the stage for a quick look at the massive audience. They were fascinated by it. They could see all the fans at the front going nuts, screaming for The Police to come on. They watched as the security guards systematically hauled girls that had fainted out of the crowd at the front, and carried them off in stretchers. They, and I too, were astonished by the sheer energy coming from the fans, and by the fact that one of the people they were screaming for was their uncle, my little brother.

When the house lights went down, the stage lights went up, and The Police hit the stage, the crowd went absolutely apeshit. The screaming was unbearable. It started out loud, and then it just got louder with each song. The band was hot, the show was amazing. Halfway through the set, I took a walk around the stadium, watching the show from various places, enjoying the vibes in the audience. I'd never felt anything quite like it. When I came back on stage, the band was just going into "Walking on the Moon." Just then, the skies cleared, and the moon came shining through, as if on cue. I looked up to the sky and shouted out loud, "Man, there's gotta be somebody up there. . . ."

CHAPTER 23

THE HARVEST

It's a big enough umbrella, but it's always me
that ends up getting wet.

—STING

THE GO-GO'S, Joan Jett and the Blackhearts, and The Police dominated the *Billboard* album charts for the better part of that year. At the same time, their respective hit songs "Our Lips Are Sealed," "I Love Rock 'n' Roll," and "Every Breath You Take" traded back and forth for the number one, two, and three positions on the singles chart. In all, FBI had fifteen bands on the charts (*Billboard*'s chart went up to two hundred): XTC, A Flock of Seagulls, Bow Wow Wow, Thompson Twins, Robert Palmer, English Beat, Oingo Boingo, Simple Minds, Soft Cell, Martha and the Muffins, UB40, and Marianne Faithfull (if memory serves me correctly), and of course The Police, Joan Jett, and the Go-Go's. By 1984, our fifth year, the agency roster had grown to a hundred bands, and our yearly gross went well into the millions.

What happened next was that I became a businessman. Yikes! I had made it to the age of thirty-five and never worn a suit. Being in the rock-and-roll business had so far allowed me to remain an adolescent. All I had to do was listen to music, hang around with musicians, and talk on the phone a lot. Suddenly I found I was running a multi-million-dollar organization, and I was to some degree responsible for a large staff and hundreds, actually thousands of artists' careers. Now I was in direct competition with the biggest agencies in the world, and they didn't stay asleep for long.

In some ways the fun had just begun for us at FBI, but in other ways the party was over. Hard work had gotten us to where we were, to be sure, but it had all been in the spirit of having fun and doing what we enjoyed doing: discovering and breaking bands. That didn't stop, far from it, but now we were forced to get a little more serious. With the growth of the roster, and the additional bookers and staff to handle it, came massive responsibilities. As the acts grew in stature and began to play arenas and stadiums, the job of booking them became much more complex, often involving more arithmetic than salesmanship. Whereas we began with band fees of a few hundred bucks, our top acts were now routinely getting a hundred thousand dollars per show, and in the case of The Police as much as half a million.

We collected deposits from promoters months in advance of the concerts (half the band's guarantee in most cases, but sometimes as much as 100 percent up front from promoters we had never worked with before), so the money that was sitting in my bank accounts at any given time was sufficient to buy a good-sized island republic. I can still remember the transformation that took place at my local bank on Fifty-seventh Street. It didn't matter to them that the money rolling in wasn't all mine. Suddenly they began to throw down the red carpet and treat me like visiting royalty every time I went in there. The bank manager would have a heart attack if he caught me standing in line like everyone else, and I'd be ushered into his private office for even the most trifling transactions. And the faces on other customers was one of astonishment, because I was always wearing raggedy old jeans and a T-shirt with some disgusting punk logo and my hair was long and often untidy—hardly what you'd expect for someone receiving such treatment. It was downright embarrassing!

I couldn't get arrested. I couldn't even get a speeding ticket. The police, the ones in blue uniform, were such big Police fans where I lived that it was impossible to get into trouble. One look at the last name on my driver's license and I'd be off the hook. "Copeland, eh? Any relation to Stewart?" More than once I was asked for an autograph or to pose for pictures in lieu of a ticket, and needless to say I was glad to oblige.

In retrospect, it's a wonder I managed to keep my head on straight, but at this stage of my life I had seen so many ups and downs that I knew to keep a handle on things financially. I kept our office overheads low, or within reason (well, okay, the gym in the office with the tiled steam room and Jacuzzi hot tub might have been a bit overboard). I kept my personal expenditures to a minimum. Considering. I bought a weekend house out on Long Island, but it was a modest place on the beach on the North Shore near Port Jefferson, not one of those fancy mansions in the Hamptons further out on the island to the south. I bought a new BMW, my first brand-new car, a beauty but not the top of the line, and a small motorboat, a piece of shit Bayliner that lasted about a year before I had to get another one. I still flew economy and took taxis. No limos and that nonsense. And I never bought cocaine!

I feel it's important to mention cocaine because I saw so many people get fucked up on it. It was impossible for me to avoid the stuff entirely; at the time its use was rampant, especially in the music business. It still is, I suppose, but not like it was in those days. People didn't know better, and it almost came with the job. You couldn't walk into a dressing room (or an office, for that matter) without someone offering you some. Suddenly pot was passé, nose candy was in. Chopping out lines replaced the rituals of rolling a joint. Fortunately for me, it didn't have the desired effect. Instead of making me loosen my tongue like most everyone else, it made me clam up and I couldn't do my business. As a result I was one of the early ones to learn to "just say no."

Meanwhile, at FBI I had Buck Williams set us up with health plans and profit sharing (and so on) for everyone in the office, and we stashed a sufficient amount as working capital before doling out the year-end bonuses. Now that I was running my own company I realized that I had a responsibility to everyone that worked for me. Above all else I had to be sure that the company weathered any unforeseeable catastrophes. And sure enough, there were a few right around the corner.

The first was personal. My wife, Connie, and daughter Chandra stayed in Macon when Paragon folded and I went to New York to form FBI until our second daughter, Barbara Lorraine Copeland, was born on October 25, 1979. Connie and the girls then moved to Manhattan where we found a small but comfortable apartment on the thirty-seventh floor of a West Side building across the street and less than one block from the office. For several years we were a picture of marital bliss. As the kids grew, however, the apartment became too crowded, and with the money I was making at that point we could certainly afford to move. So, in order to get the girls in the best schools we moved into a four-story brownstone on the East Side of town, far from the office. Simple as it may sound, that was the big mistake, the beginning of the end of our marriage. Connie married me in Macon with no way of knowing I was a workaholic. I didn't know it myself. I had a fairly normal nine-to-five job when we first met, in a sleepy town that was virtually owned by her cousin Phil Walden, who happened to be the owner of Capricorn Records and Paragon Agency. How could she have known the craziness that was coming after we wed? How could anyone? Moving to New York and building the agency, traveling all over the globe to sign acts and then booking them all over the world, kept me in the office or on the road for much of the five years we were married. Connie simply wasn't cut out for the life in the fast lane we found ourselves in. Soon after The Police played at Shea Stadium we separated, and she returned to her hometown. A year later we were divorced.

It was a heartbreaking disappointment. And I was in for another one. While my marriage was breaking up, so was my top band. In March 1984 The Police announced that they were taking a hiatus, a temporary break from each other to pursue their individual projects. But, with the exception of three free shows for Amnesty International in 1986, they never toured again. After all the work that went into getting them there, at the height of their success, they did their one big stadium tour and that was it. It hardly seemed fair, but there was nothing I could do about it. If nothing else, it showed me that I could still take nothing in life for granted.

But it wasn't the end of the world. We survived, and for the next ten years and more (FBI celebrated its fifteenth birthday in 1994) we would enjoy a roller-coaster ride in the fast lane of both the music business and the movie business. It would fill another whole book to properly chronicle the events of those years, but as you might expect they were punctuated with numerous ups and downs and roundabouts, as in all the years before. Success came late enough in my life so that I could appreciate it and not blow it, but it was too early in my life for me to be satisfied. I still had to rise to every challenge that came along, and aside from staying on the cutting edge of the new music scene, I decided to branch out into the movie business as well.

Our roster was strong enough to sustain even the loss of The Police, and every year we managed somehow to break through with another hot act, or two or three: Thompson Twins, Adam Ant, Robert Palmer, The Fixx, UB40, Midnight Oil, PIL, The Bangles, Simple Minds, Amy Grant, and so on. Sometimes bands would break up and we'd have success with the individual parts. The Smiths (one of my favorite bands of all time) broke up long before making it big, but we put singer Morrissey out with his own band and carried on, and he would eventually sell out multiple nights at the Hollywood Bowl. The English Beat split into two successful bands, General Public and Fine Young Cannibals, both of which did extremely well. And of course all three members of The Police did tours of their own after the split. Sting would eventually be earning as much on tour as were The Police in their heyday. And so would R.E.M. It took five albums and the good part of ten years, but R.E.M. indeed became one of the biggest-selling groups in the world.

I initially signed all the bands to the agency, but eventually my agents started to do some signing of their own. Anyone at the agency had the potential to become an agent. Steve Ferguson was a part-time summer intern from college who came back to work for FBI after completing college, starting out as a secretary to one of the agents. When my assistant ran off to marry the guitar player in Billy Idol's band, Ferguson volunteered to fill the slot, a ballsy move considering his lack of experience. I gave him a shot. And he was good. In no time I made him a full-fledged agent. I was just about to promote him to company vice president when ICM (whose rock department is subsidized by a powerful film department) came and stole him away with an offer of twice what I could pay him.

I never stole agents from the other big agencies. I didn't like the work ethics and bad habits they adopted at those corporate places. But that didn't stop me from hiring some of the independents. When it looked like thrash metal (or speed metal, or whatever you call it) was finally going to dethrone the heavy metal bands of the past generation, as the punks did to the rock-and-rollers, I naturally wanted to be in on it. But the band I thought would lead the way, Megadeth, was already represented by someone I knew and respected, a hard-working independent agent named Andy Somers. Somers had a handle on the whole new metal scene, having been instrumental in creating it, but he was being chipped away at by the other big agencies. Some of his big discoveries (Slayer was one) had been stolen from him, and now Megadeth was being chased by them also. I knew that Somers knew something I didn't, a new scene I wasn't in touch with. He knew he would lose Megadeth to one of the powerful agencies if he didn't do something to increase his clout. So Andy came to work for FBI, bringing his roster of new metal acts, including Megadeth, Circle Jerks, and so on.

Nine Inch Nails was a similar story a few years later, with a savvy English gentleman named Gerry Gerrard as their agent. The underground buzz on the street told me they were going to be huge, but I didn't want to steal them. I put them on a tour with Jesus and Mary Chain as "special guests" and followed that with another tour with Peter Murphy, but that was purely for my own artists' sake since Nine Inch Nails helped to sell tickets and make my shows a special event. However, seeing the crowd response convinced me they were going to be an important and influential band in the future. So I soon talked Gerry Gerrard into selling me his agency, and he came to work for FBI.

In both cases I was interested in the artists but equally interested in the talents (and ears) of the agents. Sometimes I hired agents without any acts purely because I thought they'd make great agents. John Dittmar, for instance, came from an agency in Detroit that had done well with metal acts (such as Aerosmith and The Godfathers), but it had also been whittled away by the major agencies and eventually folded. John came to FBI on a trial basis with the intention of adding more metal bands to our roster, not the thrash metal bands that Andy Somers had brought with him, but the more commercial bands of the Def Lepperd genre. I wanted to diversify our roster and I believed Dittmar could do it.

Together we managed to sign several metal bands that showed great potential, but when it came to the more established acts we didn't seem to stand a chance. In fact, we lost out whenever we were in competition with the agencies that specialized in metal acts, mainly ICM. This was because metal acts believed that the way to get a break was to get on a tour with an established metal act and win over their audience, and they were probably right. But I was convinced that we could get them on a tour as easily as any other agency, since I could go directly to the managers and record companies. I was wrong.

It turned out that the metal scene was controlled by a tightly knit clique of managers and record executives that were all in bed with each other. None of them welcomed a new face on their closely guarded turf. Dittmar and I expended an incredible amount of time and energy trying to break into their scene, but after a lot of lip-service and broken promises even I had to admit we couldn't deliver the tours. Once I came to this realization I found it impossible to put my heart into signing metal acts. They all asked if we could get them a tour with Judas Priest or someone like that, and I had to answer "no." When I suggested that we break them through the clubs like we did the new wave bands, they all looked at me like I was nuts. Most of the metal bands had been doing the clubs in cover bands for years and they didn't want to hear from that.

But we tried. After five years at FBI (1985–90) Dittmar left to form his own agency, which he called Pinnacle. I was sad to lose him and glad to help him get started in his new venture. So I tore up my contract with Badlands and the other acts John had signed to FBI, enabling him to start out with a decent roster. Over the years he built up his roster, and as proof that perseverance pays off his company now represents some of the hottest bands in the country, including Spin Doctors, Pantera, and White Zombie.

John Huie also left to form his own agency. Since before coming to New York to join FBI, John had dreamed of pursuing Christian music, and one of his first signings to FBI was Amy Grant. From there he slowly built a healthy stable of Christian music clients until

WILD THING

finally they were consuming all his energies and he decided to go on his own. His own agency lasted nearly a year before he was offered a job he couldn't refuse in California at ICM. A few years later he moved to Creative Artists Agency in Nashville, adding a host of new clients to his roster, and he is currently one of the most powerful agents in the business.

As we carried on through the eighties and into the nineties the music business went through massive changes, too many to document here, but the overall picture at the end of the day, I'm sad to say, is that too much has remained the same.

One of my main goals with FBI has been to make it easier for struggling artists to make it, to give them a better chance of success. And for a while we did. But the floodgates that were opened by the punk revolution and the new wave invasion that followed were soon closed again (at least partially) by forces beyond our control, and it seems that today things have turned a full circle. It is as hard as it ever was to break a new band. Maybe harder.

With all due respect for the many good things about MTV and the whole music video phenomenon, as far as I was concerned it turned out to be somewhat of a Trojan horse. In meetings with MTV pioneers Bob Pitman and John Sykes before MTV was launched, I eagerly agreed to provide them with videos of our bands, and to work with them to sponsor live shows that would help promote both the artist and MTV. It seemed a perfect marriage. Punk bands were making videos long before anyone else, since many of the clubs they played had video screens and this was often the only way they could get exposure. I saw videos as an exciting new art form and I recognized that a music television channel would be a powerful force in our business. I wanted FBI to be part of it. We arranged the first Annual MTV New Year's Eve Party, among other things, and we arranged for them to sponsor their first major tour—with The Police.

MTV was initially a benefit to the new up-and-coming bands, giving much-needed exposure to many who weren't getting played on radio. Be that as it may, as time progressed MTV became more and more mainstream, and it became harder and harder to get on their playlist. The main problem for me, however, was that videos became increasingly expensive to make, sometimes costing as much or more than what it cost to make the record. Michael Jackson and Madonna proceeded to up the ante by making outrageously expensive videos with massive production budgets, thereby making it necessary for other artists to do the same. When the record companies divided up the promotional pie, this money came straight out of the budget for tour support. For many bands it became a choice between going out on the road or making a video, since there wasn't enough in their budgets to do both. Bands that could tour were forced to raise their fees to cover the loss of tour support, and so ticket prices went up accordingly.

Furthermore, music fans were no longer forced to go out to clubs and concerts to investigate the new bands. Instead, they could now sit at home and watch MTV, and later VH1, and pick and choose who they wanted to see. While this may seem ideal for some, for me it was a nightmare. I chose my bands according to their merit as a live attraction, not on their ability to make a slick video. All too often, it seemed to me, a relatively mediocre band would spend the money, or their record company would spend their money, to put together the right producer and the right director and come up with a great video. The crowds would then flock to their shows only to be disappointed in their live performance. Meanwhile, some of the best live acts suffered for lack of a flashy video. This had, I believe, an immeasurably negative effect on the live touring industry overall.

MTV and VH1 cannot be blamed, of course. It was up to us—the agents, managers, promoters, and record company executives—to deal with the new situation, and to work it to our artists' advantage as best we could. Change is always for the better, as long as you are willing to accept it. A new art form was upon us and we had to work it into our programs, just as high-schoolers had to start working with computers.

The club circuit created by FBI still exists as an alternative way to break new bands without massive amounts of financial backing, but the club scene was severely crippled by the drinking age being raised to twenty-one nationwide. Aside from the fiscal effect this had on the clubs, many of which rely on the bar profits to stay in business,

WILD THING

the bands lost a huge chunk of their audience. Hell, some of the musicians themselves weren't even twenty-one.

The new breed of promoters I visualized to take over from the fat cats who weren't helpful in the beginning hardly materialized. Mostly they fell by the wayside or were assimilated into the existing promotion companies, with a few notable exceptions (Danny Eaton in Dallas, Dan Zelisko in Phoenix, and Seth Hurwitz in Washington, D.C., for example). What happened is that most of the fat cats got wise fast, and they bought out or got rid of the competition early on. Bill Graham was a good example.

Bill Graham, who once threatened my job at Paragon and who swore that I'd "never make it in dis bidness," later became one of the first of the established promoters to promote a punk show when he presented The Police in San Francisco, and thereafter he promoted all my bands in the Bay Area. But this took some doing. On my first tour west with The Police I couldn't interest Bill in promoting a show, so the closest I got to San Francisco was a show I booked at U.C.-Davis near Sacramento. But I couldn't continue to bring bands out to the West Coast and not play San Francisco, so I had no choice but to find someone, anyone, to work with. Eventually I convinced a young student at Berkeley to put on shows for the Buzzcocks and The Cramps. His name was Ken Friedman. They were successful shows but fraught with problems, mainly due to the fact that my new promoter had absolutely no experience, and I had to walk him through it over the phone from New York.

As far as Bill was concerned there was room for only one promoter in the San Francisco area, an area he considered to be everywhere north of L.A., south of Seattle, and west of Wyoming. But at first he chose to overlook Friedman's promotional fiascos in Berkeley, and he hoped Ken would just go away like he hoped this new "fad" in music would fade away. By 1978, when punk became new wave and the whole scene took off, Bill could no longer ignore it. The bomb went off when he tried to book The Cramps for their return to San Francisco and I told him I'd have to offer it to Friedman first since he did them last, a common courtesy in the business. Graham went nuclear. He shouted down the phone and called me every foul name in the book, and then made up some.

With Bill it was always a big act, and by this time I knew it. He would scream bloody murder at the top of his lungs and resort to anything to get his way. He'd make threats, lay guilt trips, bend moral points, and then try to confuse the issue with inappropriate analogies and mixed metaphors. Bill was a holocaust survivor who grew up on the mean streets of Brooklyn, and he liked a good fight.

In true Bill Graham fashion he immediately sought to stomp on his budding competition. Aside from the pressures he exerted locally, such as unleashing his staff to tear down Friedman's posters or cover them up with his own, and putting on shows that purposely conflicted with ours, Bill warned the other agencies that anyone selling a band to Friedman would be subject to his wrath, meaning their acts wouldn't get on any of his big shows, like his highly successful Day on the Green concerts. But he couldn't threaten me too much because I didn't have any bands that owed him loyalty, and by now The Police were promising to be a major act even to outsiders. Bill was obnoxious at times, but never stupid; he wasn't going to force me to give The Police to Ken Friedman, and he knew me well enough to know I'd do it if I had to.

On the other hand, I was in a dilemma myself. Of course, I certainly didn't want Ken promoting The Police. I couldn't take chances with them at this stage of their careers; they were long past being guinea pigs for all the other bands when it came to working with new promoters. Bill Graham, aside from anything else that could be said of him, was the best promoter in the world. His concerts were always events for the fans as well as for the artists backstage. His staff were the best in the country and the bands always loved playing for them. Furthermore, unbeknownst to Bill, The Cramps were bitching about working again with Ken Friedman since their last concerts were such a shambles. Ken, meanwhile, was finding it next to impossible to stay in business as a promoter when no one else would sell him acts, and I was his only supplier. That made his situation even more flaky. But I had created him, I couldn't just abandon him.

A compromise was clearly in order. In the midst of one of our shouting matches I suggested Bill stop trying to squash Friedman and hire him instead. That way, I could get my bands played in San

Francisco and he and his staff could get an education about these new bands. Bill was already aware that there really was going to be a changing of the guard, that a new generation of bands was going to be taking over for a while, and he didn't want to miss out. So Ken Friedman went to work for Bill Graham Presents.

I'm not sure Bill thanked me for it in the long run. Ken did manage to help usher Bill Graham Presents into the new wave era of music, but he never quite fit in with the rest of Bill's "family" at BGP. Eventually he talked Bill into moving him into the management side of the company, and at Bill's expense he went to England and signed three of the hottest bands around, The Smiths, Simple Minds, and UB40, coincidentally all represented by my agency. Within a few weeks of his return to America, Friedman went out on his own and formed a management company, taking those acts with him.

I developed a close working relationship with Bill over the years, booking shows in San Francisco as well as around the world. In 1982 I was approached by Steve Wozniak, the cofounder of Apple Computers, who wanted to put on a rock show. Wozniak loved rock music and had long dreamed of one day staging his own music festival featuring his favorite groups. Now that he had untold millions to spend he wanted to indulge his fantasy with a three-day festival over Labor Day weekend, and he wanted to know how much it would cost to book his favorite band of all, The Police. He loved music but he had no knowledge of the music business and had never promoted a show. I told him he could pay me half a million dollars and I still wouldn't do it.

I pulled the figure of half a million out of the air; it was many times their normal guarantee. To my surprise Wozniak was undaunted by the amount, and seemed determined to fulfill his dream at whatever the cost. I told him if he was serious he should contact a reputable promoter, someone with experience in staging such a mammoth undertaking as Wozniak had in mind. I suggested Bill Graham. Next thing I know I've got Bill Graham on the phone screaming at me.

"Half a million dollars is robbery!" he shouted. "Greed is ugly!" he screamed. "It's people like you who are going to ruin our business!"

"Bill," I replied, "I haven't said I'm going to do it yet at any price. But I do know that without The Police you don't have a festival." I had already talked with the other agents who might have acts big enough to headline such an event, and they weren't taking Wozniak seriously either. But if The Police were going to do the show it might be a different matter. It takes one major headliner to get the ball rolling, then everybody wants to jump on the bandwagon. That's just the way it works. I knew it, and so did Graham. "So I'm not going to ask how much you're making from this deal, but that's our fee."

And that's what we got. But I wasn't happy with that; just to be safe I added a "favored nations" clause to the contract, making it so that if anyone else got more our fee would go up to match it.

Bill secretly despised the idea of some "rich yuppie" buying his way into the concert business, and he seemed determined to make sure it didn't happen often. He had a field day spending the man's money. But he got the job done. Some of the other acts he signed for the show were Talking Heads, The B-52's, The Grateful Dead, The Kinks, Tom Petty and the Heartbreakers, Fleetwood Mac, and Santana. Each of the headliners at the so-called "Us Festival" received a half million dollars up front, and even bands lower down on the bill were paid several times their normal guarantees. The festival site itself cost a fortune. It was constructed from scratch in an open field in the San Bernadino Hills that turned into a huge dustbowl during the event. A huge 300-foot by 67-foot stage was constructed surrounded by enormous 50-foot video screens and a 30-foot state-of-the-art Diamond Vision screen. And although the crowd was estimated at well over 300,000 people, more than had been predicted, the festival was reported to have lost a large fortune.

But Graham and I also worked together on more serious endeavors, such as the Amnesty International tour that he coordinated with Sting and Bono from U2, and which featured a brief reunion of The Police for three of the shows. He also promoted the Band Aid and Live Aid shows that involved so many of my artists, including Simple Minds, Thompson Twins, Sting, UB40, and others.

Bill Graham promoted all of my shows in the Bay Area until his death in a fiery helicopter crash in October 1991. I will always remember him as two separate men, one a shrewd and ruthless businessman who would stop at nothing to get his way, and the other a person who genuinely cared about his profession and the environment surrounding rock and roll. Sometimes they met. Sometimes they didn't. But somehow you had to respect them both.

Bill Graham, you may note, the most famous and perhaps the most influential person in the concert business, was still waiting tables and looking for work as an actor at the age of thirty-five. His bulldog determination and the strength of his convictions finally got him to the top, further proof to me that perseverance pays off. Throughout my life I've found this to be the case.

HALFWAY TO HAPPINESS

Old man, look at my life, I'm a lot like you were . . .

—NEIL YOUNG

On January 17, 1991, after serving his country for a lifetime, and publishing three books explaining it, my father died in a little village near Oxford, England, where he lived with my mother. Still active until his death, at the age of seventy-six he was hired by the British and American authorities as a senior consultant in the investigation of the bombing of Pan Am Flight 103 over Lockerbie, Scotland.

At his funeral, held in a small church in remote Aston Rowant, England, even in my grief I couldn't help but notice the number of strangers in attendance, evidence of the lives he led that I was unaware of. I was moved by the accolades in my father's obituary, and humbled by his contribution to world events. For the first time in my life, I realized that I had taken him for granted, and it was not until that day that I began to fully comprehend the influence he had on my life.

My mother now lives in the countryside in the South of France with her ever-present dogs, and she continues to research the history of mankind. As a member of several international archaeological committees, she continues to enjoy the occasional trip to the Middle East for a dig.

My brother Miles was on the brink of bankruptcy before all those good years began. He was $400,000 in debt when he somehow managed to scrape up three grand to help Stewart's band The Police record their first album, *Outlandos d'Amour*. Since then he went on to build a highly successful multiconglomerate media company with offices all over the world.

Miles and his lovely Argentinian wife, Adrianna, currently keep three residences: what used to be our family home in St. John's Wood, London; a home in Hollywood, California; and a sprawling castle in the South of France. They have one child, a son named—what else?—Miles IV.

My sister, Lennie, resides in San Francisco with her two children, Ian and Ashley, where she makes training films for large American corporations interested in expanding their business overseas. Her book, *Going International*, is considered by experts as a textbook on the subject. She recently discovered a talent for screenwriting, and has a movie slated for release with IRS Media.

After the breakup of The Police, my younger brother, Stewart, decided to turn to more diverse musical projects, such as composing operas and recording music scores for movies and television. His first film score was for Francis Ford Coppola's *Rumble Fish*; followed by *Talk Radio* and *Wall Street* for Oliver Stone; *Wide Sargasso Sea*; *Fresh* starring FBI client Sean Nelson, Bruce Beresford's *Silent Fall*; and more recently, *Rapa Nui* for Kevin Reynolds. In television he's best known for his music score of the series *The Equalizer*. He has written three operas, and his works have been commissioned by the San Francisco Ballet, Ballet Oklahoma, the Seattle Symphony, and the Cleveland Opera. His opera *Holy Blood and Crescent Moon*, a daring tale of love between a Christian Crusader prince and a Moslem princess, received rave reviews across the country, and set attendance records wherever it played.

An avid polo player, Stewart, his wife, Fiona, and their newborn baby, Eve, spend summers in England, and winters in the hills of Hollywood. Stewart is father to four boys.

Success to the Copelands was not so much the money, but being part of the process of building new acts, new systems, and in essence, promoting transformation in the entertainment business. Noting that doors were usually closed to newcomers in the industry, we decided to stop beating on them and create new ones, resulting in IRS Records, IRS Media, and FBI agency, among others. Another component of the Copeland philosophy was to shun the master plan, because we felt it defeated the vital spontaneity required for constructive diversification in the entertainment business.

Taking risks seems to have been an essential ingredient in all of our successes. This can be said of most people I know who are successful. Nothing ventured, nothing gained, and all that. But even when we've had success we've continued to take chances, looking for new challenges. To me, challenge is the essence of life.

As far as what the future may hold in store for me, I'm sure it's anyone's guess. Like in the game Snakes and Ladders I played as a child in Cairo, you have to roll the dice and make your move, then you have to live with where you land and make the most of it. Memories, also, have a reason, and when you need them most, the sights and sounds are there, like old friends. They remind you not to take yourself so seriously, that no matter how good or bad things are, there was a time when they were better. And worse. And I guess what's true for yesterday will be true for tomorrow. In fact, I'm betting on it.

TO BE CONTINUED

WILD THING

Mission Impossible

All over this wasteland . . .
—The Mission

QUITE SOME TIME ago, early in 1986, I got a call from a literary agent at William Morris. As one of the top five full-service booking agencies in the United States, the William Morris Agency was considered by some to be my competition, at least in the areas of music and acting. But since my company, FBI (Frontier Booking International, Inc.), did not have a literary department, I was flattered to get the call.

"I hear you're working on a book," said the literary agent.

"Well, no, that's not quite true," I said. "I gather you heard that from Howard Bloom."

Howard Bloom was perhaps *the* top publicist in the music business, handling clients such as Prince, Michael Jackson, Lionel Ritchie, John Cougar Mellencamp, and Talking Heads, to name but a few. He was also the publicist for the 1985 AMC Cancer Research Center Humanitarian Award Dinner (an annual music-business fund-raiser) the year the Copeland brothers—Miles, Stewart, and I—were recipients of the award, and he had asked me to provide him with a biography for the event. He wanted a brief family history, where we grew up, and what our influences were. "Tell us how you got to be where you are," he said. Wherever that is.

Coincidentally, I'd bought a home computer for Chandra, my elder daughter, long before she was old enough to use it, and it had been gathering dust in the closet since Christmas. So I hauled it out, dusted it off, and went to work. What happened was that I got carried away with the technology of the word processor, and the marvelous things it could do. I had so much fun with it that by the time I was done, our biography was eight pages long.

I sent it over to Howard Bloom, who immediately called me and said "I can't use all this but I'd sure like to buy the rights to your book!" I told him I was flattered, of course, but he wasn't joking. "I think it's amazing that you three brothers grew up in Beirut, and now you're all in the music business together. Is there a reason you called your agency FBI, Miles called his record company IRS, and Stewart named his band The Police?" he asked.

"Well, I suppose. My father was a founding member of the CIA. The real CIA."

"Ian, I've been working on a book myself," he said, "and if you don't mind I'll send your story over to my agent and have him call you."

So now I'm on the phone with an enthusiastic Jim Stein from the William Morris Agency. I explained to him that Howard was getting ahead of himself, and although, like everyone else, I'd always fancied the idea of writing a book about my experiences, I really didn't see doing it just yet. Not with so much still going on.

"Well, think about it," said Jim, "and if you ever decide to, please let me know."

But I didn't have time to think about it then. In 1986 and 1987 I toured over eighty different groups, most of them more than once, and some of them all over the world. Apart from my regular roster of clients that were working, including Sting, R.E.M., The Bangles, Public Image Limited, Simple Minds, Siouxsie & The Banshees, The Smiths, UB40, The Cramps, Fine Young Cannibals, The Fixx, General Public, Peter Murphy, The Jesus and Mary Chain, Oingo Boingo, A Flock of Seagulls, Hoodoo Guru's, Stan Ridgway, T'Pau, Tom Verlaine, Wall of Voodoo, Screaming Blue Messiahs, Pete Shelley, and Shriekback, I bought out another agency that specialized in new-metal bands (Bandwagon Agency, owned by Andy Somers), and so now we were booking all those bands as well, like Megadeth, Testament, and Circle Jerks. On top of that, I had opened a West Coast office to handle our new and blossoming film and television division, and I was flying back and forth between offices in Hollywood and Manhattan like a yo-yo, as well as going on the road with the bands here and there and all over the place.

If ever there was a rat race, it's the agency business. But every day is different, and that's the beauty of it. Whatever else can be said about it, it is never boring. Between the bands, the managers, the record companies, the promoters, and the radio stations, everybody's trying to come up with what's never been done before, and it's the agent's job to be right in the middle of it all, making it work. It's the agent that sets up the tours, around which everything else revolves, and when something goes wrong, it's the agent that has to sort it out.

One morning, I crawled back to my apartment at 3:30 A.M. after a show at the Ritz in New York, and there was an urgent message on my machine from the road manager of a band I was touring from England called The Mission. I called the number he left for me, and a voice that answered "Police Department" turned me over to The Mission's tour manager. In a voice loaded with frustration, weariness and anger, he explained that the band's lead singer had been arrested and thrown in jail for kidnapping and corrupting a minor. It seemed that a fifteen-year-old groupie had followed Wayne, the lead singer, onto the tour bus in the course of a party following the show in New Orleans, and then passed out. She woke up on her way to Dallas, and called her parents from a rest stop just over the state line. Her parents, meanwhile, called the cops, who, upon learning the band was in another state, called the FBI—not my FBI, the other one. After the show in Dallas they were waiting for the band back at the hotel, and they nabbed Wayne as he came in with the nubile young girl.

I spent the next hour on the telephone trying to find a way to bail him out. The tour manager barely had enough money to pay the

WiLD †HinG

hotel bill, and certainly not enough to post bail for a kidnapper. It would be hours before the banks opened. In desperation, I called Danny Eaton, the promoter who had put on the show in Dallas that night, hoping he'd cough up some cash, only to learn that the band had wrecked his dressing room, spilled food all over the floor, smeared God-knows-what on the walls, broken chairs into kindling wood, ripped pillows to shreds, leaving feathers all over the place, and so on and so on.

"All that wasn't so bad," Danny said, "but one of them assholes shat on a nice cake that my mom had baked for them. Got up on the catering table in the dressing room and laid a big ol' turd right smack dab in the middle of it."

I tried to reason with him. (Remember, this was three in the morning.) I said, "The guys in The Mission wouldn't have done things like that. It had to have been the work of fans after the band left the dressing room." As convincingly as I could, I explained that pop bands stopped pulling that kind of crap years ago, back when they discovered they had to pay for it. In the end I said, "Look, just do me a favor."

"Okay, Ian," he said, "I'll bust your boy out of jail, but I'll let you in on a little secret. I don't know why you're going to so much trouble. When I talked to them just before the show they said they were voting you Asshole of the Year. They didn't have nothin' good to say about FBI."

I thanked him for the favor, then spent the rest of the night fretting about what he'd told me. The Mission was slagging the agency? No way. I finally got to sleep figuring that he'd told me that just because he was generally pissed off, and was letting off steam. Up to that point, The Mission tour had been a masterpiece of what I call "strategic booking"—that is, arranging the gigs so as to cover a maximum number of markets with the minimum amount of mileage, playing all the best venues with publicity building from one gig to the next.

It just so happened this was one tour I booked personally. In many cases I would construct and route a tour by working with my agents as a team, but I'd done this one almost entirely by myself since at this stage nobody in America had even heard of the band. I was turned on to the band by a friendly agent in London, and after listening to their tape, and liking it immensely, I flew to Amsterdam to catch their live show. I was so blown away that I determined to bring them to America. I absolutely loved the band. I truly believed in them, and by turning that on to the promoters around the country, I was able to get them top dollar headlining in the best clubs in all the major markets across America, even though the radio stations weren't playing their record and the record company was barely promoting it. The truth was, The Mission was getting as much as some of my more famous groups. Promoters were paying more than the band was worth on the basis that they should regard the fees as an investment in future dates when the band had risen to the top of the charts. In short, the promoters were trusting my track record.

I needed to get good money because the band insisted on bringing their whole entourage from Europe, including every roadie that ever worked for them in England, complete with makeup and wardrobe girl. They needed two full-size sleeper buses just for the crew. On top of that, they brought tons of equipment and their colossal cathedral backdrop, even though they were warned it would fit in few of the venues they were to be playing.

The early gigs went well enough, and The Mission seemed to be firmly on their way up, but as the tour progressed, the reports I got from the cities they played grew increasingly negative. The band, by those accounts, would play extremely well in one city, get on well with the press and promotion staff, and then be miserable in the next town and piss everybody off. They started canceling shows, on the grounds that the band members were suffering from exhaustion. That was strange enough because when we were planning the tour in my office in New York, Wayne Hussey bragged that they were "the hardest-working band in show business." He had demanded I fill every date on the tour, and wouldn't accept my explanation that we would need to keep some days off for travel, even if he *was* after James Brown's title. There were no wasted days on the tour I booked, but since I had been an agent in England for five years and in America for ten, I knew the difference between what he was used to traveling between cities and the greater distances involved in the U.S. I kept the days off where they should be, and the tour was no more grueling than hundreds of bands had done before.

After getting them bailed out in Dallas the band went on to Houston, where the promoter reported a similar scenario. The band was generally pissed off with everyone, and especially with their record company, who they didn't feel was promoting them properly. The tour manager told me that the band was seriously threatening to pull out of the Los Angeles show as a protest. That would be a disastrous mistake, so I decided to fly down to their next show and see what their problem was.

I arrived at the Prism Club in Phoenix, Arizona, long after the band should have been on stage, and I was afraid I'd missed the show when they weren't. I found a rowdy crowd shouting for the band to go on, and the band in the dressing room refusing to. They explained to me that there had been a "slight altercation" between the club's security personnel and one of their fans, and now the fan was being denied entrance to the club, even though he was on the band's guest list. Until he was let in, I was told, the band wasn't going on.

This didn't seem like more than a routine problem. In fact, I saw it as a simple chance to show off my ability to take care of such things, since I knew the club owner was eager for me to put more of my acts in his club, and therefore would be likely to cooperate. After I swore to sort it out, I went off to find the owner. He was sitting in his office with blood all over his shirt from a broken nose, which he explained was a gift from the guy on the guest list who had hauled off and punched him when he was asked politely to wait outside until the doors opened to the public. Some slight altercation! There was no question of letting the guy into the club. When I glanced over my shoulder at the four or five gorillas the manager had for bouncers, I thought it amazing that the guy was still alive.

It wasn't easy to convince the band to go on, but I finally did. But as soon as they arrived on stage they began exhorting the audience to leave the club, and never come back so long as it employed bouncers who had pig shit for brains. Understandably, the club owner and his bouncers wanted to jump up on the stage right then and there to ram the group's guitars down their throats, but, practical considerations being what they were, they let the show go on. So long as the band was on stage they were safe, giving me time to calm not only

IAN COPELAND   338

the promoter and his bouncers but also the service staff, who were threatening to walk off the job and not come back until The Mission had left Arizona. In order to reduce the promoter's temper to room temperature, I had to promise him dates on half the bands on my roster, even though most of them had long since grown out of playing clubs.

The next day I rode the bus with the band to San Diego and discovered what the problem was. In a word, drugs. They were doing them in large doses, and washing them down with lots of alcohol. The real problem was, the band thought of themselves as the bad boys of rock and roll, "The Rolling Stones as opposed to The Beatles," as the lead singer liked to say, and they were so caught up in that image they felt they had to live up to it. Night after night, town to town, it was taking its toll. The bass player, Craig, was so strung out that he reminded me of some of the crazier fuckers I'd known in Vietnam.

I was not able to reason with the band about the L.A. show, which they were indeed threatening to cancel, and the bass player nearly threw me off the bus for trying. In fact, now they were threatening to go home to England and blow off the rest of the tour. So when we arrived in San Diego, I was pleased to see the band's manager, Tony Perrin, who'd heard in London that the band was offending record company people right and left, and had flown over to have a showdown with the band. He wanted to avoid any problems in Los Angeles where they'd be seen by a large crowd and most of the major media, as well as by the record company heavies who made L.A. their headquarters. Tony Perrin was not only their manager, but a close friend to the band, like a fifth member. And if anyone could talk sense to the band, he could.

Now, this could have been a really *major* clusterfuck. The record company had arranged a special matinee show for KROQ, the radio station in L.A. that was the first one to play the band's record, and was just about the only station in the nation that was still playing it on heavy rotation. The station had co-promoted the show and was giving tickets away to their listeners; if we canceled they'd go nuclear. Not only would they discontinue playing The Mission's record, they'd likely blacklist the whole record company catalogue. When the brass at the record company caught wind that the band might

339   WILD THING

cancel, you can't imagine the pressure they put on Tony to change their minds.

Tony arrived in San Diego during the band's soundcheck, and immediately after that they had a powwow on the tour bus. The bass player insisted that I stay out. After an hour or so, Tony came off the bus looking shattered. "So, what's the verdict?" I asked him.

"They're doing the show," he said.

"Then why so glum? You should be glad."

He looked at me then, with real tears in his eyes. "In order to get them to do it," he said, "I had to promise them an ounce of cocaine."

In any case, I was glad it was sorted out, and I began to think of my own personal problems. I had arranged to meet up in L.A. with my girlfriend of three years, a young actress named Courteney Cox, who was also an FBI client. After getting a spot in the Bruce Springsteen video "Dancing in the Dark," her career started to take off, and she moved to Hollywood for a starring role in a TV sitcom called *Misfits of Science*. After that she landed another starring role in a movie called *Masters of the Universe* alongside Dolph Lundgren, and now she was playing the part of Michael J. Fox's girlfriend on *Family Ties*. We'd been living on opposite coasts for over a year now, and it seemed to me our hot romance was turning tepid. My fears were fueled further when I called her and she suggested I stay in a hotel so as not to clash with her shooting schedule. In times past, if I'd made such a suggestion, she'd nearly kill me.

Anyway, she came to the matinee, and afterward we went back to the nice new house she'd just bought out of what she'd been advanced for her latest TV series. We were just beginning to break the ice when I got a phone call from the manager of the band calling me back to their hotel. When I got there I found cops all over the place, and my luggage down in the lobby along with that of the whole band. Craig, the bass player, had come back to the hotel from the matinee show, having first consumed at least one bottle of Jack Daniels, and had thrown a fit, and his boots, at the people at the reception desk because they wouldn't give him his room key, which they'd have been glad to do except that he couldn't remember his room number, and refused to give them his name. Instead, he caused such a scene they called the cops and had everyone ejected from the hotel, myself included.

We managed to check the band into another hotel, but the guys were so pissed off at the drunken bass player that when they finally got him into a bed, the whole show, complete with road crew, checked out of *that* hotel and into another one, without leaving any messages. When the bass player woke up he thought the band had gone home to England, so he packed his bags, went to the airport, and took the first plane to London.

With that news I figured the tour was over, and I'd be faced with a lot of phone calls to a lot of promoters who'd gone to great expense just to put this band on for me. But fortunately, Wayne Hussey, the band's leader, was a real trouper. "The show must go on," he said. The two remaining sold-out L.A. shows were canceled, and so were some of the other shows in California, but with a lot of hustling, and by using up any time I had hoped to spend with Courteney, I was able to salvage most of the tour by craftily rescheduling the dates, and, with a week of rehearsals, the band continued on, with their multi-talented soundman standing in for the bass player. And, to crown it off, as a gift from heaven in the name of an agent named Jonny Podell, my ex-boss at Paragon, I was able to get them on the Psychedelic Furs arena tour, a perfect way for them to play in front of larger audiences, and thus sell more records.

Unfortunately, I was not able to salvage the relationship with Courteney, and we agreed to a "trial separation," as if we weren't separated enough already. I climbed aboard the plane back to New York, on the late-night red-eye flight, feeling like the hogs ate me. Having checked to see that the flight was virtually empty, I booked an economy seat so I could stretch out on four seats in the back, and hopefully get some much-needed sleep. Instead, some guy sat down in my row, and asked me, "Hey man, where're you from?"

"I was born in Damascus," I told him, "but my hometown's Beirut." It was a big mistake. I should have said "New York" and left it at that. Instead of getting any sleep, I ended up telling him half my life story just to explain. His next question was "So, what do you do for a living?" That took up the rest of the flight. When we arrived at JFK after talking all the way, he said to me: "Holy shit, man! You should write a book."

I was surprised at the airport by a beautiful model whom I had

WILD THING

been introduced to at a party a few weeks earlier. She not only surprised me by showing up, she came in a long stretch limo, with champagne on ice. On the way into the city, I got on the car phone and called the William Morris Agency. I asked for Jim Stein.

"Jim," I said, "let's go to work."

BAND LIST: FBI MOST WANTED—1979–1994

The following is a list from A to Z of the bands represented by FBI (1979–1994) compiled from advertised agency rosters and year-end statements. My regrets to any artists that may have been unintentionally omitted:

Adam Ant
Adorable
Adrian Belew
A Flock of Seagulls
Alice Donut
Alien Sex Fiend
Alley Cats
Al Stewart
Alvin Lee
American Girls
Amy Grant
Andy Fraser
Andy Prieboy
Andy Summers
Animal Logic
Anti-Nowhere League
APB
A Split Second
Aswad
Australian Crawl
B–52's
Bad Brains
Badlands
Bananarama

Bangles
Barry Diamond
Black Sabbath
Black Uhuru
Bow Wow Wow
Brian James
Burn Baby Burn
Burning Spear
Buzzcocks
Cabaret Voltaire
Charlie Peacock
Chelsea
Chiefs of Relief
China Crisis
Circle Jerks
Clock DVA
Comateens
Concrete Blonde
Cro-Mags
Crossfire Choir
Daisy Chainsaw
Dark Angel
Dave Wakeling
David Broza

Dennis Brown
Dessau
Destruction
Dez Dickerson
Die Warzau
Difford and Tilbrook
Dirty Looks
D.O.A.
Doctor and the Medics
Donna Destri
Donny Osmond
Dread Zeppelin
Dreams So Real
Dream Syndicate
D.R.I.
Easterhouse
Echo and the Bunnymen
Eddie and the Hot Rods
Eek a Mouse
E*I*E*I*O*
808 State
Einsturzende Neubauten
Europeans
Fashion
Fine Young Cannibals
Fingerprintz
Flat Duo Jets
Flesh for Lulu
Flotsam and Jetsam
Flying Pickets
Foetus Inc.
Food For Feet
Front Line Assembly
Fun Boy Three
Gang Green
Gang of Four
Gary Clail
Gary Numan
Gaye Bykers on Acid
G.B.H.
General Public
Genitorturers
Go-Go's
Grand Funk
Green Jellÿ
Gwar

Havana 3AM
Heaven 17
Hoodoo Gurus
House of Schock (Gina Schock)
Howard Devoto
Hunters and Collectors
Iggy Pop
Illustrated Man
In The Flesh
Joan Jett & the Blackhearts
Joe "King" Carrasco & the Crowns
Joe Strummer
John Cale
John Foxx
John Otway
Jools Holland
Joshua Kadison
Joy Division
Julian Cope
Katrina and the Waves
Katydids
Kid Creole and the Coconuts
Kids in the Kitchen
King Diamond
King Sunny Ade
Kissing the Pink (KTP)
Klark Kent
Klaus Nomi
Kreators
Laibach
Legal Reins
Legendary Pink Dots
Let's Active
Lime Spiders
Lizzy Borden
Loop
Lords of the New Church
Lucky Seven
Machines of Loving Grace
Magazine
March Violets
Marianne Faithfull
Mari Wilson
Marshall Crenshaw
Martha and the Muffins (M&M)
Meat Beat Manifesto

Meat Loaf
Megadeth
Michael Gregory
Michael W. Smith
Midnight Oil
Mikey Dread
Milltown Brothers
Ministry
Mi-Sex
Mo-Dettes
Monochrome Set
Morbid Angel
Morrissey
Native
Ned's Atomic Dustbin
New Order
Nick Heyward
Nina Hagen
Nine Inch Nails
999
No Doubt
Nona Hendrix
Nuclear Assault
Oingo Boingo
Overkill
Over the Rhine
Pale Saints
Patty Donahue & the Waitresses
Penetration
Penguin Cafe Orchestra
Pere Ubu
Peter Himmelman
Peter Murphy
Peter Tosh
Pete Shelley
Petra
Phranc
Pigbag
Plastics
Pop Will Eat Itself
Psychedelic Furs
Public Image Ltd.
Pylon
Rank & File
Ranking Roger
Rebel Pebbles

Red Hot Chili Peppers
Red House Painters
Re-Flex
R.E.M.
Renaissance
Ride
Robert Palmer
Robin Lane and the Chartbusters
Rosie Vela
Royal Crown Revue
Sacred Reich
Saffron
Sanctuary
Savatage
Screaming Blue Messiahs
Sea Level
7 Seconds
Severed Heads
Sheep on Drugs
Shona Laing
Shriekback
Simple Minds
Siouxsie & the Banshees
Sister Double Happiness
Skafish
Sly & Robbie
Social Distortion
Soft Cell
Something Happens
Special Beat
Split Enz
Squeeze
Stan Ridgway
Steel Pulse
Stewart Copeland
Stiff Little Fingers
Sting
Stryper
Supreme Love Gods
SVT
Swans
Swimming Pool Q's
Sword
Testament
Test Department
The Accused

WILD THING

The Aquanettas
The Blue Aeroplanes
The Bolshoi
The Boo Radleys
The Cadillac Tramps
The Call
The Cavedogs
The Colourfield
The Connells
The Cramps
The Creatures
The Cure
The Dead Boys
The Dickies
Thee Hypnotics
The (English) Beat
The Exploited
The Fall
The Fixx
The Fleshtones
The Fuzztones
The Gun Club
The High
The Human League
The Jack Rubies
The Jesus & Mary Chain
The Levelers
The Lilac Time
The Lurkers
The Members
The Nils
The Only Ones
The Plimsouls
The Police
The Proclaimers
The Producers
The Professionals
The Ramones
The Rattlers
The Rockats
The Ruts
The Samples
The Screaming Tribesmen
The Selecter
The Sextants

The Silencers
The Slits
The Smiths
The Soup Dragons
The Specials
The Stranglers
The Sweet
The Three O'Clock
The Truth
The Untouchables
The Wailers
The Wolfgang Press
Third World
Thompson Twins
Timbuk 3
Tim Scott
Tom Robinson
Tom Verlaine
T'Pau
Trouble
Trouble Funk
29 Palms
UB40
U.K. Subs
Ultravox
Uncle Green
Underground Lovers
Urban Verbs
Velvet Elvis
Venom
Voice Farm
Voivod
Wall of Voodoo
Wazmo Nariz
Wednesday Week
We've Got a Fuzzbox, and We're
    Gonna Use It
Will and the Bushmen
Winter Hours
Wishbone Ash
XTC
Y Kant Tori Read? (Tori Amos)
Young Gods
Z

INDEX

A

A&M Records, 233, 238, 239, 240, 244, 262–63, 280
Ace, 173–74
Adam Ant, 284, 319
Aerosmith, 320
A Flock of Seagulls, 292–93, 305, 315, 334
Agency for the Performing Arts (APA), 271
Albert Hall, 12
Algonquin Hotel, 260
Al Hamra Bowling Alley, 50
Alice Cooper, 183, 248, 251*n*
Allman Brothers Band, 198, 213, 215, 219, 231, 232
Alternative Television, 210
American Community School, 49–50
American Embassy Beach Club, 53
American Talent International (ATI), 269, 271
American University in Cairo, 278
Amnesty International, 327
"Anarchy in the U.K.," 204
Anchor Records, 174
Animal Logic, 172*n*
Animals, 127
Apollo 11, 144
Apple Computers, 326
Apple Records, 159
Apted, Michael, 28
Argus, 159
Arista, 292
Arlington Cemetery, 154
Armatrading, Joan, 184, 187
Ashley (niece), 330

Associated Booking Corporation (ABC), 271
"As Tears Go By," 181
ATI (American Talent International), 269, 271
Atlanta Rhythm Section, 213
Average White Band, 175, 176

B

B–52's, 247–48, 261, 327
Baalbek, 37
Baigert, Michael, 34*n*
Bamyeh, Mustafa, 88–89, 92–93
Band Aid, 327
Bandwagon Agency, 335
Banfield, Phil, 179
Bangles, 297, 299–301, 319, 334
Bangs *see* Bangles
Banks, Pete, 183
Bannon, Vince, 240
Barcelona, Frank, 261
Bauer, John, 219
BBC World Service, 51
Beacon Theater, 295
Beard, Danny, 228, 240
Beat, *see* English Beat
Beat Exchange, 300
Beatles, 51, 159, 193, 289, 303
Beck, Jeff, 178–79
Bedrossian, Berge, 88–89, 90
Beirut, 22, 36–37, 45
Ben-Menashe, Ari, 252
Beresford, Bruce, 330
Berry, Bill, 213–15, 226, 230, 231, 232, 235, 260, 297–302, 308
Berry, Chuck, 87
Bicknell, Ed, 168–69, 170–71, 174, 180, 225–26

Big Brother and the Holding Company, 125
Billboard, 271, 306, 315
Bingenheimer, Rodney, 273
Birmingham Southern College, 48
Black Knights, 52
Black Uhuru, 285, 306
Blake, 131, 135, 139
"Blank Generation," 206
Blasband, Rebecca, 24, 25–26
Blondie, 248, 292
Bloom, Howard, 333–34
Blotto, 268
Boardwalk Records, 291
Boberg, Jay, 289, 300
Bob Marley and the Wailers, 284
Bolting, John, 183
Bolting, Ray, 183
Bolton, Jimmy, 20
Bolton, Michael, 24
Bondi Beach, 22
Bon Jovi, 196*n*
Bono, 327
"Boogie 'Til You Puke," 224
Bottom Line, 268, 273
Bow Wow Wow, 284, 297, 315
Boyd, Doreen, 172–73
Boykin, Robert, 246
Boyle, Jack, 219
Brazil, 14
Brendel, Steve, 159
Brigati, Eddie, 162
Brinsley, Tony, 183
Brisbane, 21
Broken English, 182
Brooks, Elkie, 177
Brooks, Garth, 25
Brown, Dennis, 285
Brown, James, 205, 208, 215

Brunel University, 173
Bruscoe, Charlie, 220, 222
BTM Records, 180, 191, 196, 199, 200, 202, 223
Buck, Peter, 229, 232, 298
Buffalo Springfield, 162
Burton, Pamela, 265–66, 268, 295–96, 310
Buzzcocks, 205, 207, 246, 264, 289, 324
Byblos, 37

C

Cale, John, 247, 256, 257, 264, 265
Campbell, Lady Georgina, 202–3, 204, 207
Canned Heat, 75
"Can't Stand Losing You," 209, 239, 285
Capricorn Records, 215, 225, 226–27, 231, 235, 253, 318
Caravan, 187, 190, 191, 193, 194–96
Carousel, Le, 50, 56
Carrack, Paul, 173
Carrasco, Joe "King," 301
Carrier Dome, 304
Carroll, David, 240
Carter, Jimmy, 231, 251–52
Casey, William, 252
Cassidy, David, 17
Cat Iron, 183–85, 242
Cauldron, 22
Caviano, Ray, 196
CBGB's, 242, 273
Chapman, Ernest, 178–79
Charlie Daniels Band, 198, 213, 215, 218, 224
Chelsea, 205, 206, 209, 228, 264

Cherry Vanilla, 238
Chiang Kai-shek, 277
China, People's Republic of, 14, 28
Chronic Town, 301
Chupa, John, 131, 132, 135
Circle Jerks, 320, 335
Clarke, John Cooper, 283
Clash, 205, 207, 248, 249, 250–251, 253
Climax Blues Band, 167, 176, 187, 191, 198, 202, 223
"Cohen, Lieutenant," 125, 128–29, 130–31, 135
Colaiuta, Vinnie, 12, 20
College Event, 173
Collins, Art, 24
Coltham, Eddie, 65, 66, 67, 69, 145–46, 148
Connie (groupie), 162
Cooley, Alex, 219
Copeland, Adrianna (sister-in-law), 330
Copeland, Barbara Lorraine (daughter), 260, 266, 314, 318
Copeland, Chandra (daughter), 253, 314, 318, 334
Copeland, Connie (wife), 253, 260, 266, 318
Copeland, Elizabeth Lorraine Adie (mother), 35, 49–50, 55, 58, 59, 75–76, 78, 92, 93, 329–30
Copeland, Eve (niece), 330
Copeland, Fiona (sister-in-law), 330
Copeland, Lorraine Leonora "Lennie" (sister), 35, 46–47, 55, 75, 76, 93, 148, 154, 330

Copeland, Miles (brother), 12, 19, 23, 24, 26, 33, 35, 47–48, 49, 55, 58–59, 69, 70, 75, 76, 91–92, 93, 142, 157–61, 166–167, 168, 172–73, 176, 180, 183, 184, 185, 187, 190, 191, 192, 193, 196, 197, 198, 201–202, 203–4, 206, 209–10, 219–220, 223–24, 233, 237, 238, 247–48, 251, 261–62, 265, 269, 275, 277–79, 280, 289–290, 294, 299–301, 305–06, 311–12, 313, 330, 333, 334
Copeland, Miles (father), 33–36, 41, 45–46, 47, 48, 49–50, 55, 58, 59–60, 70, 75, 76–77, 78, 92, 93, 94, 145, 146, 149, 175, 202, 251–52, 259, 329
Copeland, Miles, IV (nephew), 330
Copeland, Stewart (brother), 27, 28, 33, 46–47, 53, 75, 78–79, 93, 163*n*, 165, 183, 186, 201, 202, 204, 206, 207–8, 209, 228, 237, 238, 305, 309, 312, 317, 330, 333, 334
Coppola, Francis Ford, 330
Corbett, Cecil, 219
Cormier, Gary, 240
Costa Rica, 15
Costello, Elvis, 286, 292, 294
Cottage, 235
Country Joe and the Fish, 103, 187
Cox, Courteney, 310, 340, 341
Craig (bassist), 339, 340
Cramer, Jim, 248–50
Cramer, Wayne, 162
Cramps, 261, 264, 275, 289, 324, 325, 334

WILD THING

WILD THING

Acknowledgments

Thanks are not enough, but, thanks anyway:

To Howard Bloom, whose idea it was to write the book. To my agent, Jim Stein, for selling the idea. To my publisher, Bob Asahina, for buying the idea, and to everyone at Simon & Schuster, especially Sarah Pinckney, John Paul Jones, Virginia Clark, Felice E. Javit, Victoria Meyer, and Melissa Roberts, for turning it into reality.

To Ahmed "Blondie" Mamlouk, Buck and Patti Williams, Russell La Mont, Tom Najemy, Ron Jaragosky, Davin Seay, Courteney Cox, Theresa Lowery, Gail Zappa, Paula Leone, Megan Edwards, Deborah Lin, Ben Pollock, Brent Smith, Gabe Bloom, Eddie Katz, Lucrezia Mangione, and everyone who provided me with research, advice, constructive criticism, or otherwise helped me write the book. Thanks for all your input and immoral support.

To Miss Bullin, my teacher at Manor House School in Beirut, Lebanon. To Platoon Sergeant Cleophas Atwater, my drill instructor at the U.S. Army Training Center, Infantry, Fort Dix, New Jersey. To the memory of John Sherry, who gave me my first shot in the music trade as a rookie booker at his agency in London; and to Ed Bicknell, who took me under his wing. To Alex Hodges, who brought me to America and trained me as an agent in Macon, Georgia. To Jerry Moss, who loaned me the money to start my own agency in New York, and to Jane

Friedman who convinced me to go for it. Thanks for the faith.

To Connie. Thank you for Chandra and Barbara, and for being such a wonderful mother.

To Miles, Lennie, Stewart, Mom, and most of all my Dad, not only for getting me to the present, and for helping me sort through the sometimes sordid details of my past, but for lending me the wisdom to try and make more of the future. Thanks for everything.

Photo Credits